Excel for the Math Classroom

by Bill Hazlett with Bill Jelen

Holy Macro! Books

Excel for the Math Classroom
© 2007 Tickling Keys

All rights reserved. No part of this book may be reproduced or transmitted in any form or by any means, electronic or mechanical, including photocopying, recording, or by any information or storage retrieval system without permission from the publisher.

Every effort has been made to make this book as complete and accurate as possible, but no warranty or fitness is implied. The information is provided on an "as is" basis. The authors and the publisher shall have neither liability nor responsibility to any person or entity with respect to any loss or damages arising from the information contained in this book.

Written by:
Bill Hazlett with Bill Jelen

Edited by:
Linda DeLonais

On the Cover:
Design by Shannon Mattiza, 6'4 Productions.

Published by:
Holy Macro! Books
PO Box 82
Uniontown, Ohio, USA 44685

Distributed by:
Independent Publishers Group

First printing:
November 2006.
Printed in the United States of America

Library of Congress Data
Excel for the Math Classroom/Bill Jelen and Bill Hazlett
Library of Congress Control Number: 2006931384

ISBN-10: 1-932802-15-0
ISBN-13: 978-1-932802-15-3

Trademarks:
All brand names and product names used in this book are trade names, service marks, trademarks, or registered trade marks of their respective owners. Holy Macro! Books is not associated with any product or vendor mentioned in this book.

Table of Contents

Dedications .... a
Acknowledgements .... a
About the Authors c
Preface .... e
Calculation Basics 1
    Using the Touch-Typing Method (Addition) 1
    Using the Mouse Method (Subtraction) 3
    Using the Arrow Key Method (Addition and Subtraction) 5
    Entering Multiplication Problems 9
    Entering Division Problems 10
    Entering Fraction Problems 10
    Using Parentheses to Control the Order of Operations 11
    Calculating Squares, Cubes, Square Roots, Cube Roots 12
    Adding a Column of Numbers 15
    Calculating an Average 17
Printing Grid Paper 19
    Opportunity 19
    Solution and Overview 19
    Creating the Solution 19
    Using the Application 22
        Adding Gridlines 22
        Configuring Print Settings 26
        Saving the Document 30
        Printing the Grid Paper 30
    Excel Extras 31
        Making Larger Grids 31
        Isometric Grid Sheets 32
Cartesian Coordinate Grids 35
    Opportunity 35
    Solution and Overview 35
    Creating the Solution 35
    Using the Application 40
    Excel Extras 40
        Grids with Points or Lines 40
        Handout Sheet 42

Table of Contents

Multiplication Tables 45
Opportunity 45
Solution and Overview 45
Creating the Solution 45
- Using the Fill Handle to Extend a Series 46
- Copying a Range on its Side 46
- Entering a Single Formula for Many Cells 47
Using the Application 49
Excel Details 49
- Simplifying Dollar Sign Entry in Absolute and Mixed References 49
- More Cool Fill Handle Tricks 50

Math Exercise Sheets 53
Opportunity 53
Solution and Overview 53
Creating the Solution 53
- Basic Math Facts: Adding Two Terms with an Answer Under 10 54
Using the Application 58
- Keeping the Worksheet from Changing 58
- Adapting for Multiplication 59
- Creating an Answer Key 60
Excel Details 62
- Subtracting with Two-Digits Without Regrouping 62
- Expressing Problems That Go Across the Page 63
- Avoiding Duplicate Problems 65

Arithmetic Facts Quiz 67
Opportunity 67
Solution and Overview 67
Creating the Solution 67
Using the Application 73
Excel Extras 73

Homework Checker 75
Opportunity 75
Solution and Overview 75
Creating the Solution 75
Using the Application 78
Excel Details 79
- Adding Color Based on a Result 80
- Where Did They Go Wrong? 84

Magic Squares 87
Opportunity 87
Solution and Overview 87
Creating the Solution 87
Using the Application 97
Excel Extras 98

Coordinate Grid Matching 99
- Opportunity 99
- Solution and Overview 99
- Creating the Solution 99
- Using the Application 116
- Excel Extras 116

Math Art 117
- Opportunity 117
- Solution and Overview 117
- Creating the Solution 117
  - String Art 117
  - Tessellations 121
- Using the Application 124

Candy Bar Fractions 127
- Opportunity 127
- Solution and Overview 127
- Creating the Solution 127
- Using the Application 141

Math Facts Game 143
- Opportunity 143
- Solution and Overview 143
- Creating the Solution 143
- Using the Application 158

Secret Code Maker 159
- Opportunity 159
- Solution and Overview 159
- Creating the Solution 159
- Using the Application 165
- Excel Extras 165

Probability with Coins or Dice 167
- Opportunity 167
- Solution and Overview 167
- Creating the Solution – Tossing a Coin 168
- Using the Coin Toss Application 177
- Creating the Solution – Rolling a Die 177
- Using the Roll the Die Application 183
- Excel Extras 183

Table of Contents

Demonstrating and Comparing Fractions with Charts 185
- Opportunity 185
- Solution and Overview 185
- Creating the Solution 185
  - Making a Worksheet Not Look Like Excel 189
  - Customizing a Chart 190
- Using the Application 195
- Excel Extras 195
  - Pie Chart with Only One Section Filled in 195
  - Pie Charts Showing Difference between Two Fractions 196

Finding Maximum Area and Volume 201
- Opportunity 201
- Solution and Overview – Farmer's Fence 201
- Creating the Solution 202
- Using the Application 209
- Excel Extras 210
- Solution and Overview – Popcorn Box 211
- Creating the Solution 212
- Using the Application 218

Solving Systems of Equations 219
- Opportunity 219
- Solution and Overview 219
- Creating the Solution 219
- Using the Application 231
- Excel Extras 232

Index 235

Dedications

Bill Hazlett:

To my best math kids: Benjamin, Nathan, Ryan, and Caitlin; to Michelle and Mike, Ross and Amanda; and of course, Arlene

Bill Jelen:

To Jane Eckstein and Messers. Irwin, Krcelik, Bosu, and Bevington

Acknowledgements

Bill Hazlett

Many thanks to Bill Jelen for agreeing to collaborate with me on this book. Thanks also to Linda DeLonais for her editing skills and patience. Thanks to Olaf Stackleburg, Ed Dubinsky, and all the other talented instructors of IFSMACSE at Kent State University (1989-92) for introducing me to the wonders of spreadsheets and mathematics. Thanks to Tom Dryfuse for his help in co-writing the curriculum for our "Computer Problem Solving" class at Vermilion High School, from which some of the ideas for this book came. Thanks to William Masalski and NCTM for publishing the first book on using the spreadsheet as a teaching tool in the math classroom, and for giving me additional ideas to adapt for this book. Thanks to Kathy Staats and Denise Sheffield at Revere Hillcrest Elementary for helping me with ideas for the lower grade levels.

Bill Jelen:

Thanks to Bill Hazlett for asking me to contribute to this edition.

Dedications and Acknowledgements

About the Authors

Bill Hazlett

Wm. J. (Bill) Hazlett graduated from the Ohio State University in 1971 with a B.S. of Ed. degree in industrial arts and mathematics. In 1982, he received the M.Ed. degree from Bowling Green State University. Most of his career was spent as a middle school/high school teacher in Vermilion, Ohio, where he taught industrial arts, mathematics, and computer classes in grades 7-12.

After 30 years in the classroom, he retired in 2001. He now teaches part-time for the University of Akron in the Summit College Department of Developmental Studies.

Bill Jelen

Bill Jelen is the host of MrExcel.com. You can find him on TechTV in Canada and Australia, on his daily video Excel podcast or doing a seminar for your local teacher's association. He is the co-author of 15 books about Excel, including Excel for Teachers, Pivot Table Data Crunching, and Special Edition Using Excel 2007.

About the Authors

Preface

This book was born out of a desire to help teachers teach their students math by being engaged in its study, and by showing teachers how they can custom-build visual examples of some of the concepts they are trying to get across to their students. Microsoft Excel is an extremely powerful spreadsheet with literally hundreds of built-in mathematical, statistical, and other functions to accomplish the mundane calculations encountered in the world of business. However, the Excel program has tools and features hidden in arcane menus that do not enable self-discovery. A person using Excel often thinks, "there MUST be a way to do this, but where would they have hidden it?".

Our hope is that this book will help you to discover more features available in Excel and your students to become better at mathematics by using Excel. If you are also inspired to alter, refine, or completely redesign what you will find in here, even better. And, if you would rather not spend a lot of time trying to learn Excel, you can download all these files in their completed state by going to the "secret" web page at http://www.MrExcel.com/mathfiles/html .

One final note to Mac users: all of our screen shots were done using the Windows version of Excel 2003. Instructions for the Mac should be similar, except that the Windows right-click on the Mac is accomplished by holding down the Control key on the keyboard while clicking on the right mouse button.

Bill Hazlett

Bill Jelen

.

Calculation Basics

Excel is great at doing math. When Dan Bricklin conceived of the first spreadsheet in 1978, he envisioned a calculator where you could set up a math problem, but then scroll backwards in time and change the terms in the problem to see a new answer. Along with Bob Frankston, he developed VisiCalc – a Visible Calculator. Since VisiCalc in 1979, all spreadsheets have been able to calculate.

This section will teach you the basic math operators and the functions available for demonstrating classroom math.

There are at least three common methods of entering formulas. In the first three examples below, you will learn these three methods of entering formulas. You can then choose whichever method is the easiest for you.

Using the Touch-Typing Method (Addition)

Figure 1 shows a story problem. You want to enter a formula in cell B6 that will add cells B4 and B5.

Figure 1

Solving an addition story problem in Excel with touch-typing

	A	B	C	D	E
1	Josh had twenty Pokemon cards. He bought 10				
2	from Zeke. How many does he have?				
3					
4			20		
5		+	10		
6					

1. Start your formula with an equals sign.
   With the mouse, single click in cell B6 to move the cellpointer to that cell. Every formula must start with an equals sign, so type the equals sign to start entering the formula.

Excel for the Math Classroom

Calculation Basics

Figure 2

Always start a formula with an equals sign.

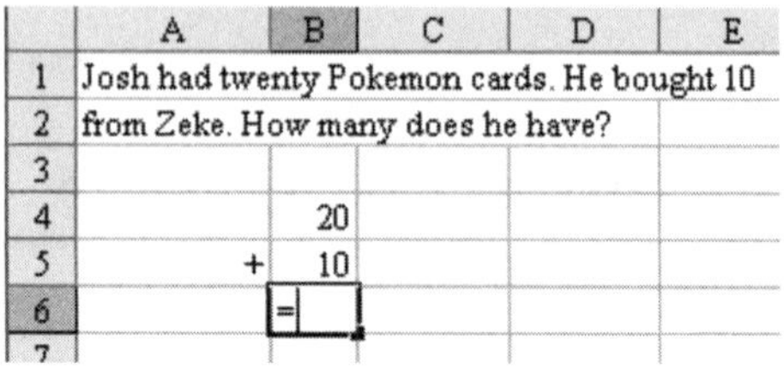

2. Type in the rest of the formula.
   In this example, you will use the *Touch-typing* method of entering the formula. Without typing any spaces, finish typing the formula as follows:
   B4+B5

Figure 3

Using a formula to add values in two cells

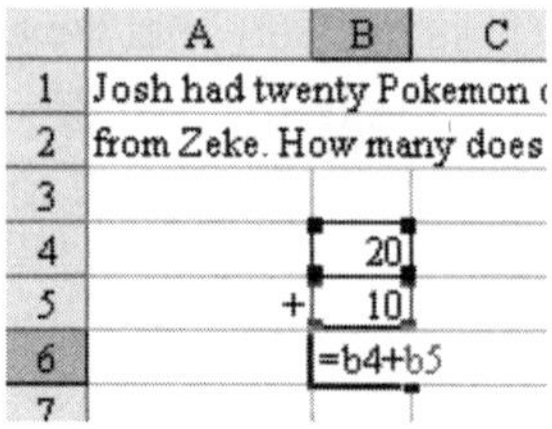

3. Press Enter to tell Excel that the formula is complete.
   When your screen looks like Figure 3, press the Enter key on the keyboard. After you type Enter, Excel will calculate that the sum is 30. Excel will also move the cellpointer down one cell to B7.

Figure 4

Pointer automatically moves down one cell when calculation is done.

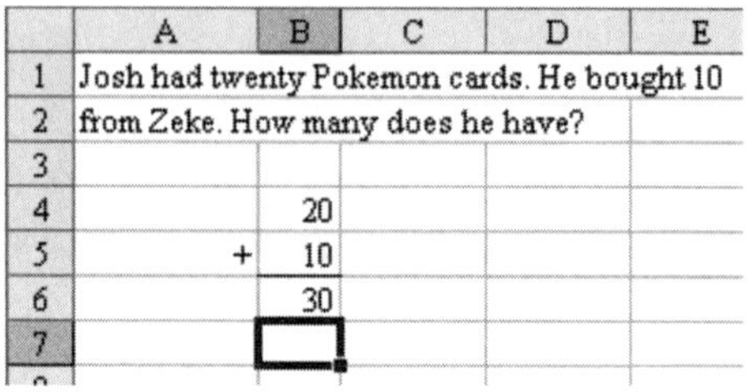

4. Look at the formula.
   Press the Up arrow one time to move the cellpointer back to cell B6. When B6 is selected, look at the formula bar just above the spreadsheet. Although

the spreadsheet shows a value of 30 in the cell, the formula bar reveals that this cell actually contains a formula of =B4+B5.

Figure 5

Formula bar displays the formula used to derive the value in a cell.

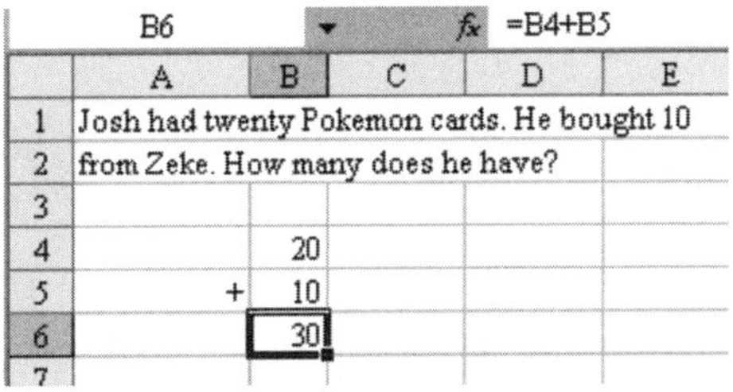

5. See how the formula result changes when the elements change.
   Here is the "miracle" of spreadsheets. Move the cellpointer up to cell B4 and type a different number instead of the 20. Type 200 and press Enter. The cellpointer will move down to cell B5, but all formulas that reference B4 in the entire worksheet will instantly recalculate. Thus, cell B6 becomes 210.

Figure 6

A formula's value automatically updates when any cells referenced in that formula change.

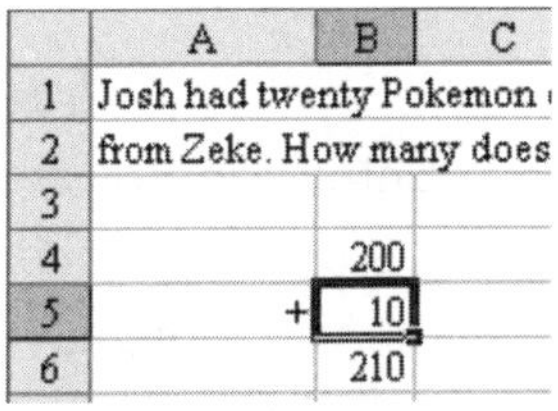

Using the Mouse Method (Subtraction)

Figure 7 shows a subtraction story problem. In this case, you will want to set up a formula that subtracts B5 from B4. In this example, you will use the *Mouse method* for entering parts of the formula.

1. Start your formula with an equals sign.
   As before, you have to type the equals sign on the keyboard to start the formula.

Calculation Basics

Figure 7

Formulas start with an equals sign

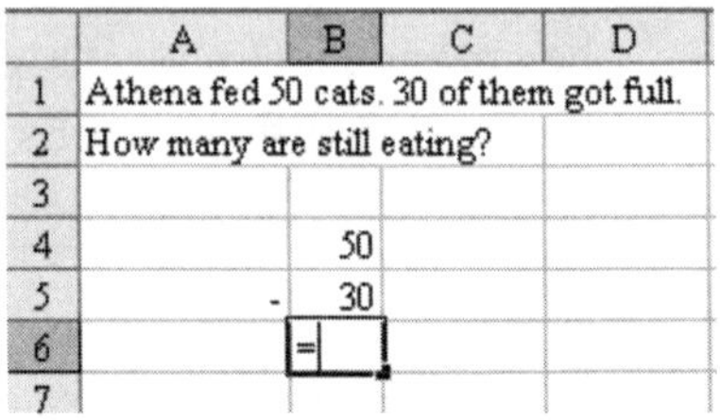

2. Select the first term.
   After typing the equals sign, use the mouse to touch cell B4. Because you are in formula entry mode, the formula in cell B6 automatically types B4 for you.

Figure 8

Solving a subtraction problem in Excel using the mouse

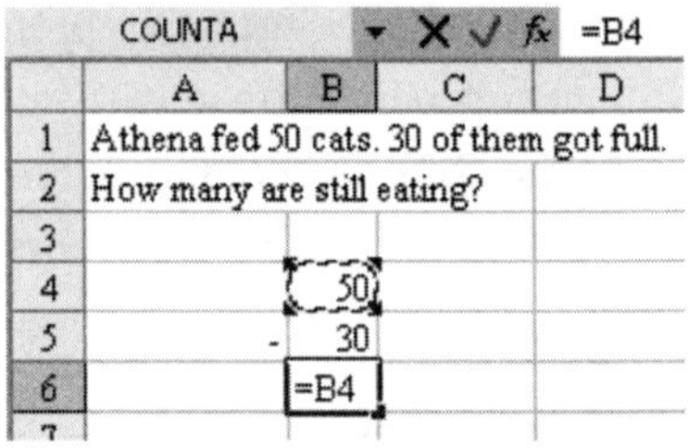

3. Enter a minus sign.
   Now, back on the keyboard, type the minus sign. Notice that when you type the minus sign, the flashing dots around B4 become a solid blue color. Excel is waiting for you to touch another cell with the mouse.

Figure 9

A solid blue box indicates that Excel is waiting for your input.

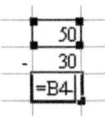

4. Select the second element.
   With the mouse, touch the 30 in cell B5. Excel will enter B5 in the formula.

Excel for the Math Classroom

 *Tip:*

If your keyboard has a numeric keypad, the upper right keys on the keypad will let you type the common operator keys without using the Shift key.

Figure 10

Excel automatically enters the cell location you click on with the mouse.

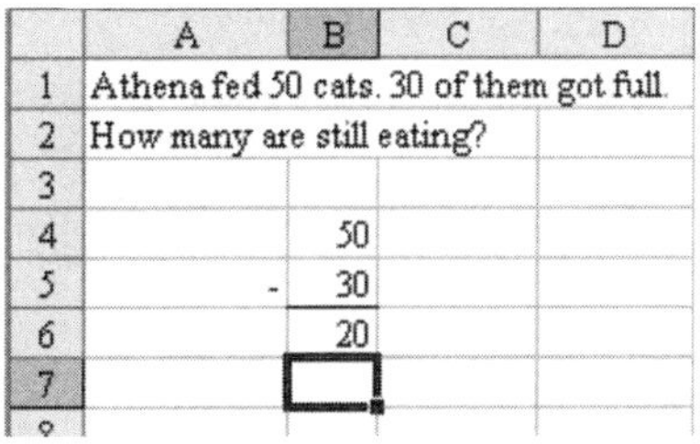

	A	B	C	D
1	Athena fed 50 cats. 30 of them got full.			
2	How many are still eating?			
3				
4		50		
5		- 30		
6		20		
7				

5. Press Enter to tell Excel that the formula is complete.

   When you type the Enter key, Excel calculates the result.

Figure 11

Excel calculates the result and automatically moves the cursor down one cell.

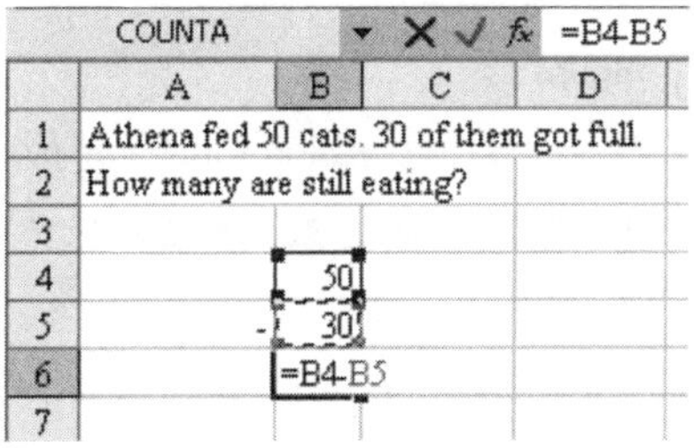

	A	B	C	D
1	Athena fed 50 cats. 30 of them got full.			
2	How many are still eating?			
3				
4		50		
5		- 30		
6		=B4-B5		
7				

If you are comfortable using the mouse, this technique of entering formulas is fairly quick and easy.

Using the Arrow Key Method (Addition and Subtraction)

The next story problem requires both addition and subtraction. The *Arrow key method* was introduced in 1981 by Lotus 1-2-3. The method became very popular for accountants who hated typing obscure cell references like B4 and AJ62. This was before computers typically had a mouse (the first Macintosh didn't come out until late 1983).

Calculation Basics

1. Start your formula with an equals sign.

   As shown in the image below, type an equals sign in cell B7.

   Figure 12

   Solving a subtraction problem in Excel using the arrow keys

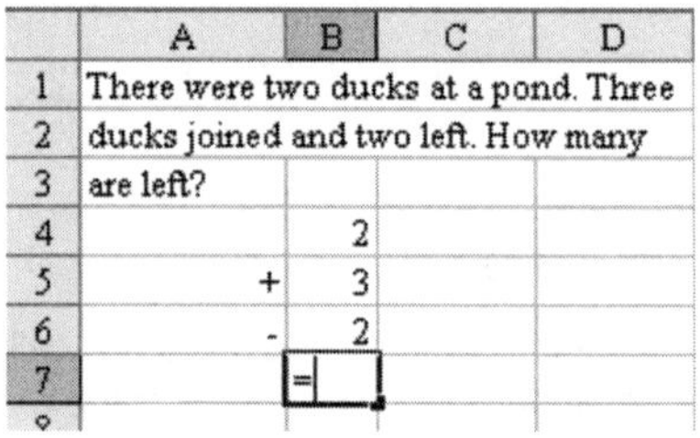

	A	B	C	D
1	There were two ducks at a pond. Three			
2	ducks joined and two left. How many			
3	are left?			
4			2	
5		+	3	
6		-	2	
7		=		

2. Select the first element.

   a. Using the arrow keys on your keyboard, type the Up arrow key three times. After the first press of the Up arrow key, the screen will think that you want to start your formula as =B6.

   Figure 13

   Screen after pressing the Up arrow key once

   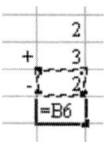

   b. That is OK. Ignore the screen and press the Up arrow key a second time. Now the screen thinks that you must want to start your formula with =B5.

   Figure 14

   Screen after pressing the Up arrow key twice

   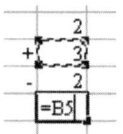

   c. Again, ignore what is on the screen and type the Up arrow key one more time. Now the screen suggests that your formula should start with =B4. This is correct.

Figure 15

Screen after pressing the Up arrow key thrice

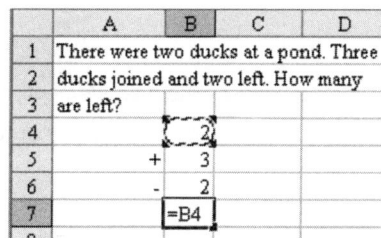

3. Enter a plus sign to the first element.

   The next part is a little tricky. In your formula, you want to add B5 to the formula. Type the plus sign on your keyboard. This tells Excel that you are accepting the B4 portion of the formula and that you are ready to enter another cell. Instead of a flashing box around B4, you now have a solid box around B4. Here is the tricky part: as soon as you type the plus sign, Excel returns the focus back to the original cell location of B7.

Figure 16

The flashing box turns solid blue when you accept a portion of the formula by typing the plus sign

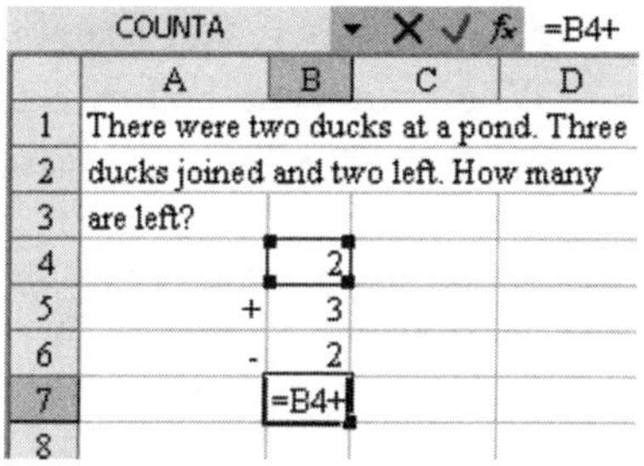

4. Select the second element.

   You want to point to the 3 in cell B5 now. Many people trying this method for the first time think that they should type the Down arrow to move down from B4. This is not correct. You actually have to type the Up arrow twice to move up from cell B7 to B5.

   Type the Up arrow twice and Excel will propose a formula of =B4+B5.

Calculation Basics

Figure 17

Excel proposes the next element in the formula

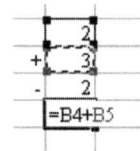

5. Enter a minus sign and select the third element.
    Next, type the minus sign on the keyboard. Excel will return the focus to the original location of B7. Press the Up arrow one time to subtract B6 from the formula.

Figure 18

Selecting the next element

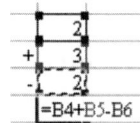

6. Press Enter to tell Excel that the formula is complete.
    When you type Enter, Excel calculates an answer of 3. Move the cellpointer back to B7 to examine the formula in the Formula bar.

Figure 19

Completed formula

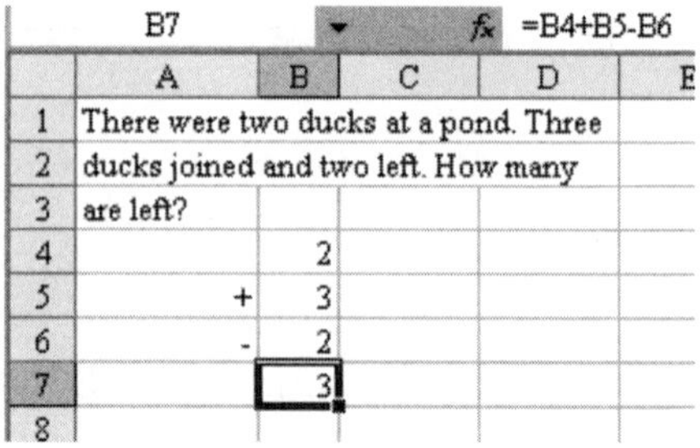

Now that you have learned the three methods for entering formulas, you can use whichever method suits you the best. In the remaining sections of this chapter, you will see the formulas to use for various mathematical operations. You can use whichever method you prefer for entering these formulas.

 Note:

Once you get used to the arrow key method, it is the absolute fastest way to enter formulas. The act of moving your hands from the keyboard to the mouse then back to the keyboard is relatively slow. The process to enter the formula above requires only nine keystrokes, and many of those are repetitive strokes of the Up arrow.

Entering Multiplication Problems

Problems requiring multiplication use the Asterisk key for the multiplication operator. Type an asterisk using the Shift+8 keys or the Asterisk key on the numeric keypad.

Yes – it would be a lot easier if they used the X key for multiplication, but then it could become confusing whether the X was referencing a cell location, as in X2, or was meant to multiply by 2.

Figure 20

Multiplication problems use an asterisk

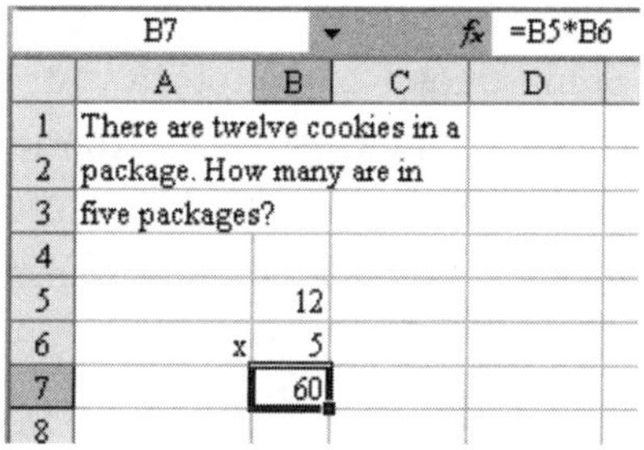

Entering Division Problems

There are two slash signs on the keyboard. File paths in Windows typically require the backslash, located above the Enter key. Luckily, division problems require the forward slash, located on the same key as the question mark. The image below shows a division problem.

Figure 21

Division problems use a forward slash

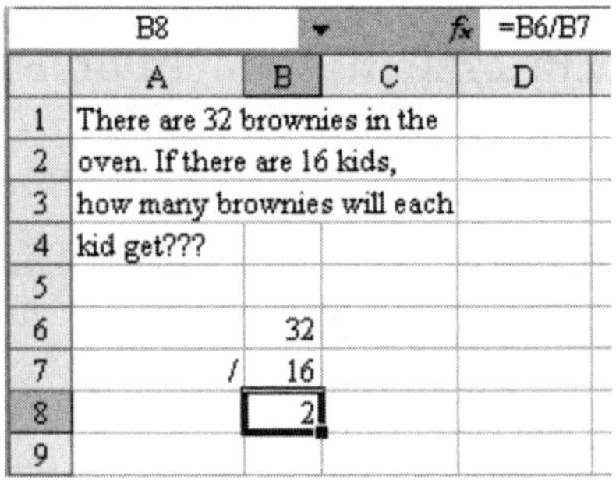

Entering Fraction Problems

Sometimes Excel expects your students to understand higher mathematical concepts, such as that a fraction is really a division problem. That is, one-ninth is actually one divided by nine. For fractions in Excel, enter the numerator, the forward slash, and the denominator, as seen in the formula bar in Figure 22.

Figure 22

Expressing fractions as division problems

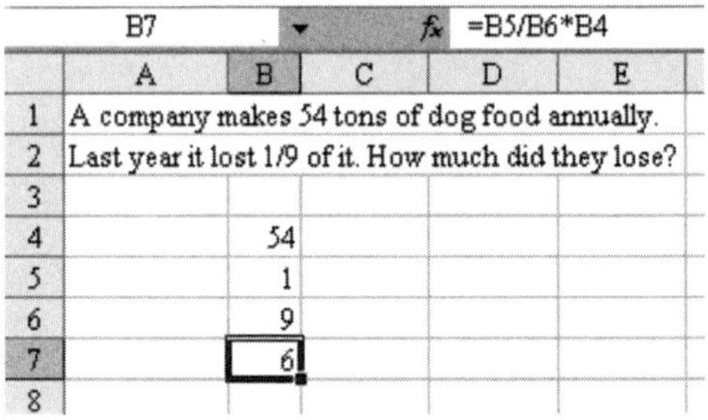

Using Parentheses to Control the Order of Operations

When it comes to math operating signs in an Excel formula, Excel understands and uses the order of operations correctly. It does not necessarily move from left to right within the formula. Instead, it follows the old mnemonic phrase "Please Excuse My Dear Aunt Sally": Parentheses (P) and other grouping symbols take precedence, followed by Exponents (E). Next, Multiplication (M) and Division (D) are done in order from left to right, and then Addition (A) and Subtraction (S), also from left to right. The only exception is that if you use a minus sign in front of a number, Excel assumes it to be a negative number first before performing any other operation. If your students understand how to calculate correctly using the order of operations, then they should have few problems writing formulas.

A very simple word problem can explain how this works.

> Jimmy brought 4 candy bars to the club house.
>
> Calvin brought 2 candy bars.
>
> Suzy brought 6 candy bars.
>
> They agreed to split the candy bars equally. How many candy bars does each club member get?

The obvious solution is to add the numbers together and divide by 3. However, using the formula =4+2+6/3 results in the wrong answer of 8. To fix this, you need to enclose the addition in parenthesis so that Excel knows to do the adding first, followed by division. The formula =(4+2+6)/3 gives the correct result of 4.

Excel for the Math Classroom

Calculating Squares, Cubes, Square Roots, Cube Roots

Excel has the tools to figure out exponents and roots. However, it might be a bit confusing to figure out the third or fourth root of a number.

The following problem tests the student's knowledge of the Pythagorean Theorem. The student has to square the length of both legs of a right triangle, sum the squares, and then take the square root.

The formula in C6 to square 122 is =B6^2. In Excel, the carat (^) is used to raise a number to a power.

Figure 23

Using a carat to raise a number to a power

 Tip:

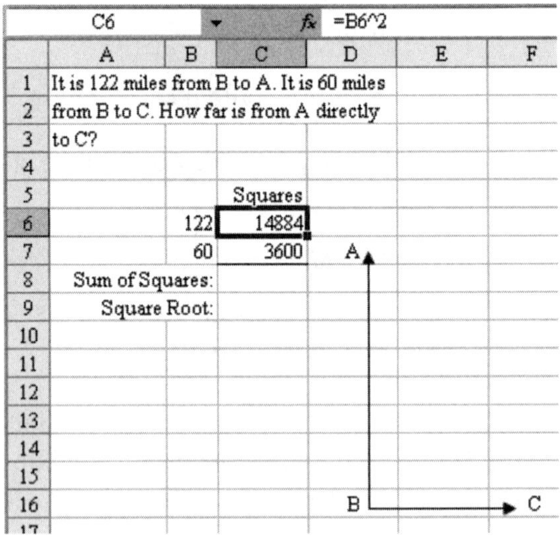

You can type a carat by holding down the Shift key and pressing 6.

Look at Figure 24. The formula in C7 is =B7^2. The formula in C8 is =C6+C7. In cell C9, you want to take the square root of cell C8. There are two ways to do this.

First, Excel offers a built in function to calculate square roots.

1. Type =SQRT followed by an open parenthesis to start the function.

2. Using the mouse, touch cell C8. Type the closing parenthesis.

This formula suggests that it is about 136 miles from A to C.

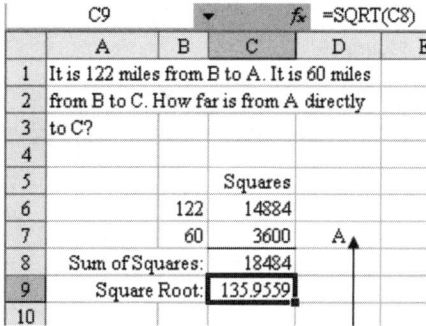

Figure 24

Taking a square root using SQRT

C9 =SQRT(C8)

	A	B	C	D	E
1	It is 122 miles from B to A. It is 60 miles				
2	from B to C. How far is from A directly				
3	to C?				
4					
5			Squares		
6		122	14884		
7		60	3600	A	
8	Sum of Squares:		18484		
9	Square Root:		135.9559		
10					

At some point in the future, much later than eighth grade, your students may learn that taking the square root of a number is the same as raising the number to the one-half (1/2) power.

Thus, the alternate formula for C9 is =C8^(1/2), as shown in Figure 25.

Figure 25

Taking a square root using exponents

C9 =C8^(1/2)

	A	B	C	D
1	It is 122 miles from B to A. It is 60 miles			
2	from B to C. How far is from A directly			
3	to C?			
4				
5			Squares	
6		122	14884	
7		60	3600	A
8	Sum of Squares:		18484	
9	Square Root:		135.9559	
10				

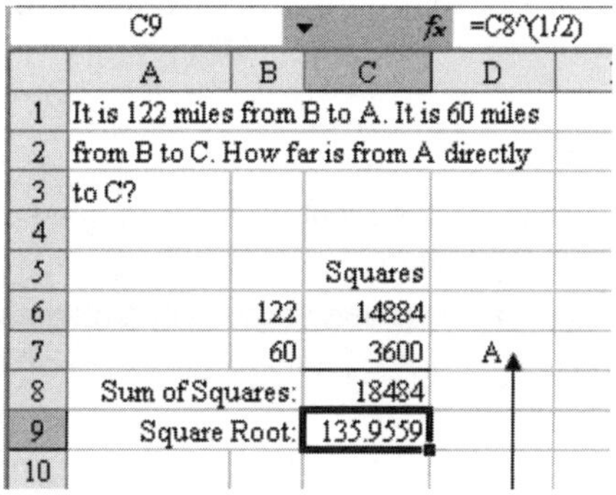

In the next problem, the student is to determine the volume of a cube that is 25 feet on each side. The volume is the length raised to the third power. Again, the carat is used for an exponent.

Calculation Basics

To raise B6 to the third power, use =B6^3.

Figure 26

Raising to the third power using a carat

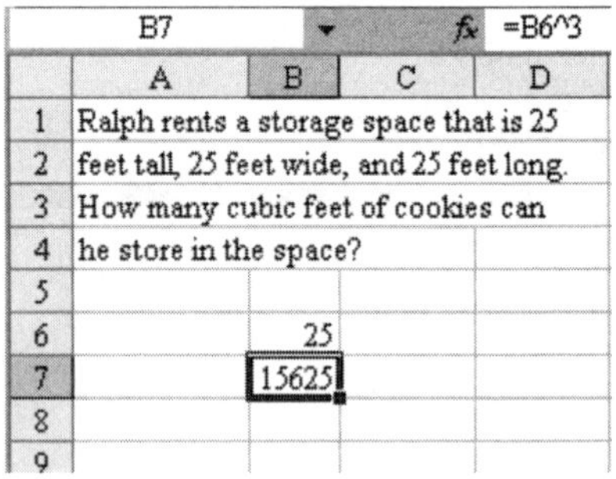

The converse problem is trickier. In the following problem, the student would have to take the cube root of 3375. Excel does not offer a Cube Root function like the SQRT function for square roots.

Thus, your student is going to have to use the alternative form of =B5^(1/3) in order to take a cube root. This may be confusing for the student, but it is easier than figuring out cube roots by hand!

Figure 27

Taking a cube root using a carat and a fraction

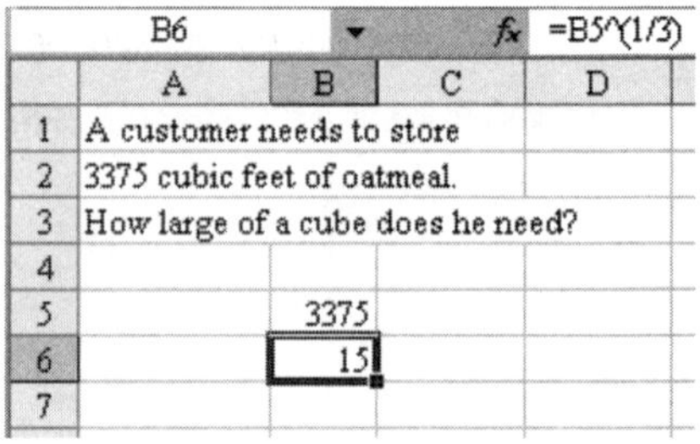

Calculation Basics

Adding a Column of Numbers

Consider the problem in the next image. You might be tempted to use a very long formula such as =B5+B6+B7+B8+B9+B10+B11 to calculate the total.

Figure 28

Adding a column of numbers

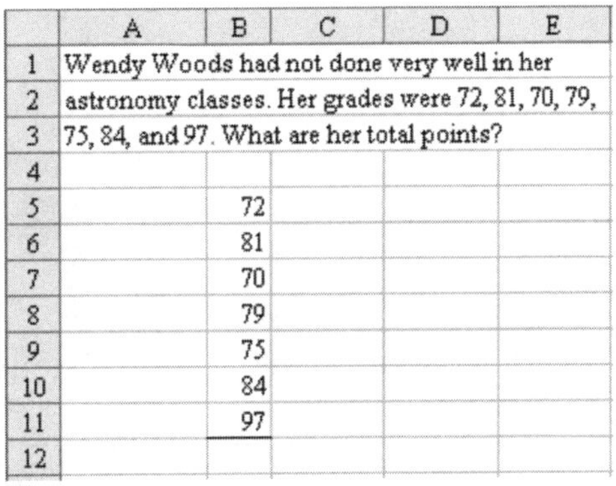

	A	B	C	D	E
1	Wendy Woods had not done very well in her				
2	astronomy classes. Her grades were 72, 81, 70, 79,				
3	75, 84, and 97. What are her total points?				
4					
5		72			
6		81			
7		70			
8		79			
9		75			
10		84			
11		97			
12					

There is a much faster way. Excel offers a SUM function for totaling several cells. Because summing a column of numbers is such a popular task among accountants, Microsoft provided a shortcut key to enter sums.

1. Locate the AutoSum button.
   Place the cellpointer in cell B12. Look on the Standard toolbar for a Greek letter Sigma (Σ). This is the AutoSum button. See Figure 29 below.

Figure 29

AutoSum button shortcut for summing cells

2. Select the range to sum.
   With the cellpointer in B12, press the AutoSum button. Excel will use its IntelliSense and propose a formula to sum the range from B5:B11. The program even draws a flashing box around the range that it is proposing to sum.

Calculation Basics

Calculation Basics

Figure 30

Proposed range to sum

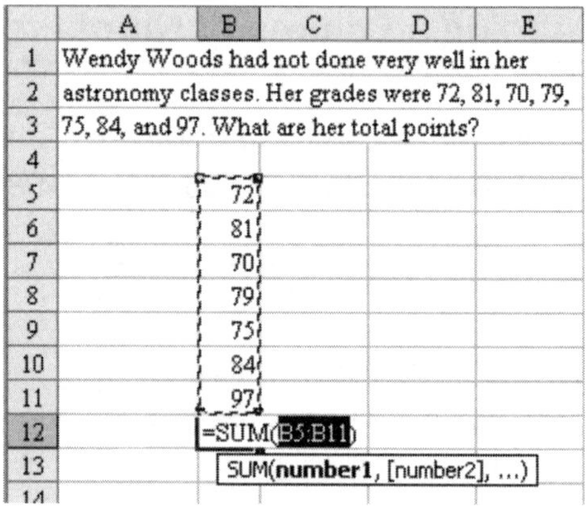

	A	B	C	D	E
1	Wendy Woods had not done very well in her				
2	astronomy classes. Her grades were 72, 81, 70, 79,				
3	75, 84, and 97. What are her total points?				
4					
5		72			
6		81			
7		70			
8		79			
9		75			
10		84			
11		97			
12		=SUM(B5:B11)			
13		SUM(**number1**, [number2], ...)			
14					

3. This is the correct range, so simply type Enter to sum this column.

Figure 31

Summing of a column of numbers

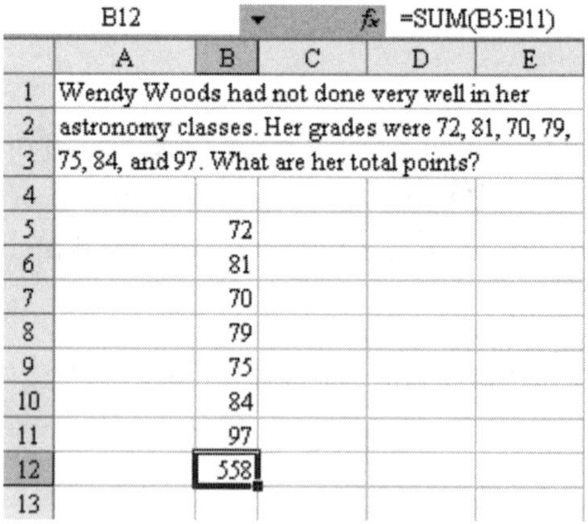

B12　　　　　ƒx　=SUM(B5:B11)

	A	B	C	D	E
1	Wendy Woods had not done very well in her				
2	astronomy classes. Her grades were 72, 81, 70, 79,				
3	75, 84, and 97. What are her total points?				
4					
5		72			
6		81			
7		70			
8		79			
9		75			
10		84			
11		97			
12		558			
13					

Calculating an Average

In the next problem, you need to figure out the average of a column of numbers.

Figure 32

Taking the average of a column of numbers

	A	B	C	D	E
1	Wendy Woods had not done very well in her				
2	astronomy classes. Her grades were 72, 81, 70, 79,				
3	75, 84, and 97. What is her average score?				
4					
5		72			
6		81			
7		70			
8		79			
9		75			
10		84			
11		97			
12					

Take a look at the AutoSum button in Figure 33. To the right of the button is a dropdown arrow. This dropdown arrow will allow you to quickly enter formulas that will let you Average, Count, and find the smallest or largest value.

Put the cellpointer in B12. Select the dropdown arrow next to the AutoSum button and choose Average.

Figure 33

Selecting Average from the AutoSum dropdown menu

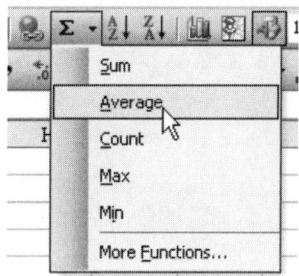

The result: Excel will enter a formula using the **AVERAGE** function to calculate the average.

Calculation Basics

Calculation Basics

Figure 34

Finding the Average of a column of numbers

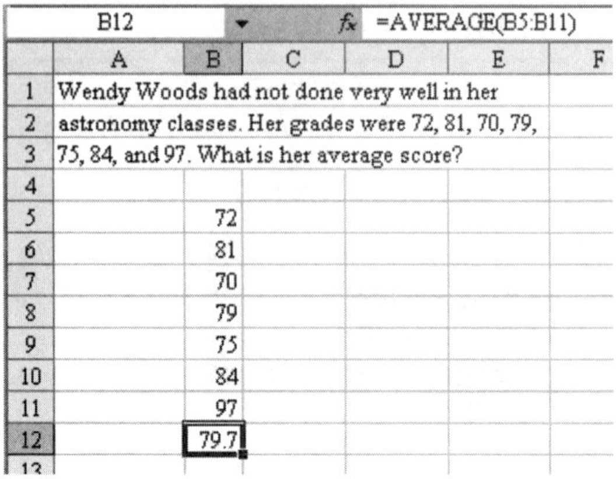

	A	B	C	D	E	F
		B12		f_x =AVERAGE(B5:B11)		
1	Wendy Woods had not done very well in her					
2	astronomy classes. Her grades were 72, 81, 70, 79,					
3	75, 84, and 97. What is her average score?					
4						
5		72				
6		81				
7		70				
8		79				
9		75				
10		84				
11		97				
12		79.7				
13						

Excel for the Math Classroom

Printing Grid Paper

Opportunity

You need some grid paper for math class or for mapping or for art class. You realize that you have run out of grid paper in your supply cabinet. The school doesn't have any. Or – you have grid paper with five squares per inch, but you need grid paper with two squares per inch for your younger students.

Solution and Overview

By its nature, Excel is the world's largest sheet of grid paper. With 256 columns and 65,536 rows, it is fairly easy to convert a blank Excel spreadsheet into a printed sheet of grid paper.

Creating the Solution

The main problem is that Excel's cells are rectangular instead of square. This is fairly easy to resolve.

1. Adjust the row height.
   Open a blank Excel worksheet. To the left of cell A1 is a gray box with the row number 1 in it. Below the number for row 1 is another gray box with the number 2 in it.

   a. Hover your mouse pointer over the line between the gray 1 and the gray 2. When your mouse is in the right position, the mouse pointer will change to a horizontal line with arrows pointing up and down as shown below.

Printing Grid Paper

Printing Grid Paper

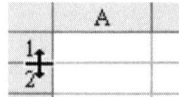

Figure 35

Mouse pointer with vertical arrows indicates that you are ready to change the row height

b. When the mouse pointer looks like the one in the figure above, left-click the mouse without moving it up or down. A tooltip appears showing that your rows have a height of 12.75, which corresponds to 17 pixels. You will want to remember the 17 pixels figure. (This will be different on each computer, based on your default font).

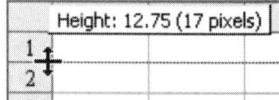

Figure 36

Finding row height in pixels

2. Next, you will want to adjust all of the columns to be 17 pixels wide. There is an easy way to do this. To select all of the cells on the worksheet, click the gray box above and to the left of cell A1. This will highlight the entire spreadsheet.

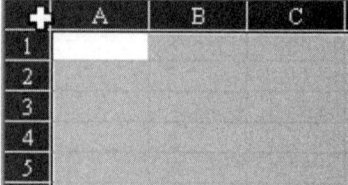

Figure 37

Selecting the entire spreadsheet

a. Position the mouse between the gray A column header and the gray B column header. When the mouse is resting just on the line between the A header and the B header, the cursor will change to a vertical line with arrows pointing left and right.

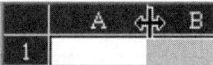

Figure 38

Mousepointer indicates that you are ready to change the column width

b. When the mouse pointer looks like the figure above, left-click the mouse and slowly drag to the left. The tooltip will show that you are starting at 56 pixels.

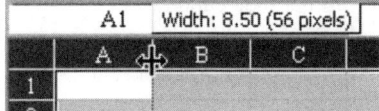

Figure 39

Starting to change column width

c. As you drag to the left, the width of the column will narrow. When you have reached 17 pixels, release the mouse button.

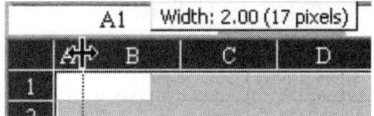

Figure 40

Stop dragging when column width is equal to row height

Because you selected all of the cells, changing the width of column A will change the width of all columns. You have now created cells that are perfectly square.

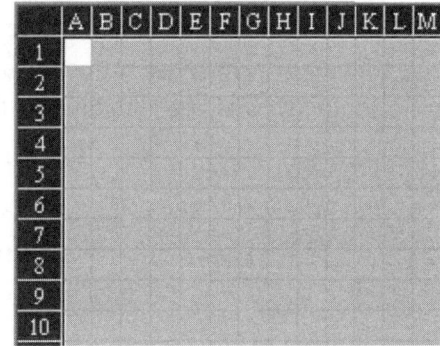

Figure 41

Spreadsheet filled with square cells, 17 pixels on a side

Printing Grid Paper

Using the Application

Printing Grid Paper

Even though you will be drawing gridlines, Excel expects there to be something inside of the cells. When you later try to print or use Print Preview, Excel will complain that there is nothing to print.

Figure 42

Prompt indicating nothing to print

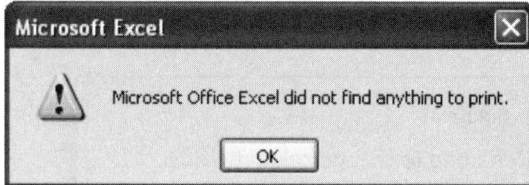

To prevent this objection from Excel, enter a single spacebar character in cell A1 of the spreadsheet.

Adding Gridlines

In order to print the grid paper, you will have to either turn on gridlines or add borders to the cells. It is easier to turn on gridlines (see Formatting with Gridlines on page 26) but you have more control when you use borders.

Formatting with Cell Borders

1. Open the Format Cells dialog box.
   While you have all cells selected, type Ctrl+1 (in case it is hard to read in this font, that is the numeric "one" key while you are holding down the Ctrl key). Ctrl+1 is the shortcut to display the Format Cells dialog box.

2. Format the border.
   The Format Cells dialog has six tabs across the top. Choose the Border tab.

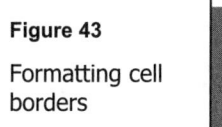

Figure 43

Formatting cell borders

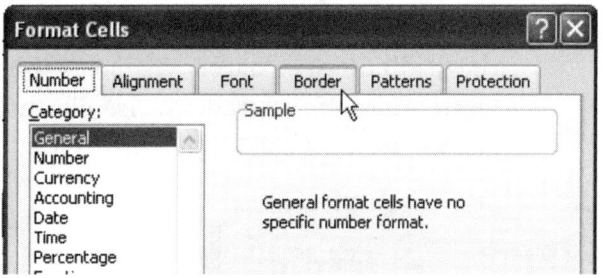

Printing Grid Paper

 Note:

As shown in the next figure, the Border tab of the Format Cells dialog contains three sections. Be sure to make selections in the Line section on the right before touching anything in the Presets or Borders sections.

Figure 44

Border tab options

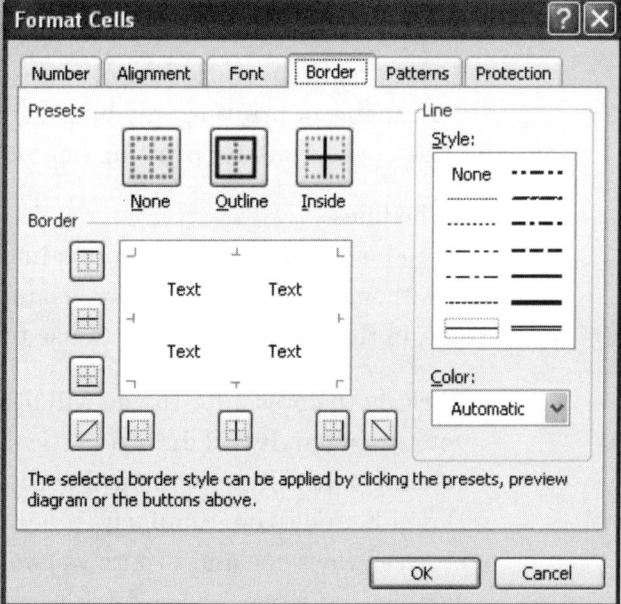

a. Choose the Line Style.
The Line section offers 15 different line styles. You can choose to use the default thin solid line (the last choice in the left column), or any of the dotted line styles.
You choice will depend on the project.

Excel for the Math Classroom 23

If your students are drawing a floor plan of their room, you might want the gridlines to be barely visible. A thin dotted line might be the most appropriate. If the students are plotting points on an XY coordinate, you might want solid lines throughout.

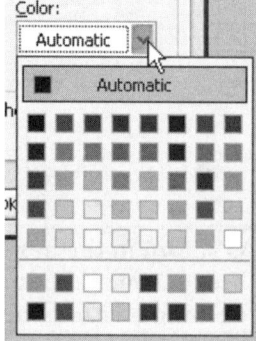

Figure 45

Color dropdown menu

b. Set the line color.

    The Color dropdown offers 56 colors. If your classroom has a laser printer capable of printing only black, then one of the three gray options might be appropriate for printing lighter lines.

c. Draw the lines.

    Once you have selected a color and a line weight, it is time to draw the lines. Although the Border section would let you draw any combination of lines, in this case it is easiest to use the Presets section.

    i. Clicking the preset for Inside will draw borders between all cells in your selection. It will draw a vertical border between column A and column B. It will draw vertical borders between B and C, C and D, D and E, and so on. Similarly, it will draw horizontal borders between rows one and two, rows two and three, rows three and four, rows four and five, and so forth.

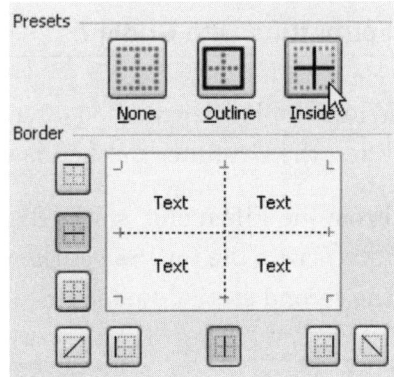

Figure 46

Using the Inside Preset icon

ii. The Inside preset will not draw the border around the outside of the selection. So, you will not have a vertical border to the left of A or a horizontal border above row 1. To draw the border around the outside of the selection, choose the Outline preset icon. This will complete the grid paper.

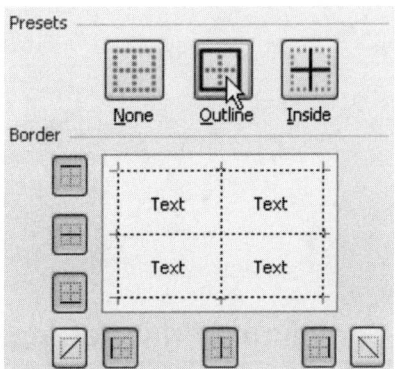

Figure 47

Using the Outline Preset icon

d. Choose OK to close the Format Cells dialog.

Printing Grid Paper

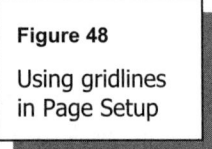
Printing Grid Paper

Formatting with Gridlines

While the Border method offers control over the line weight and color of the lines, the Gridlines method is simpler for basic grid paper.

From the File menu, select Page Setup. In the Page Setup dialog, there are four tabs across the top. Select the right-most tab called Sheet. On the Sheet tab, in the second section under Print, click the checkbox for Gridlines.

Figure 48

Using gridlines in Page Setup

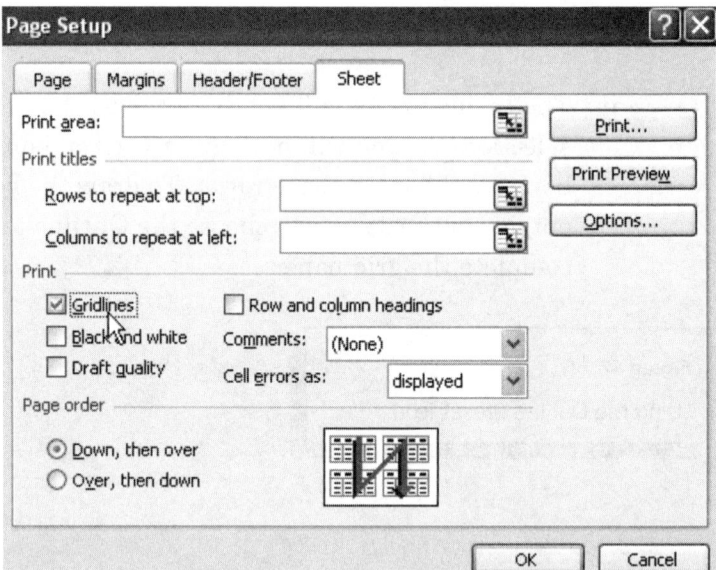

Configuring Print Settings

Whether you used the Gridlines option or Borders, you will want to make some settings to the Page Setup to maximize the printed area on the page.

1. Set the margins.
   From the menu, select File → Page Setup. On the Page Setup dialog, choose the Margins tab. The default margins on the page might be one inch at the top and bottom, three-fourths of an inch on the left and right.

Printing Grid Paper

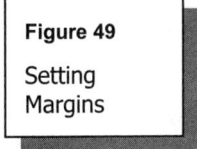

Figure 49

Setting Margins

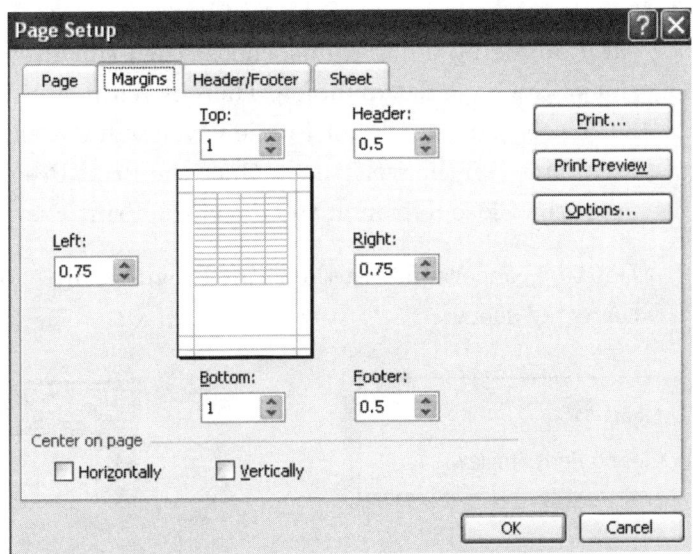

Click the down arrow on the spin buttons to change the top, bottom, left, and right margins to 0.25.

Figure 50

Changing default margin settings

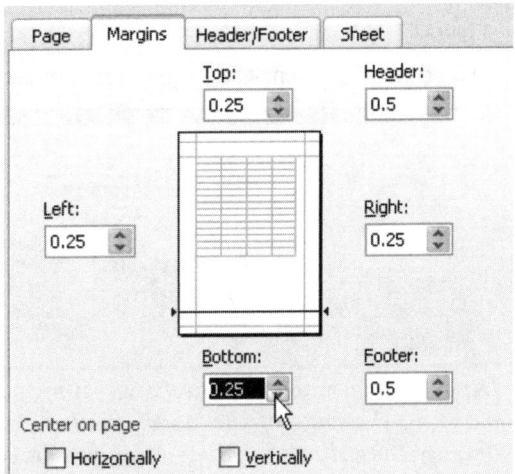

Printing Grid Paper

2. Locate the boundaries of the first page.

   After adjusting the margins, choose the Print Preview button on the right side of the Page Setup dialog. There is really nothing for you to preview, but by choosing the Print Preview, you will force Excel to draw in the page break lines on the worksheet. Once the Print Preview has been displayed, press the Close button at the top of the Print Preview window.

   Don't be concerned that the Print Preview only shows one box. This will be corrected soon.

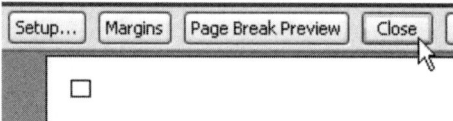

Figure 51

Closing Print Preview

   a. In the midst of the gridlines on your worksheet, you will see one vertical line that represents the right edge of the first printed page. On my computer, this line occurs around cell AN.

Figure 52

Dotted vertical line indicates right border of page

 Tip:

Depending on your border settings, it may be impossible to distinguish the darker line marking the edge of the page. In this case, select View → Page Break Preview to display these lines in blue. After you have determined the edge of the page, choose View → Normal to return to Normal mode.

b. If you scroll down several rows, you will eventually see a darker horizontal line around row 59. This is the bottom of the printed page.

Figure 53

Dotted horizontal line shows bottom border of page

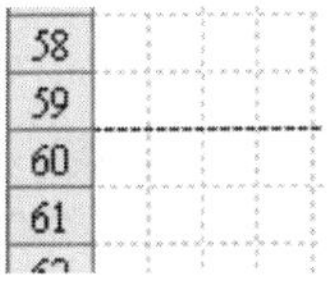

3. Set the print area.
   As mentioned previously, Excel looks at all of these seemingly empty cells and is not sure why you would want to print them. You need to explicitly tell Excel to print the entire page of borders.

   a. In the preceding images, the last cell on the first page is AN59. Earlier in this section, you entered a single spacebar character in cell A1. Now, you need to select cell AN59 and enter a single spacebar in that cell.

   b. Finally, make sure that you don't print more than one page. Click in cell AN59 and drag up to cell A1 to select the range of A1:AN59. With this range selected, go to the File menu and select Print Area → Set Print Area.

Printing Grid Paper

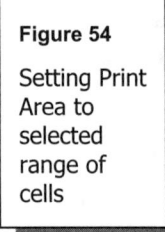

Figure 54

Setting Print Area to selected range of cells

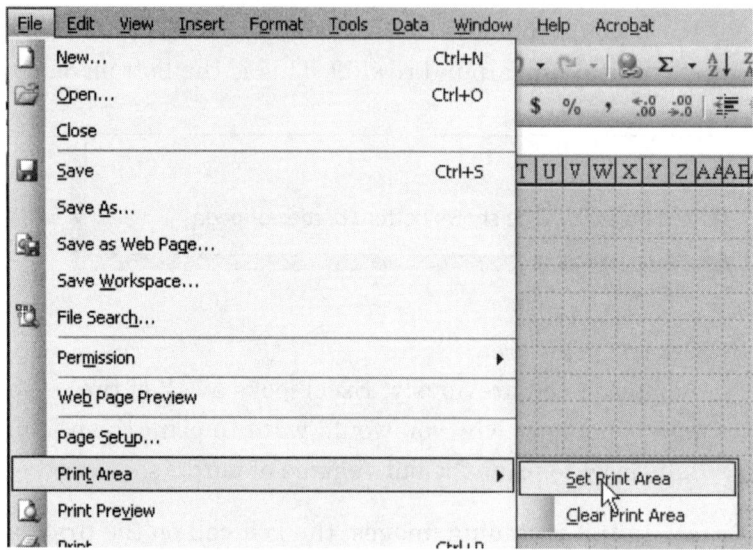

Saving the Document

Use File → Save As to save the document as Gridpaper.xls. This makes sense, because you will certainly need to use grid paper again throughout the year or next year and you wouldn't want to have to repeat these steps again.

Printing the Grid Paper

You probably know that you can print a single copy of the worksheet by using the Printer icon in the Standard toolbar. But what if you want to print 25 copies? Rather than clicking the Printer icon 25 times, just tell Excel to print 25 copies at once.

1. From the menu, select File → Print to display the Print dialog.

Printing Grid Paper

Figure 55

Selecting desired number of copies

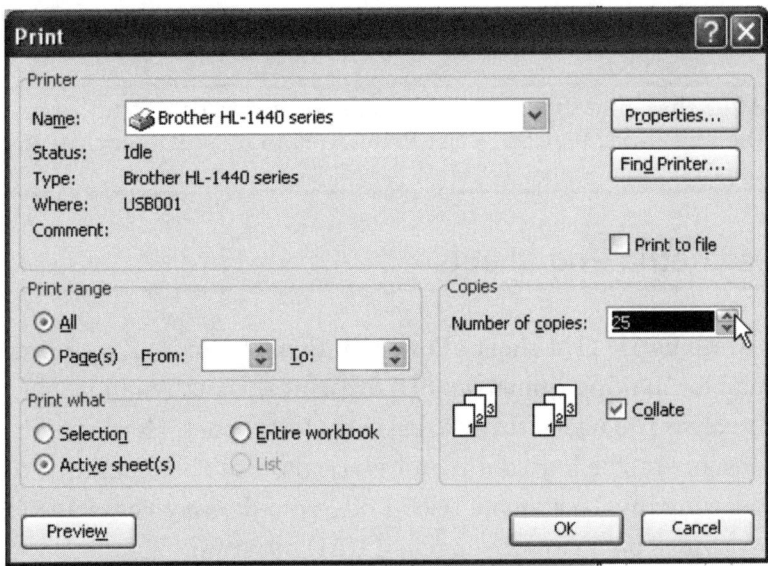

2. Click and hold the upward-pointing part of the spin button near the Copies setting until you have specified the correct number of copies. You can also select the number block and type in the desired number of copies.

3. Click OK to print 25 copies of the grid paper.

Excel Extras

Use the following instructions to modify your grid paper.

Making Larger Grids

The instructions above will create grid paper with approximately five squares per inch. For younger students, you might wish to create grid paper with larger grids. Select all of the cells and adjust the row height and column width to about 48 pixels. This will produce squares that are approximately half an inch square.

Note:

After changing the grid size, it is important to do a Print Preview, and then adjust the File → Print Area → Set Print Area to include just the range that will fit on the first page.

Isometric Grid Sheets

An isometric grid sheet allows you to make an XYZ coordinate grid or a sketch pad for making isometric (3D) drawings. Usually, an isometric drawing involves the use of three axes, each 120° apart. However, the grids in Excel are designed to be horizontal and vertical only. The technique to make this type of drawing involves an old trick I discovered many years ago for doing 3D drawings on a two-dimensional CAD program.

You will need to set up row and column sizes so that the diagonal distance across a cell is twice the row height. This will mean that the area inside of a cell is made from two 30-60-90 right triangles. Remember that the hypotenuse of such a triangle (the diagonal of the cell) is twice the length of the smallest leg (the height of the cell). In isometric drawings, the length and depth of an object are laid out along two lines drawn at 30° to the horizon. You won't be able to get this exactly, but a row height of 15 pixels and a column width of 26 pixels will give a diagonal length of 30.0167, which is close enough for sketching purposes!

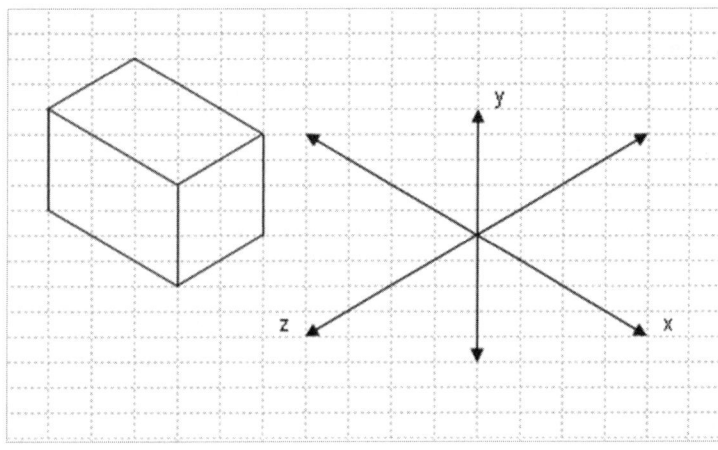

Figure 56

Isometric grids are useful for 3D drawings

1. Set the row height.
   Using the techniques in making the original grid paper, highlight columns A through AB and change the width to 26 pixels. Highlight rows 1 through 67, and change the height to 15 pixels.

2. Format the borders.
   Highlight cells A1 through AB67. Press Ctrl+1 and select Border. On the right side, you have a choice of line styles and color. Under Style, select one of the dashed lines. (With my printer, the second one down on the left side gave me the look I wanted.)

   Next, click on the down arrow next to the word Automatic, and select the lightest gray color, which should be Gray 25%. When the box closes, select Outline and Inside from the Presets at the top of the dialog box, and then click OK. *Do not click anywhere on the worksheet.*

Printing Grid Paper

Printing Grid Paper

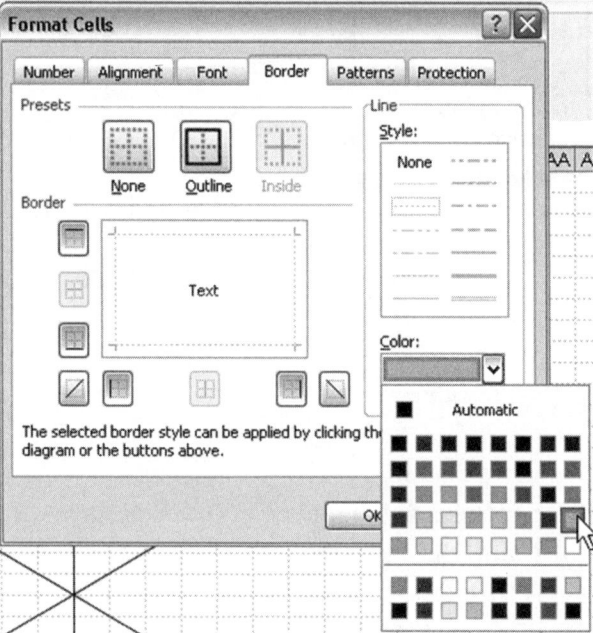

Figure 57

Selecting border placement and color

3. Set the print area.
   With the grid area still selected, click on File → Print Area → Select Print Area.

4. Set the margins.
   Select File → Page Setup → Margins. Set all four margins for the minimum margin your printer allows. (On mine, that's .25.) Now, click Print Preview to see if the entire grid will fit on one sheet of paper.

   The idea is to make the grid as large as possible without running off the edges. Make adjustments by deleting rows and/or columns from the center of the grid. If the grid is too small, add rows or columns, again from the center, to maintain the row/column size and the grid color. When it looks right, print out a sample, and then save your worksheet as Isometric Grid.

 Note:

One horizontal unit on the paper is approximately equal to two diagonal units. With a little practice, you and your students will be sketching geometric solids with ease.

Cartesian Coordinate Grids

Opportunity

There are times when you need a few sheets of grid paper for sketching or graphing activities, or times when you would like to be able to insert a small Cartesian coordinate grid into a test or quiz written in Word. There are all sizes and types available in books and workbooks, but cutting them out and taping them to a document before printing is a big hassle. You may also want a handout sheet with the same size grids on them for homework assignments.

Solution and Overview

By adjusting row and column widths and using borders, you can create any size grid you want, up to a full page. And, by using the drawing tools, you can create a grid with arrows on the x- and y-axes, or add points or lines to the grid. You can then copy and paste these grids into a Word document.

You will make a small 16 x 16 grid, with arrows on the ends of the x-axis and the y-axis.

Creating the Solution

1. Set the column width so that it is the same as the row height.
    Start with a blank Excel worksheet. Move your mouse cursor on the line between the 1 and 2 in the row headings until it changes into a plus sign with horizontal arrows. See Figure 58 on the following page. When you left-click your mouse, you will see "Height 12.75 (17 pixels)".

Cartesian Coordinate Grid

Figure 58

Plus sign cursor with vertical arrows indicates that you are ready to change the row height

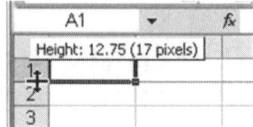

Cartesian Coordinate Grids

Click on the gray box with the A in it at the top of column A. Left-click and drag to the right, and watch as Excel counts the columns for you (1C, 2C, etc). When the count reaches 16C (column P), stop.

2. Set the row height.
Now, move your cursor to the line between A and B in the column headings until it changes into a plus sign with vertical arrows. You will see "Width: 8.43 (64 pixels)". Click on the plus sign and drag to the left until it reads "Width: 1.71 (17 pixels)". All of the highlighted columns will now have the same width.

Figure 59

Setting columns to the same width

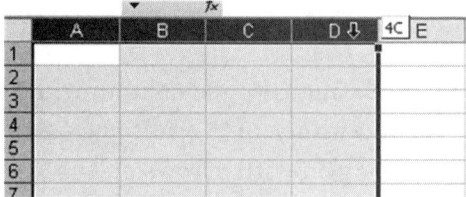

3. Select the grid area.
Place your cursor in cell A1. Click and drag to highlight over to column P and down to row 16.

4. Format the grid area.
Press Ctrl+1 (that's the Ctrl key and the number 1) to access the Format Cells dialog box; select the Border tab. On the right side of the dialog box, under Style, make sure that the bottom line in the left column is highlighted. Now, at the top, under Presets, click on Outline and Inside, and then click OK. You now have a basic coordinate grid that measures from −8 to +8 along both the x- and y-axes.

Figure 60

Selecting border presets for Cartesian coordinate grid

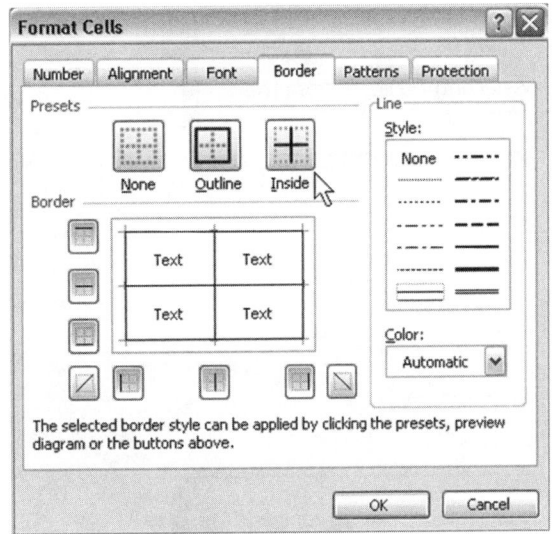

5. Prepare to draw the axes.

   To make the axes more visible, you will use Excel's Drawing tools.

   a. First however, zoom in a bit so you can see what you are doing. Select View from the drop down menus, and then Zoom. Click on 200%, and then OK.

Figure 61

Increasing magnification to make drawing easier

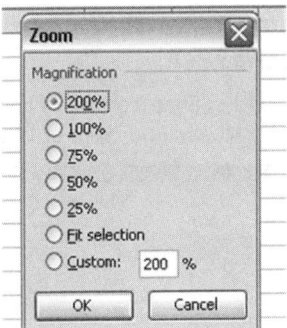

   b. If the Drawing toolbar is not visible, select Toolbars from View and click on Drawing. The Drawing toolbar will now be visible at the bottom of the screen.

Excel for the Math Classroom

Cartesian Coordinate Grid

Cartesian Coordinate Grids

Figure 63

Selecting Toolbars from the View menu

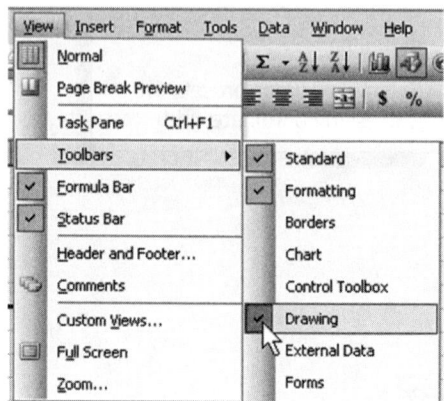

Figure 62 Drawing toolbar

c. On the Drawing toolbar, click on the word Draw on the left end, and then click on Snap. Next select To Grid. This will make all lines start and end in line with the worksheet grid.

Figure 64

Using Snap To Grid to line up start and end point of lines

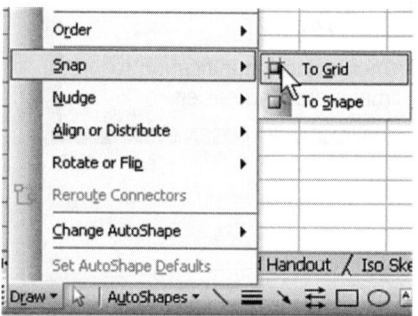

38   *Excel for the Math Classroom*

Cartesian Coordinate Grids

6. Draw the x-axis.

    Click on the word AutoShapes, select Lines, and then click on the double arrow line. Your cursor should now be a small plus sign. Move the cursor to cell A8, click on the bottom line of the cell, drag to cell P8, and let go. You should now have a double arrow line to indicate the x-axis. Change the line thickness by clicking on the Line Style icon on the Drawing toolbar (three horizontal lines) and select 1½ point.

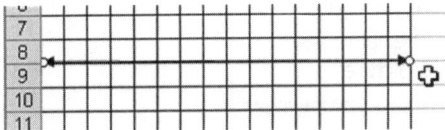

Figure 65

Selecting double arrow line format

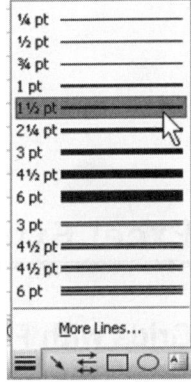

Figure 66

Selecting line thickness

7. Draw the y-axis.

    Repeat Step 6, except start the arrow at the right edge of cell H1 and drag down to H16. Click anywhere off the grid to turn off Drawing tools.

8. Select View from the drop down menus, and then Zoom. Click on 100%, and then OK. Save your worksheet as Coordinate Grid.

Cartesian Coordinate Grid

Using the Application

Cartesian Coordinate Grids

To insert this graph into a Word document, highlight cells A1:P16, and select Edit → Copy (shortcut: Ctrl+C). Move to your Word document. Select Edit → Paste Special → Picture (Windows Metafile). Excel will insert the grid into your Word document. It is now technically a picture, so you can move or resize it within the document. Just be sure to resize using one of the corner diagonal arrows to retain the correct proportions. And, as with any picture, you can have Word align text to the left, right, or around your coordinate grid.

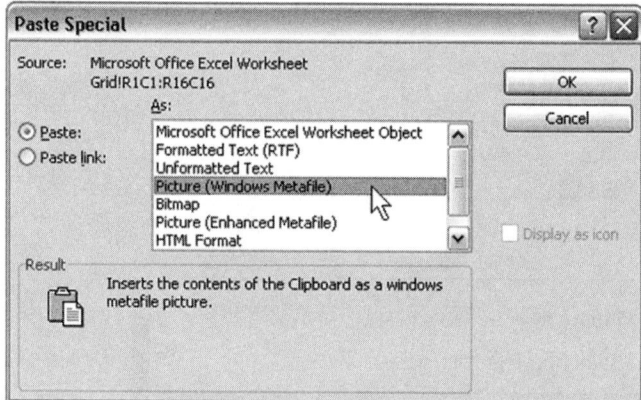

Figure 67

Using Paste Special to insert a picture

Excel Extras

Grids with Points or Lines

If you want to get fancy, you can also use the Drawing tools to place points or lines on the graph before inserting it into Word. For lines, use the same process that you used to place the axes on the grid. For points, use the Oval tool to make a small circle.

1. Draw a small circle.
   First, turn off Snap To Grid, or you won't be able to make a circle smaller

than the cell you start in. Next, click on the Oval icon in the Drawing toolbar (right next to the rectangle). Click anywhere on your grid, keep the left mouse button down, and drag around.

2. Adjust the size of the circle.
    By adjusting the size of the two axes, you can make a very small circle. It does eventually reach a minimum size, which should be about right.
    If you are having difficulty seeing what you are doing, use View and Zoom to adjust the screen to 200%. When the circle is the right size, release the mouse button and you will have a small circle surrounded by four circular grab handles.

3. Add color to the circle.
    Use the Fill Color tool to make the dot black instead of transparent. Find the Paint Bucket icon in the Drawing toolbar. If it has a bar of black underneath it, simply click on it and the circle you just made will turn black. If it is some other color, click on the small arrow to the right of the paint bucket to select black from the color palette.

Figure 68 Selecting shape and fill color of a dot

4. Move the circle into place and label.
    Move your cursor over the black circle. When it changes to a plus sign with four arrows, left click and move your point to where you want it on the grid. Click on one of the cells near it, and type in a letter to label it. If you want, keep the dot off to the side of your grid before saving. Then, by using copy and paste, you can make as many circles as you need for a particular Word document.

Cartesian Coordinate Grid

Handout Sheet

To make a handout sheet with six grids per side, do the following:

1. Select and copy the grid.
   Highlight the grid, and copy it by pressing Ctrl+C. Click on cell A18 and press Ctrl+V (paste); then click on cell A35 and press Ctrl+V.

2. Copy and paste the first column of the grid.
   Highlight all three grids on the left, and press Ctrl+C. Click on cell R1, and press Ctrl+V.

3. Set the column width.
   Unfortunately, using copy and paste does not adjust column width. However, you can copy column widths using Paste Special. Once again, highlight the three grids in the first column and press Ctrl+C. Click on cell R1. From the drop down menu, select Edit → Paste Special → Column Width and press Enter.

4. Highlight all six grids, and then select File → Print Area → Set Print Area.

5. Adjust the margins to fit.
   From File → Page Setup → Margins, adjust all the margins to .5", and center both horizontally and vertically. Click on Print Preview, and see what you have. Depending on your specific printer, this should work, but you may want to adjust margin spacing, or the amount of space between the grids on the worksheet.

Cartesian Coordinate Grids

Figure 69

Grid Handout with six grids per side

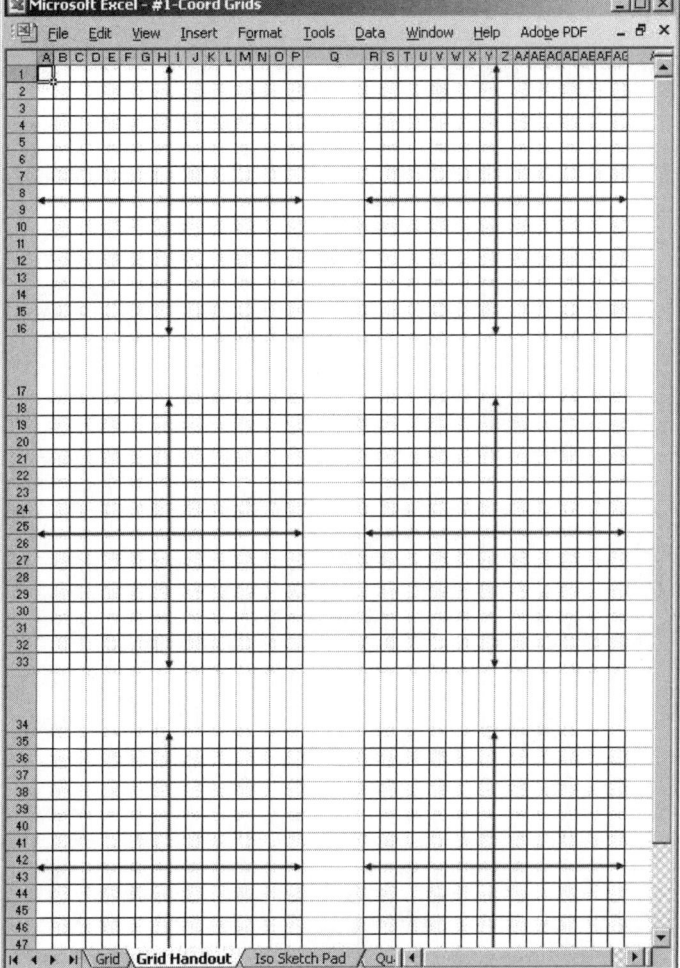

Cartesian Coordinate Grids

Excel for the Math Classroom 43

Cartesian Coordinate Grid

Cartesian Coordinate Grids

Multiplication Tables

Opportunity

Bill Jelen's classic example for demonstrating the various types of mixed references is to create a multiplication table. Although you probably have access to a multiplication table that you can photocopy, this exercise will demonstrate both the AutoFill option and how to use mixed cell references.

Solution and Overview

You will use some efficient tools to create the multiplication table. AutoFill lets you type the first few cells in a series and then extend the series. Transpose lets you turn a range on its side. Finally, you will build one formula that handles the entire multiplication table.

Creating the Solution

This process involves two operations:

- Extending a series using the fill handle
- Transposing a range by copying it on its side

Using the Fill Handle to Extend a Series

1. Start with a blank Excel workbook. Leave cell A1 blank.

2. Enter the first two elements of a series.
   In cells A2 and A3, type the numbers "1" and "2". Select a range containing both cells. In the lower right corner of the selection, there is a square dot known as the Fill Handle. With the mouse, grab the fill handle and drag down to row 13.

Figure 70

Selecting the fill handle

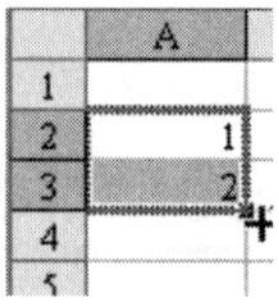

3. Extend the series.
   As you drag, a tooltip appears showing the numbers that will be entered in the last cell. When you get to row 13, the tooltip indicates that the series will extend to 12. Release the mouse button to enter 1 through 12 in the cells.

Copying a Range on its Side

1. Copy the range.
   After using the fill handle, the range of A2:A13 will be selected. Use Ctrl+C to copy that range. Move to cell B1.

2. Transpose the range.
   From the menu, select Edit → Paste Special. In the Paste Special dialog box, choose the checkbox for Transpose. The process of transposing will turn data that goes down a column to data that goes across a row.

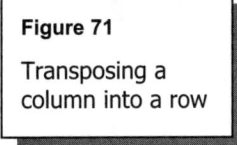

Figure 71

Transposing a column into a row

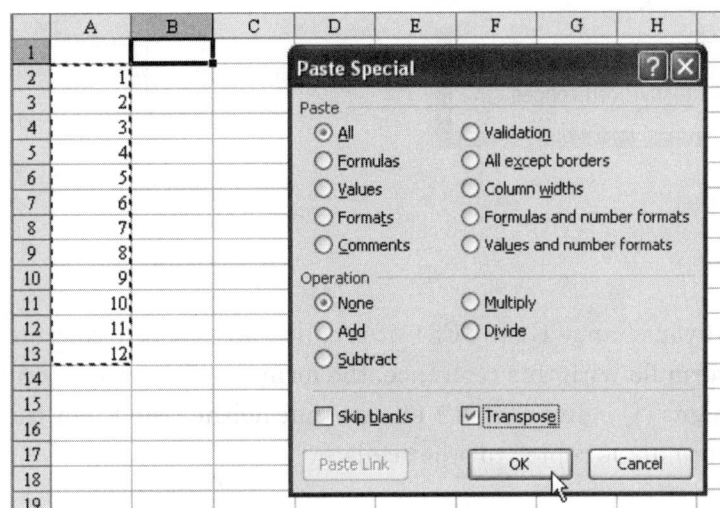

Entering a Single Formula for Many Cells

With a little thought, you can usually write one formula that can be copied to many cells. If you think about the formula that is needed to populate the interior of the multiplication table, you could express it this way:

For any cell, multiply the number found in row 1 above the cell with the number found in column A to the left of the cell.

One such formula would be =C1*A5, as shown in cell C5.

Figure 72

Formula multiplying two cells

While the preceding formula will work just fine in cell C5, it will not work when you copy the formula to any other cell in the table. Figure 73 shows the formula after it has been copied to D6. The reference that used to point to C1 is now pointing to D2. The reference that used to point to A5 is now pointing to B6. This is called a *Relative* reference and it is by design in Excel.

Multiplication Tables

Figure 73

Relative references

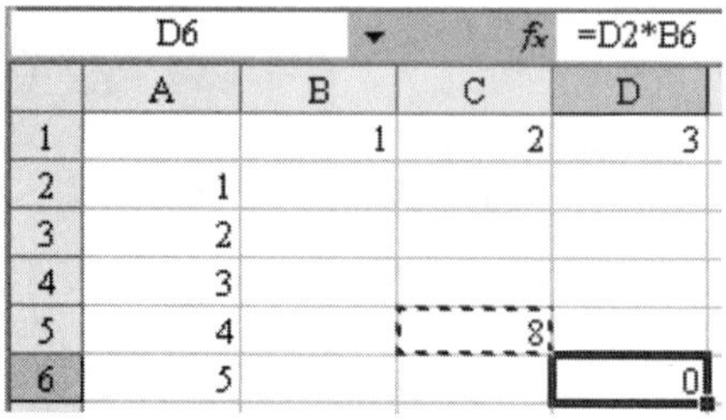

	A	B	C	D
1		1	2	3
2	1			
3	2			
4	3			
5	4			8
6	5			0

D6 — fx =D2*B6

If you change C1 to $C$1, it is called an *Absolute* reference. When you copy a formula with this reference, the formula will always point to cell C1. The dollar signs ($) before C and 1 ensure that neither the C nor the 1 will change as the formula is copied to other cells.

Sometimes, you need a reference that is partially absolute. This is called a *Mixed* reference and has only a single dollar sign.

If you place the dollar sign before the column letter, then the column letter will be fixed but the row number will change as you copy the formula down the rows. In our current example, the portion of the formula pointing at column A would need a dollar sign before the A.

If you place the dollar sign before the row number, then the row number will be fixed, but the column letter will change as you copy the formula across a range. In our current example, the portion of the formula pointing at row 1 would need a dollar sign before the 1.

1. Select the range.
   Move the cellpointer to cell B2. While holding down the Shift key, use the Down- and Right-arrow keys to select the range of B2:M13.

2. Enter the formula.
   Any formula that you type will start to appear in cell B2. Type the following formula: =B$1*$A2

3. Copy the formula throughout the range.
   Then, instead of pressing Enter by itself, type Ctrl+Enter to put a similar formula in the entire selected range.

Figure 74
Mixed references

	A	B	C	D	E	F	G	H	I	J	K	L	M
1		1	2	3	4	5	6	7	8	9	10	11	12
2	1	1	2	3	4	5	6	7	8	9	10	11	12
3	2	2	4	6	8	10	12	14	16	18	20	22	24
4	3	3	6	9	12	15	18	21	24	27	30	33	36
5	4	4	8	12	16	20	24	28	32	36	40	44	48
6	5	5	10	15	20	25	30	35	40	45	50	55	60
7	6	6	12	18	24	30	36	42	48	54	60	66	72
8	7	7	14	21	28	35	42	49	56	63	70	77	84
9	8	8	16	24	32	40	48	56	64	72	80	88	96
10	9	9	18	27	36	45	54	63	72	81	90	99	108
11	10	10	20	30	40	50	60	70	80	90	100	110	120
12	11	11	22	33	44	55	66	77	88	99	110	121	132
13	12	12	24	36	48	60	72	84	96	108	120	132	144

B2 • ƒx =B$1*$A2

Multiplication Tables

Using the Application

Print the sheet out and allow your students to study from it.

Excel Details

Simplifying Dollar Sign Entry in Absolute and Mixed References

The process of entering the dollar signs in a reference can be simplified by using the F4 key. As you are entering the formula, pressing F4 immediately after typing the reference will change the reference from relative to absolute; that is, A2 would change to $A$2. Press F4 again to change to a mixed reference where only the row is held constant – A$2. Press F4 again to change to a reference where only the column is fixed – $A2. Press F4 once more to toggle back to the relative reference of A2.

Thus, the shortcut for entering the formula in B2 is as follows.

1. Type an equals sign.

2. Type the Up-arrow to move to B1.

3. Press F4 twice to lock just the row.

4. Type the Asterisk key on the numeric keypad.

5. Type the Left-arrow to move to A2.

6. Type the F4 key three times to lock just the column number.

More Cool Fill Handle Tricks

At the start of this chapter, you used the fill handle to extend a series starting with 1, 2. The fill handle can automatically enter many types of data in a range of cells.

1. Type "Sep" into a cell. Select the cell. Click on the fill handle and drag down or to the right.

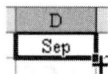

Figure 75 Dragging the fill handle

Excel will automatically fill in months of the year. As you drag, a tooltip will indicate the last month to be filled in. When you release the mouse button, the selected number of months will appear.

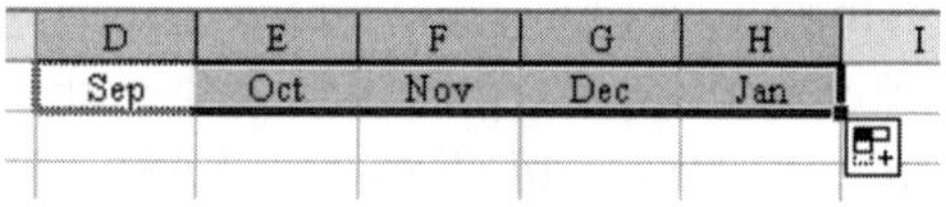

Figure 76

Months filled in automatically

2. Type "1st Period" into a cell, then select the cell and drag the fill handle; Excel will type the remaining periods.

Figure 77

Class periods filled in automatically

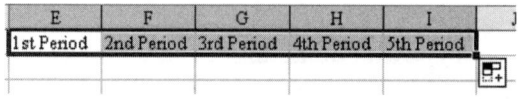

3. There is a neat trick with days or dates. If you type "Monday" into a cell and drag the fill handle, you will get the days of the week.

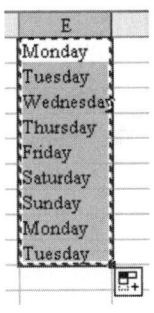

Figure 78
Days of the week filled in automatically

4. As a teacher, though, try this trick. Type "Monday" into a cell. Select the cell. Right-click the fill handle and drag.

Initially, the tooltip shows Tuesday, Wednesday, Thursday, Friday, Saturday, Sunday, etc.. However, when you release the mouse pointer, you are given a drop-down menu. Choose Fill Weekdays.

Figure 79
Selecting Weekdays from Fill dropdown menu

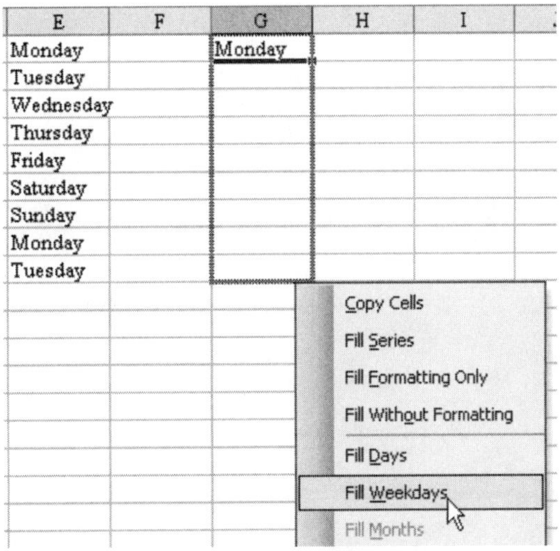

Multiplication Tables

Instead of giving you all the days of the week, Excel will repeat Monday through Friday.

Figure 80

Weekdays filled in automatically

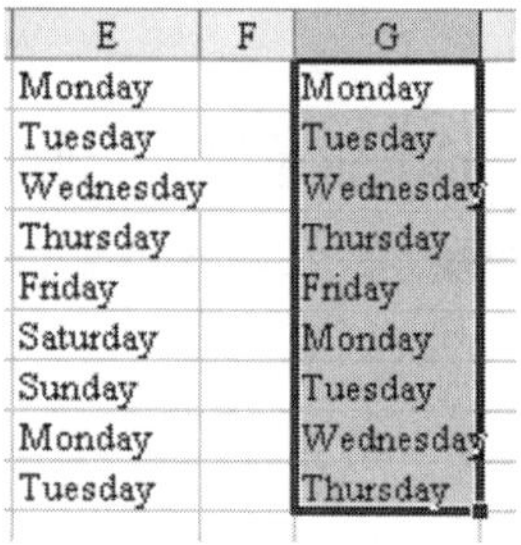

5. The fill handle "right-click and drag trick" also works with dates.

Figure 81

Dates filled in automatically

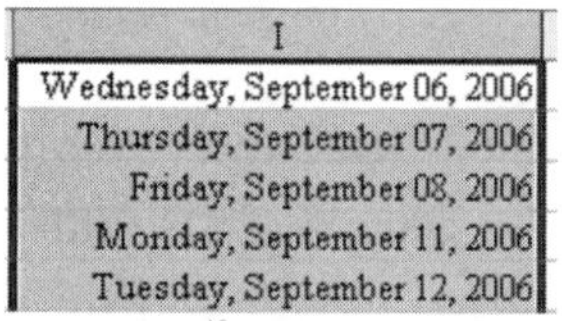

Math Exercise Sheets

Opportunity

You've been using the same math exercise sheets for years. Some of the kids are starting to memorize the answers. Can you use Excel to create new drill sheets for math facts?

Solution and Overview

Excel has a couple of functions to generate random numbers. Using a combination of these functions will produce a fresh exercise sheet every time. You can even create different sheets for each student in the class, avoiding the urge to cheat.

Creating the Solution

Excel offers several hundred different functions ready for use. The program also ships with another 150 obscure functions that you can make available to Excel. As it turns out, this chapter will use the RANDBETWEEN function, which is in that collection of 150 functions.

RANDBETWEEN, the function you will use to generate the random numbers, is not a standard Excel function. It is, however, part of something called the Analysis ToolPak.

This is how to make the Analysis ToolPak available for use on your computer.

1. Open Excel.

2. From the Tools menu, select Add-Ins. When the dialog box opens, click on the boxes next to Analysis ToolPak and Analysis ToolPak – VBA. Click OK to exit.

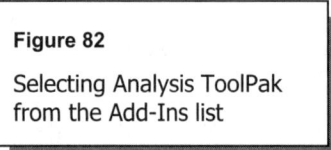

Figure 82

Selecting Analysis ToolPak from the Add-Ins list

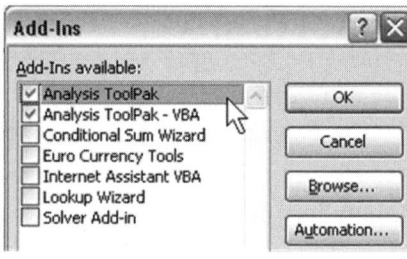

Once you have enabled the Analysis ToolPak, you will be able to use any of the 150 extra functions on that computer.

Basic Math Facts: Adding Two Terms with an Answer Under 10

Say that you want to create a worksheet of addition problems. You want the problems to appear in a large font so that your first graders will have space to write the answer. You would like perhaps 15 different problems on the paper.

You will use the RANDBETWEEN function. To use this function, specify two numbers as arguments in the function and separate the two arguments with a comma. For example, =RANDBETWEEN(1,20) would return a random whole number between 1 and 20, inclusive.

1. Enter the following formula in cell B2: =RANDBETWEEN(1,8)

Figure 83

Finding a random number from 1-8

2. In cell B3, you want to find a random number such that the answer will not exceed 9 – actually, a random number between 0 and (9-B2). Luckily, either

Excel for the Math Classroom

argument in the function can be a reference to another cell instead of a number. To handle any case, enter the following formula in cell B3:
=RANDBETWEEN(0,9-B2)

Figure 84

Finding a random number between 1 and 6

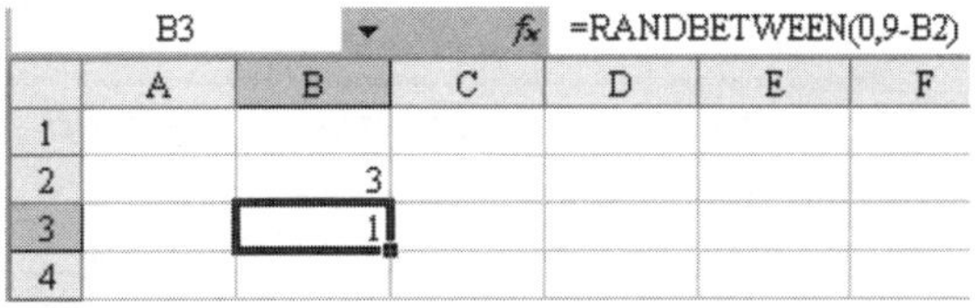

Note:

Every time that you enter a new value or press the F9 key, Excel will recalculate all of the formulas on the worksheet. This includes generating new random numbers. Thus, as you enter the formula in B3, the value in B2 will probably change. To test that the logic is working, press the F9 key several times and you will see that you continually get new problems whose total is less than 10.

3. Add a line under the second term.

   Before making a whole sheet of these problems, take some time to get the first problem correctly formatted. With the cellpointer in B3, choose the bottom border button in the Formatting toolbar.

Figure 85

Adding a line below the second number in an equation

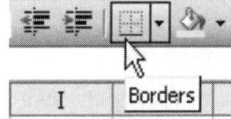

This will add a line across the entire length of the bottom of cell B3. I think using the Borders icon for a bottom border is better than using the Underline icon, which would only extend the underline as far as the digits in the cell.

4. Enter a plus sign to the left of the second term.

   In cell A3, enter a quotation mark and a plus sign. The quotation mark will not appear in the cell, but serves as an indicator to Excel that this is a text entry and that you want the entry to be right-justified.

 Tip:

When you wish to enter numbers or mathematical operators in a cell, you need to either prefix them with an apostrophe for left justification, a quotation mark for right-justification, or a carat for centered.

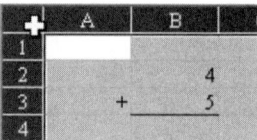

Figure 86

Adding a plus sign to a problem

5. Change the font to a larger size.

   Select all of the cells in the worksheet by clicking the gray box to the left of the "A" heading above column A.

   While all of the cells are selected, choose a large font size such as 24 from the Font Size selector on the Formatting toolbar. This should make the font large enough for your young students to be able to write an answer below the problem.

Figure 87

Increasing the font size

6. Copy and paste the first problem into the first row.
   Now that you have one problem set up, you will want to copy those formulas. Select cells A2 through B3. Type Ctrl+C to copy the cells to the clipboard.

   a. Click in cell D2 and type Ctrl+V to paste the cells from the clipboard.

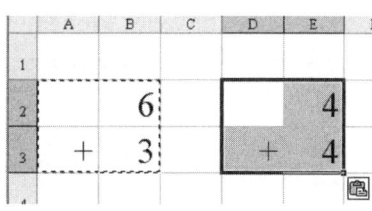

Figure 88

Copying the problem formula

   b. Click in G2 and type Ctrl+V to paste a third column of problems.

7. Copy and paste the first row of problems into subsequent rows.
   Now that you have one complete row of problems set up, select cells A2:H3 and type Ctrl+C to copy the formulas for all three problems.

   a. Click the mouse in A6 and type Ctrl+C to paste three more problems on the worksheet.

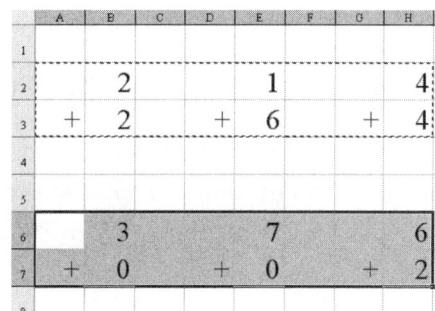

Figure 89

Copying a complete row of formulas

   b. Click in A10 and type Ctrl+V to paste a third row.
      Click in A14 and type Ctrl+V to paste a fourth row.
      Click in A18 to paste a fifth row of problems.

8. Make a place for student signatures.
   In cell A1, type NAME: followed by a long series of underline characters.

Using the Application

Every time that you type the F9 key, you will generate a new set of problems. If you wish to give every student a different problem sheet, you can repeat these steps:

1. Press the F9 key to generate new problems.

2. Choose the Printer icon in the Standard toolbar.

Although it may seem tedious, you can quickly generate 25 different worksheets in only about a minute.

Keeping the Worksheet from Changing

What if you have the perfect set of problems and you want to use these same problems again for a pretest/posttest situation? In this case, you will want to turn off the automatic Excel calculation.

1. From the menu, select Tools → Options. The Options dialog is one of the busiest in Excel, with 13 different tabs.

2. Choose the Calculation tab, usually the second tab along the bottom row. In the Calculation tab, choose the option button for Manual and uncheck the box for Recalculate Before Save.

Math Exercise Sheets

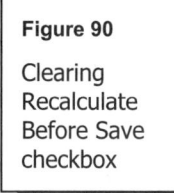

Figure 90

Clearing Recalculate Before Save checkbox

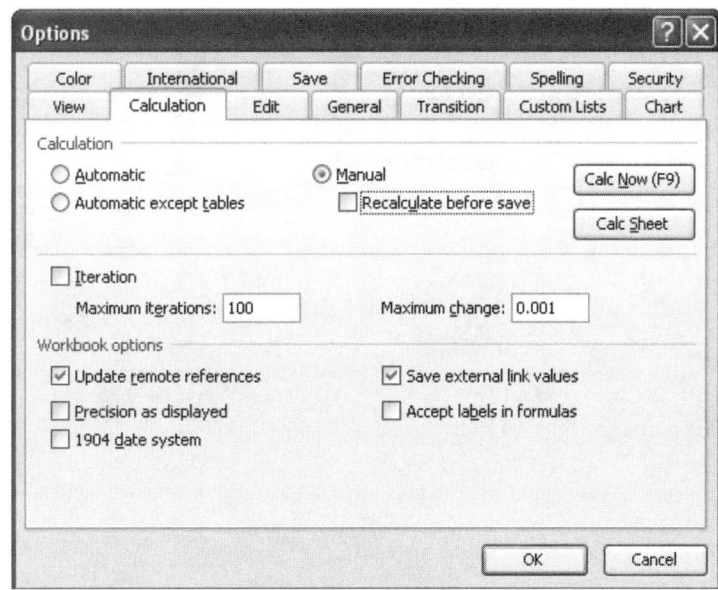

With these calculation settings, the current set of problems will stay constant until you press the F9 key again.

Adapting for Multiplication

Your older students need a sheet of two-digit multiplication problems.

1. The formula for both terms can be =RANDBETWEEN(10,99). For the older students, you might not need a 24 point font; adjust the font to 18.

2. Adjust column width.
   If you make columns A, C, D, F, G, I, J, L, and M narrower, you can fit five problems across the sheet.

3. Insert a blank row between problems.
   The students will need more space between each problem in order to show their work. Put the cellpointer in row 6 and choose Insert → Row from the menu to insert an extra blank row between the problems. You can fit 25 problems on a single page.

Math Exercise Sheets

Figure 91

Adapting the worksheet for multiplication problems

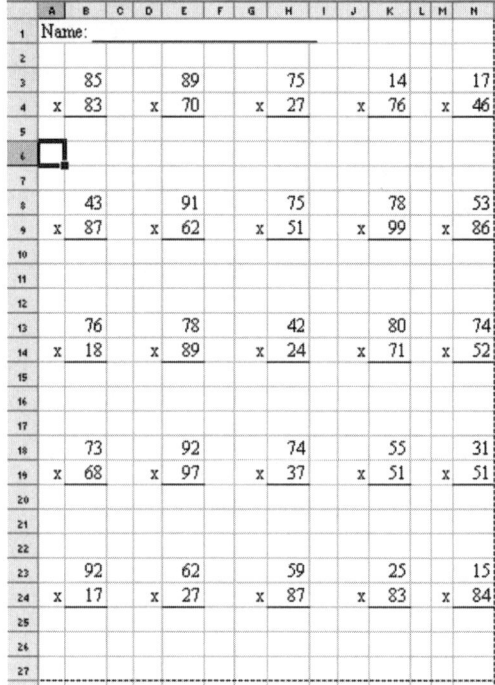

Creating an Answer Key

It would be helpful to have an answer key for the preceding multiplication example. As you enter the first problem, you can set up a formula to produce the answer for the problem.

1. Enter the following formula in cell B5: =B3*B4

Figure 92

Calculating the answer to a multiplication problem

Excel for the Math Classroom

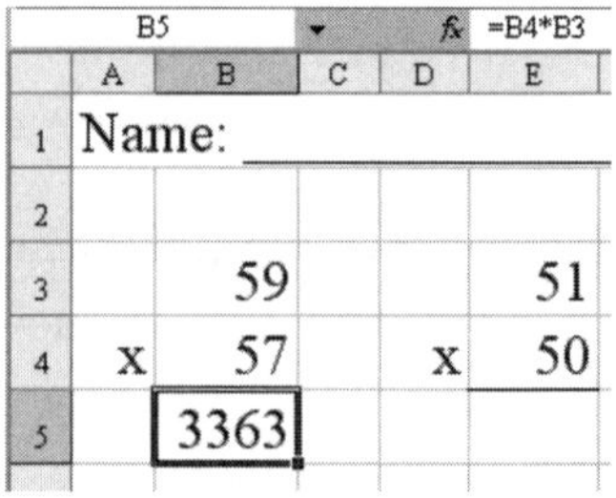

2. Hide the answer.
   Select the cell containing the answer. Look on the right side of the Formatting toolbar. There is a blue A above a red rectangle. This is the font color tool. To the right of the tool is a small down arrow. Click on the down arrow to access a pallet of colors. Choose white from the pallet. This will make the answer disappear on the screen and from the printed page.

   However, when you select all of the cells, Excel highlights the cells in a blue color, allowing the white answers to appear on your screen.

Figure 93

Hidden answers display only on your screen

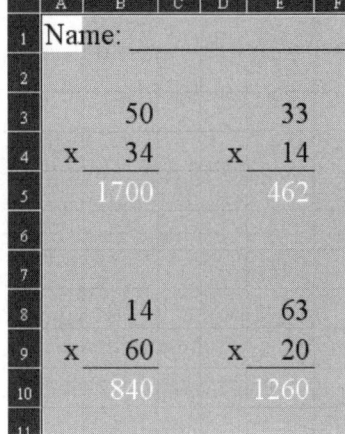

Math Exercise Sheets

Excel Details

The addition and multiplication problems above are fairly straightforward. Those of you who want to delve a little deeper will enjoy these exercises to create more complex worksheets.

Subtracting with Two-Digits Without Regrouping

This is one of the more difficult worksheets to create.

1. Enter the formula for the first term.
    The formula for the top number is fairly straightforward. You want a two-digit number between 10 and 99 so use the following formula and enter it in cell B2 as shown below: =RANDBETWEEN(10,99)

Figure 94

Using RANDBETWEEN to determine the first Term in a subtraction problem

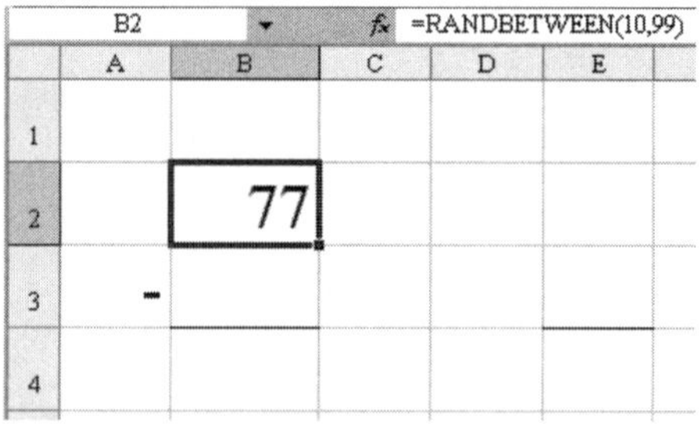

2. Enter the formula for the second term.
    The bottom number is far more complex. You need the digit in the ones position to be between 0 and the digit in the ones position of the number in B2.

    a. To find the digit in the ones position, use the following formula:
        =MOD(B2,10)
        The MOD function is a Modulo function. It basically returns the Remainder after dividing the second argument into the first argument. Thus, the formula to find the first digit of the second term is as follows:
        =RANDBETWEEN(0,MOD(B2,10))

b. Next, you have to figure out a formula for the tens position of the second number. You want this number to be between 1 and the digit in the tens position of the first number. To find the number in the tens position of B2, use the following formula: =INT(B2/10)
The INT function will calculate 77 divided by 10, drop the fractional portion, and just return the whole integer. The formula for the tens position is as follows: =RANDBETWEEN(1,INT(B2/10))

c. To put these two formulas together, you have to multiply the second formula by 10 and add it to the first formula, as shown below. Enter the following formula in B3:
=10*RANDBETWEEN(1,INT(B2/10))+RANDBETWEEN(0,MOD(B2,10))

Figure 95 shows a portion of a page full of these problems.

Figure 95

Worksheet with randomized subtraction problems

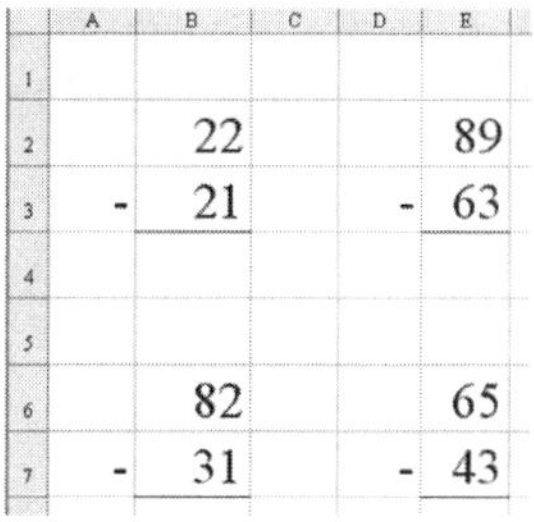

	A	B	C	D	E
1					
2		22			89
3	-	21		-	63
4					
5					
6		82			65
7	-	31		-	43

Expressing Problems That Go Across the Page

For variety, you might sometimes wish to build problems that read across the page. This is possible with Excel but requires a bit of trickery.

Figure 96 shows a worksheet with several pairs of =RANDBETWEEN(1,20) formulas in columns A and B.

Figure 96

Worksheet with pairs of random numbers between 1 and 20

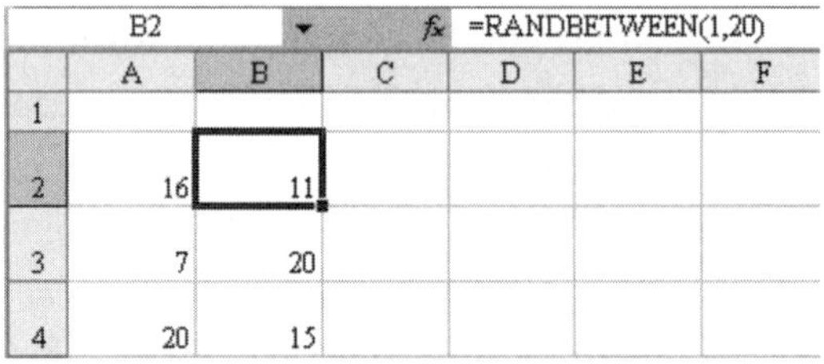

Figure 97 shows a formula that concatenates the value in A with a plus sign, then the value in B, then an equals sign, and several underscore characters to provide a place for the student to write the answer.

Figure 97

Adding plus signs and underscores for student's answers

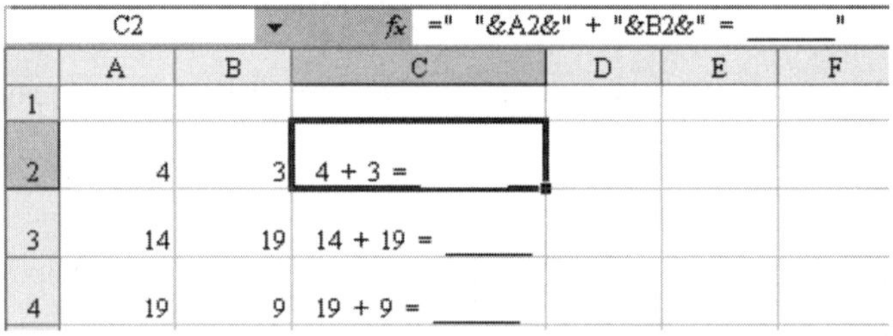

To join a value with text, use the concatenation operator – the ampersand (&). If you want to join a value with a *Literal*, such as the equals or the plus sign, you have to include the literal in double quotes.

 Caution!

There is one annoying "bug" that shows up as you enter this formula. Notice in the above figure that there is a space on either side of the plus sign. You generally have to hold down the Shift key to type the plus sign. You may accidentally continue to hold down the Shift key when you type the spacebar after the plus sign. Unfortunately, Shift+Spacebar is an Excel shortcut to select the entire row. If you suddenly see your formula change to Figure 98, you inadvertently typed Shift+Spacebar instead of just the Spacebar. Simply type the Backspace to get rid of the 3:3 entry.

Figure 98

Result of holding down Shift key while pressing Spacebar

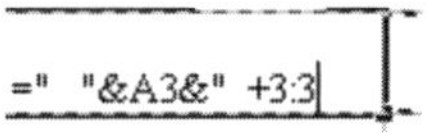

Before printing the worksheet, you will want to hide columns A and B. Select any range of cells such as A1:B1. From the menu, select Format → Columns → Hide. Excel will hide columns A and B from view.

Figure 99

Hiding columns A and B

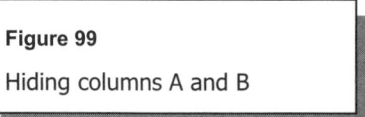

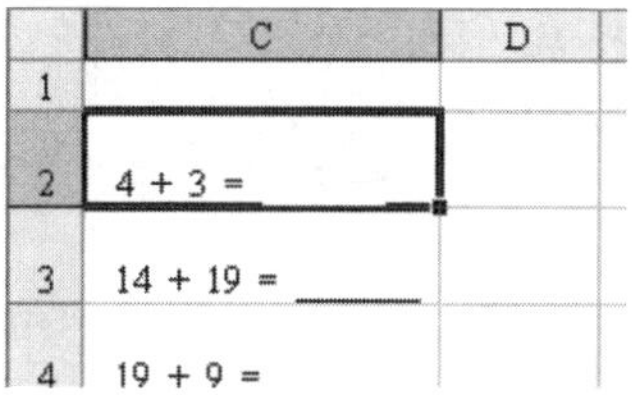

 Tip:

To unhide all columns, select the gray box above row 1 and select Format → Columns → Unhide.

Avoiding Duplicate Problems

In the worksheets described so far in this chapter, it is likely that the same problem may randomly appear on the worksheet. If you absolutely want to ensure no duplicates, use the No Duplication worksheet in the downloadable worksheets. (Sample files can be downloaded from this secret page: http://www.MrExcel.com/mathfiles.html)

Math Exercise Sheets

Figure 100 No Duplication worksheet

	A	B	C	D	E	F	G	H	I	J	K	L
1	Enter 10 Numbers for the top figure here:											
2		1	2	3	4	5	6	7	8	9	10	
3												
4	Enter 10 Numbers for the bottom figure here:											
5		1	2	3	4	5	6	7	8	9	10	
6												
7	Rand	Rank	The formulas here will generate the possible problems									
8	0.40318	61	1	1			NAME:					
9	0.04235	95	1	2								
10	0.65172	38	1	3				9			6	
11	0.5363	47	1	4			+	4		+	8	
12	0.38897	62	1	5								
13	0.70347	32	1	6								
14	0.19712	88	1	7				3			2	
15	0.82707	21	1	8			+	1		+	2	
16	0.95349	7	1	9								

This worksheet accepts 10 possible first numbers and 10 possible second numbers. Formulas down column C and D build all possible pairs of these numbers. The RAND function in A assigns random numbers to the 100 possible problems. The RANK function in B finds the top 15 problems. Then, VLOOKUP formulas in the printable area of the worksheet pull out the numbers for the top 15 problems.

Arithmetic Facts Quiz

Opportunity

Each of your students is at a different stage in learning their multiplication (or addition) facts. You would like to be able to quiz them at their own level, without having to come up with six or more individual quizzes each week. You can have Excel generate the numbers randomly and then have each student enter the addend or multiplier they are working on.

Solution and Overview

You will have Excel create four quizzes to a side in landscape mode, with 10 to 20 questions in each quiz. Each time the quiz is printed, the numbers will be scrambled. Students will write in the number on whose facts they are working.

Creating the Solution

1. Format the page as landscape mode.
   Open a new file. From the File menu, select Page Setup, and then the Page tab. Click on the radio button labeled Landscape.

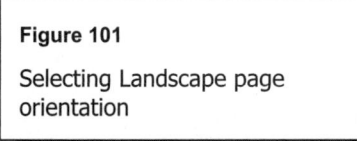

Figure 101

Selecting Landscape page orientation

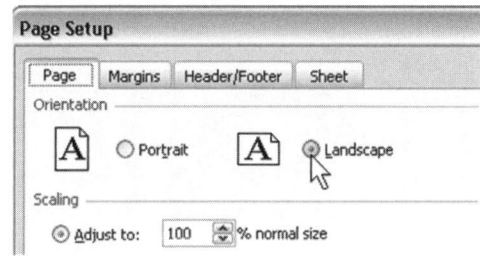

2. Set the margins.

   Now click on the Margins tab. Set the top and bottom margins to 1" and the left and right margins to 0.5". At the bottom, click on the box next to the word "Horizontally" to center the quizzes on the page. Click OK to close.

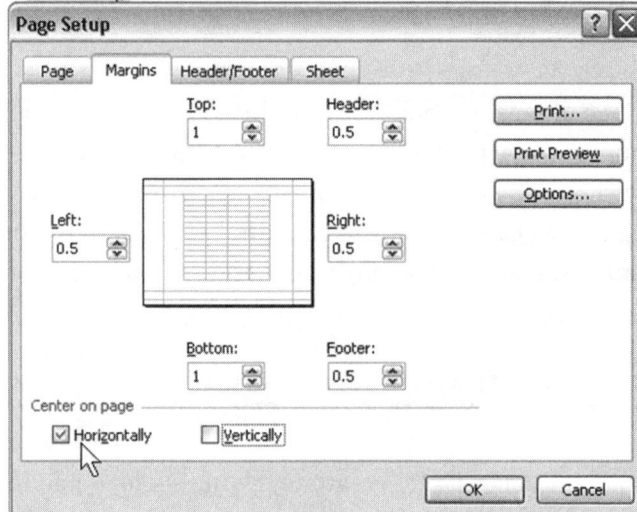

Figure 102

Setting Margins

3. Select and format a range.

   Click on cell A4, hold down the left button, and drag down and to the right to cell B15. Let go, and the range A4:B15 should be grayed in.

   a. Right-click inside the gray area; select Format Cells and click on the Border tab. Under Presets, click on both Outline and Inside. Click OK to exit.

Figure 103

Formatting cell borders

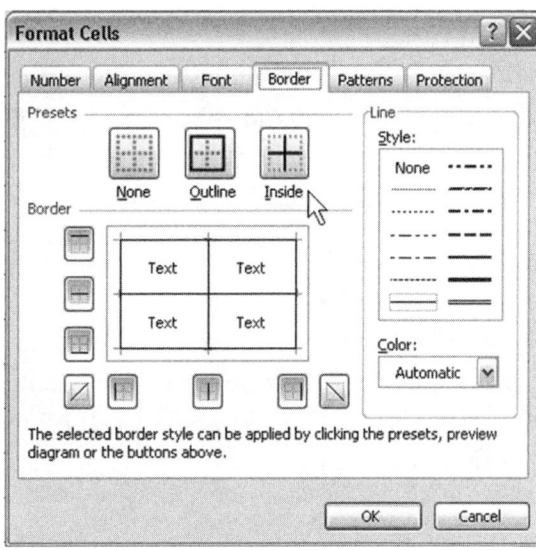

b. Now click on cell A1, hold down the left button and drag down and to the right to cell B15. Again, right-click and select Format Cells. Select the Font tab, and choose Arial as the Font, and change Size to 20. Last, select the Alignment tab. Under Text alignment, change both Horizontal and Vertical to Center. Click OK to exit.

Figure 104

Centering text alignment

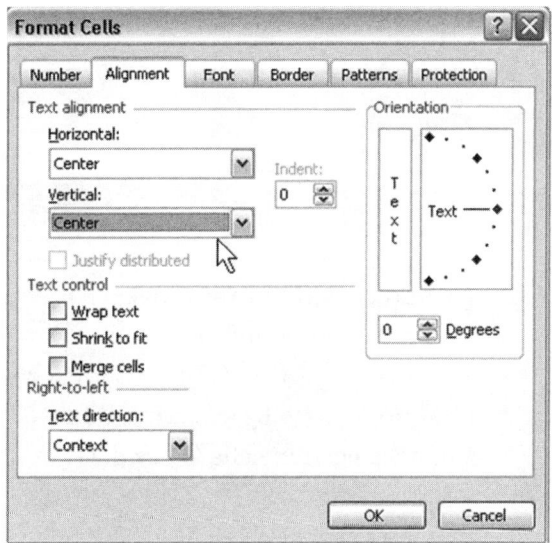

4. Add a border.
    Click on cell A1, and drag to the right to also select cell B1. Right-click in the grayed area and select Format Cells, and then the Border tab. On the left edge, select the third box down to put a border on the bottom edge of the two cells, and then click OK.

5. Add a place for student's name.
    Click on cell A2, and drag to the right to select cell B2. Right-click, select Format Cells, and then the Alignment tab. Under Text alignment, Horizontal, click on the arrow and select Center. Under Text Control, select Merge cells. Click OK to exit. Select cell A2 again. Type in the word **Name** and then press Enter.

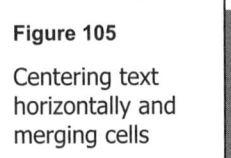

Figure 105

Centering text horizontally and merging cells

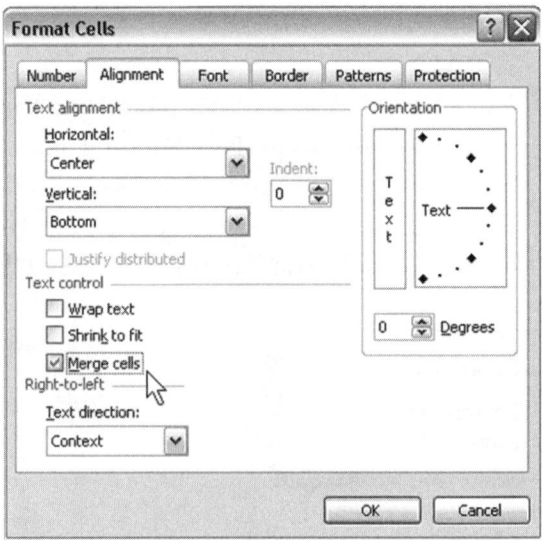

6. Copy and paste the first range.
    Click on cell A1, and drag down and to the right to select the range A1:B15, and copy by selecting Edit → Copy (or press Ctrl+C). Move the mouse to cell D1, and paste by selecting Edit → Paste (or press Ctrl+V). Paste twice more, once each in cells G1 and J1.

7. Set column width.
   Click in the box at the very top of column C (the one with the C in it). Right-click anywhere in column C and select Column Width. In the box that appears, type in 15 and click OK. Repeat for columns F and I.

Figure 106

Setting column width

8. Set up the numbers that will be displayed as questions on the quiz and tell Excel how to display them randomly.
   This example uses the numbers zero through ten (0 – 10), but you can change this later if you want fewer or more numbers.

   a. Go to cell S5, type in the number zero (0), and press Enter. Put your cursor on the fill handle (the small square in the lower right corner) of cell S5. Right-click and drag down to S15. Release the right button, and select Fill Series. The cells will fill with the numbers 0 – 10.

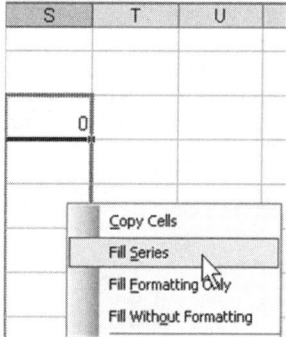

Figure 107

Using the fill handle and the right-click menu to fill a series

   b. In cell R5, type in the following formula: =RAND() and then press Enter. A random decimal number will appear. Left-click on the fill handle in R5, drag down to R15, and release. Each of these cells will have a ran-

Excel for the Math Classroom

Arithmetic Facts Quiz

dom decimal in it. Every time you press the F9 key, these numbers will change.

c. In cell Q5, type in the formula: =RANK(R5,$R$5:$R$15) and copy it down through cell Q15 (following the same procedure as in Step 8b). This formula ranks the random numbers from 1 to 11, based on their size relative to each other.

d. In cell P5, type in the number one (1). Follow the process in Step 8b to enter the numbers 1 – 11. These are, in effect, the question numbers.

e. When finished, you can view all the formulas in columns Q and R by pressing Ctrl+` (Grave). The Grave is just to the left of the number 1 at the top of your keyboard on the same key with the Tilde (~). Your worksheet should look like this:

Figure 108

Using Ctrl+` to view all formulas

P	Q	R	S
1	=RANK(R5,$R$5:$R$15)	=RAND()	0
2	=RANK(R6,$R$5:$R$15)	=RAND()	1
3	=RANK(R7,$R$5:$R$15)	=RAND()	2
4	=RANK(R8,$R$5:$R$15)	=RAND()	3
5	=RANK(R9,$R$5:$R$15)	=RAND()	4
6	=RANK(R10,$R$5:$R$15)	=RAND()	5
7	=RANK(R11,$R$5:$R$15)	=RAND()	6
8	=RANK(R12,$R$5:$R$15)	=RAND()	7
9	=RANK(R13,$R$5:$R$15)	=RAND()	8
10	=RANK(R14,$R$5:$R$15)	=RAND()	9
11	=RANK(R15,$R$5:$R$15)	=RAND()	10

Tip:

Ctrl+` toggles in and out of Show Formulas mode. To return to a normal spreadsheet, press Ctrl+` again.

f. Next, you will use the VLOOKUP formula. VLOOKUP has Excel look at a value in a particular cell, go to a specified table of values, and return a value based on the instructions that you give. In cell A5, type in the following formula and then use the fill handle to copy it down to cell A15: =VLOOKUP(P5,$Q$5:$S$15,3,FALSE)

In plain language, this formula tells Excel to look at the number in P5 (which is 1), and then find that number somewhere in column Q. Excel then counts over three columns (column Q gets included in the count), finds the number in column S, and puts that number into cell A5. Every time you press F9, the numbers in column A will change as the ranks in column Q change.

g. In cell D5, type in the following: =A5
Use the fill handle to copy that formula down to cell D15. While the cells are still grayed in, press Ctrl+C. Move your cursor to cell G5, press Ctrl+V (paste), and then paste into cell J5.

h. If you want to use this as an addition quiz, put a plus sign (+) in cells A4, D4, G4, and J4 (Remember to precede the plus sign with a single apostrophe!). For multiplication, use a capital X.

Using the Application

Pressing the F9 key changes the quiz. If you are giving the same quiz to all of your students, enter the number (in B4, E4, H4, and K4) which is to be added or multiplied to the numbers in the quiz. If you want to have each student work at their own level, leave those cells blank. When you give the students the quiz, tell them the number to write into the top right hand box (next to the operation sign).

Excel Extras

This quiz can be expanded to up to 20 questions with a little bit of work. (You can fit more on the page if you decrease the row height and font size.) If you have your students learn their multiplication tables up to 12, for example, you would need to extend the border formatting by two rows. You would also need to alter the formulas you originally wrote in cells A5 and Q5 to take into account the extra rows and to extend the values in columns P, R, and S.

1. In rows P and S, right-click and drag down to extend the series you previously made in each column. If your students are learning up to the twelves, add two more numbers.

2. In row R, copy down the formula two extra rows.

3. Click on cell X5. Push the F2 key to enter into Edit mode. In the formula in the cell, change the "$R$15" entry so that the 15 is a 17. Copy this new formula down to row 17. Some of the cells in the worksheet may now contain ### instead of numbers, but don't worry.

4. Click on cell A14, keep the left mouse button down, and drag to the right and down to cell K15. Copy this range of cells and paste into cell A16. Again, you will have cells with ###, but we'll fix this next.

5. In cell A5, change the $S$15 so that the 15 is a 17. Copy this new formula down to row 17. The ### should now be gone.

 Tip:

Pound signs (###) indicate that the column is too narrow to display the cell entry. To automatically adjust the column width, double-click the line between the columns in the header row. The column to the right will automatically adjust to accommodate the cell contents in that column.

 Note:

Have you visited the "secret" web page at http://www.MrExcel.com/mathfiles/html? You will find a terrific application there called "EXCEL-lent Math Facts Practice" whose structure is beyond the scope of this book – easy to use, but hard to build. Download and use it with our compliments.

Homework Checker

Opportunity

Do you allow your students to check their math papers with a calculator? Excel can offer a fun way to check the students' papers. You can either build a worksheet where they can plug in the problems and get the answer, or where they can plug in the problem along with their answer, and Excel will indicate if the answer is correct or not.

Solution and Overview

The beauty of the visible calculator invention is that you can scroll back in time, change any previous cells, and then all future calculations will automatically recalculate. It is fairly simple to set up a formula that multiplies two cells. Your students could plug in the terms from a sheet of math problems and the spreadsheet would show them the correct answer.

If you want to be less direct about the process, you could set up a logical formula to test if the student's answer to the problem matches the real answer. In this case, rather than seeing the right answer, they simply know that they got the problem wrong and it is up to them to work through the problem again.

Creating the Solution

1. Format font and set column width.
   Start with a blank spreadsheet. Select all cells by typing Ctrl+A. On the Formatting toolbar, set the font size to 24 points. Use Format → Column → Width and set the columns to a width of 15.

2. Enter title and directions.
   In cell A1, type a title as follows: **Room 4 Magic Homework Checker**
   In cells A3 and A4, enter these directions: **Enter the terms of your multiplication problem in the yellow boxes below.**

3. Format term cells.
   Move the cellpointer to cell B6. On the Formatting toolbar, you will see a paint bucket above a colored rectangle. This is the Fill Color tool. Next to the tool is a dropdown arrow. Select the dropdown arrow to see a pallet of colors. Choose a light yellow color.

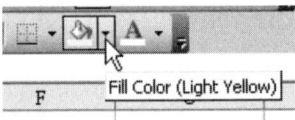

Figure 109

Locating Fill Color dropdown

a. Near the Fill Color icon is a Borders icon. Again, there is a dropdown next to this icon.

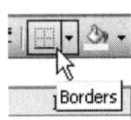

Figure 110

Locating Borders icon dropdown

b. Choose the dropdown arrow and then select the thick border to draw a box around cell B6.

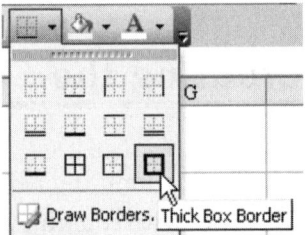

Figure 111

Selecting a thick box border

Tip:

After you select a color from the Fill icon or a border from the Border dropdown, the tool on the Formatting toolbar will change to the selected border style. You can then apply the same border to other cells with a single click.

4. Enter a multiplication operator (X).
   In cell C6, type a carat (^) and a capital X. This will center a multiplication sign in cell C6.

5. Copy the cell format for second term.
   You will want to put a yellow box in D6. There is an easy way to copy formatting from one cell to another. Select cell B6. Type Ctrl+C to copy. Select cell D6. From the menu, choose Edit → Paste Special. In the Paste Special dialog, choose Values and click OK.

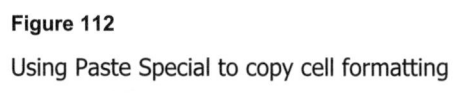
Figure 112
Using Paste Special to copy cell formatting

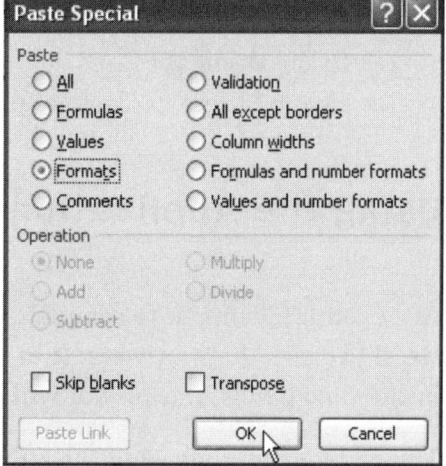

6. Add an equals sign (=).
   In cell E6, type ^= to center an equals sign in the cell. With the cellpointer in E6, press the B icon in the Formatting toolbar to make the equals sign bold.

Homework Checker

7. Enter the multiplication formula.
   In cell F6, you will want to put in a formula to multiply B6 by D6. Type the following formula: =B6*D6

 Tip:

If your answers will likely exceed 1000, then you might want to format cell F6 to include commas.

8. Format the multiplication formula cell.
   Select cell F6. Select Format → Cells from the menu. On the Number tab, you will have to make three adjustments.

   a. First, in the Category list, change from General to Number. This will cause options for decimal places and the 1000 separator to appear.

   b. Check the box for Use 1000 Separator(,).

   c. In the Decimal Places field, type the down arrow on the spin button to switch to zero (0) decimal places.

Using the Application

After your students have completed their math worksheets, allow them to use Excel to check their answers. If they type in the terms from their math problem in the yellow cells, the answer will appear in F6.

The problem with allowing the student to check their answer with a calculator or with this Excel solution is that the student is directly given the answer. In the Excel details section, you will learn how to modify the worksheet to guide the students without giving them the answers.

Excel Details

1. Add an answer cell.

   You can modify the worksheet used above to be less direct. In the figure below, the students are presented with new directions. They are to enter the terms of the multiplication problem in the yellow boxes and their answer in the green box. Set up a green box in cell F6. Remove the formula in F6 by typing a number in the cell.

Figure 113

Replacing a formula with a number

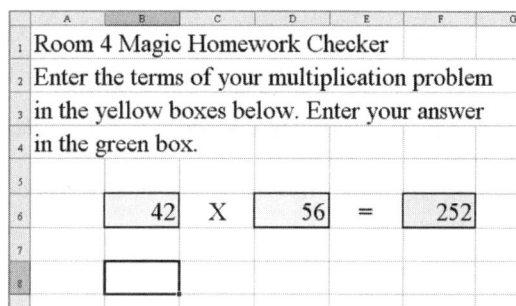

The goal now is to build a formula in B8 that will check to see if the answer is wrong or correct. Excel offers the IF function. There are three arguments to the IF function.

> ➢ The first argument is some logical test. In this case, you will check to see if B6*D6 is equal to the answer typed in F6.

> ➢ The second argument is the text or formula to use if the logical test is true.

> ➢ The third argument is the text or formula to use if the logical test is false.

 Note:

If the second or third argument contains a formula, you can leave off the opening equals sign. If these arguments contain text, the text must be in double quotes.

Homework Checker

2. Enter the resulting IF formula as follows: =IF(B6*D6=F6,"Right!","Try again."

Figure 114

IF formula will inform students whether or not their answer is correct

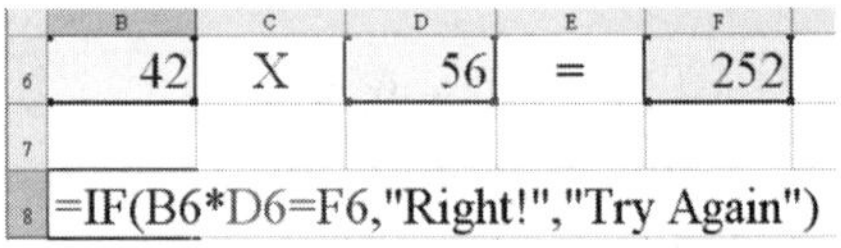

	B	C	D	E	F
6	42	X	56	=	252
7					
8	=IF(B6*D6=F6,"Right!","Try Again")				

a. If the students enter a wrong answer, cell B8 will advise them to try again.

Figure 115

"Try Again" response to an incorrect answer

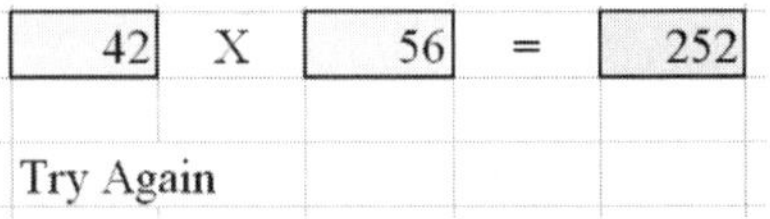

42	X	56	=	252
Try Again				

b. If they enter the correct answer, cell B8 will advise them that it is correct.

Figure 116

"Right!" response to a correct answer

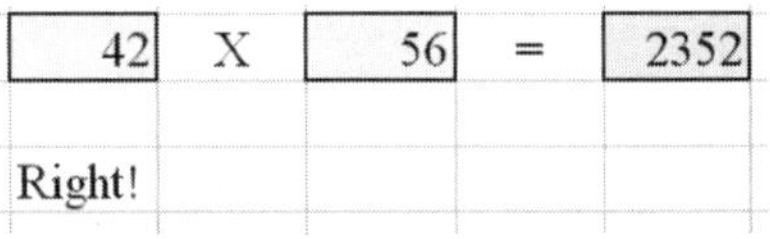

42	X	56	=	2352
Right!				

Adding Color Based on a Result

You can jazz up the worksheet a little bit. Back in Excel 97, Microsoft added something called *Conditional Formatting*. Conditional formatting allows you to change the formatting of a cell or group of cells based on conditions that you set. In this case, you will change the cell color.

1. Initiate conditional formatting.
   Select cell B8. From the menu, choose Format → Conditional Formatting. The Conditional Formatting dialog initially looks like Figure 117. There are a couple of adjustments required to set up the formatting.

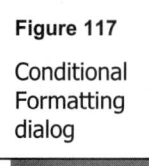

Figure 117

Conditional Formatting dialog

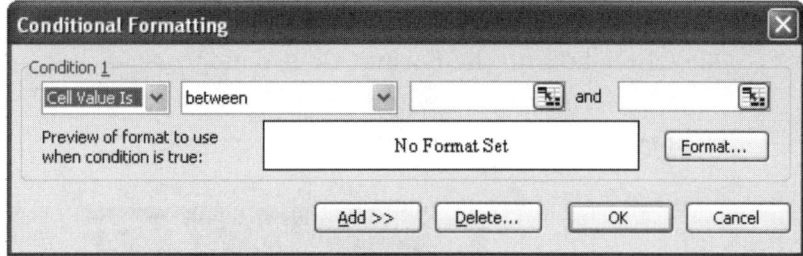

2. Set conditional formatting parameters for the first condition.

   There is a dropdown that contains the word "between". Select the arrow on the right side of this dropdown to see your other choices. Choose "equal to" from the dropdown.

Figure 118

Selecting Cell Value condition to be "equal to"

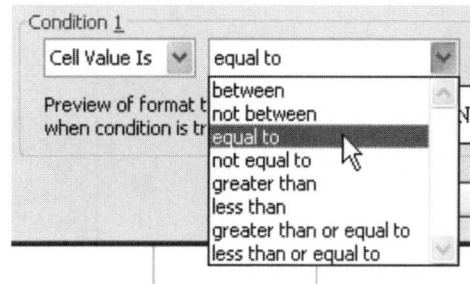

a. After you choose equal to, the two boxes on the right side of the dropdown change to a single box. Type the word "Right!" in that box as shown in Figure 119.

Figure 119 Setting "equal to" value

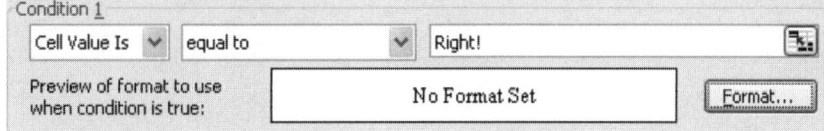

b. Click the Format… button in the lower right area of the dialog. There are three tabs on the Format Cells dialog, one each for Font, Border, and Patterns. Choose a green color on the Patterns tab and change the font color to blue on the Font tab.

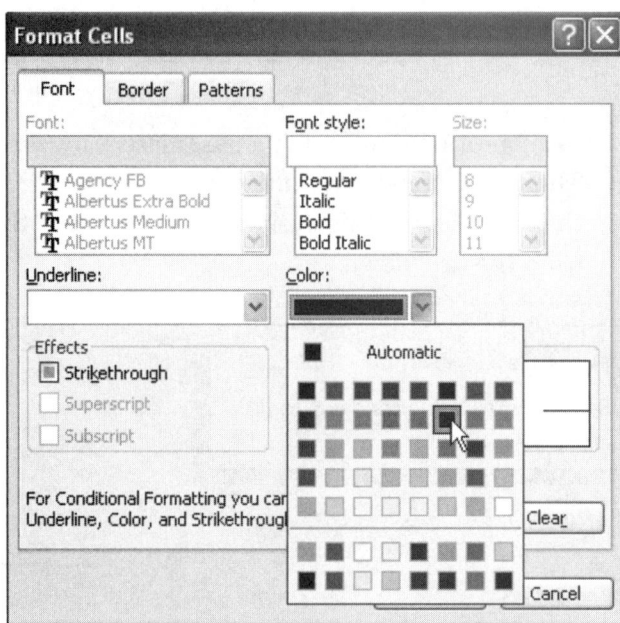

Figure 120

Selecting color and pattern formats for correct answers

3. Add a second conditional format and set parameters.
   You have now set up a format for when the answer is correct. You can add a second condition to handle the answer if it is not correct. On the Conditional Formatting dialog, choose the Add… button to add a second condition.

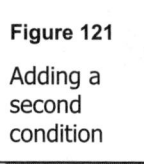

Figure 121

Adding a second condition

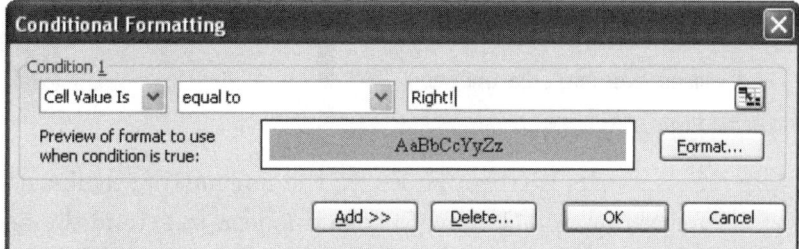

Note:

You can only add second and third conditions. Although many people would like this feature to handle four or more conditions, Microsoft has not yet accommodated this need.

Figure 122

Formatting the second condition

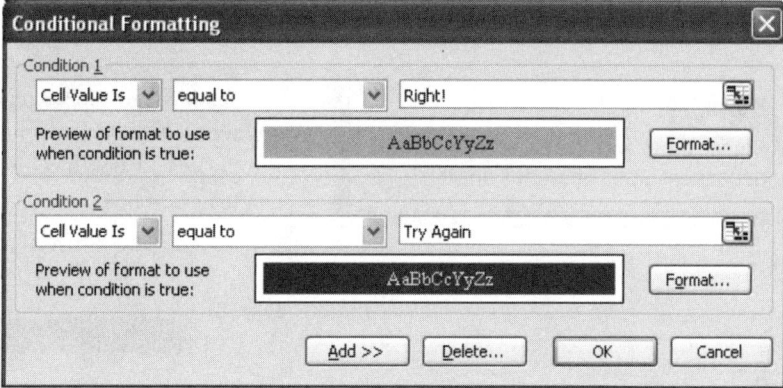

a. Set up the second condition similar to the first. Choose a yellow font on a red background.

b. Click OK to close the Conditional Formatting dialog. Cell B8 looks great when the answer is **Right!**, but the text in **Try Again** is too long.

Homework Checker

Figure 123
Text spilling over into adjacent cell

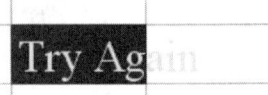

c. Select cells B8 through F8. In the Formatting toolbar there is an icon for Merge and Center. Choose this icon to extend the text and formatting in B8 to the entire range of five cells.

Figure 124
Using Merge and Center to handle overflowing text

The resulting spreadsheet offers a large box with either green positive or red negative feedback for the student.

Figure 125
Spreadsheet with text and formatting dependent upon student's answer

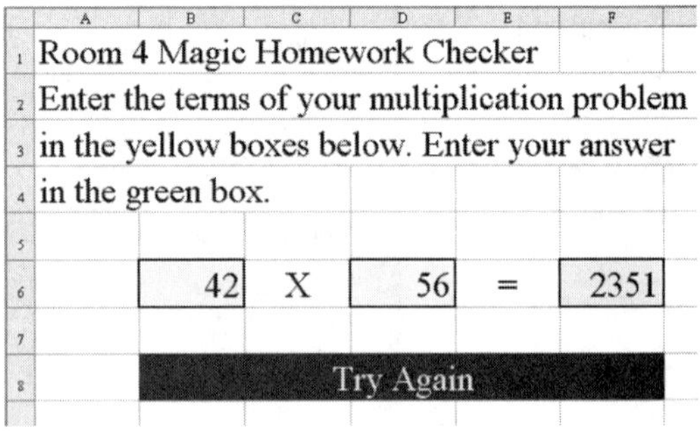

Where Did They Go Wrong?

The final example in this chapter is a worksheet to help the students figure out where they went wrong. To multiply two three-digit numbers, the students will actually perform three multiplication problems and one addition problem. The worksheet below identifies the correct answer for each step of the problem. Your students can compare this with their work to figure out why they had the wrong answer.

Figure 126

Worksheet showing the correct intermediate steps to answer a multiplication problem

```
         321
    x    456
        1926
       16050
      128400
      146376
```

When the students type new numbers into the original problem, the worksheet recalculates to show them the new intermediate results.

Figure 127

Worksheet showing revised intermediate steps

```
         789
    x    654
        3156
       39450
      473400
      516006
```

The following screen shot is taken in Excel's Show Formulas mode. Look on your keyboard. On the upper left side, just above the Tab key and to the left of the 1 key is a key with a tilde (the squiggly thing above an "n" in some Spanish words) and a reverse apostrophe or grave. To turn on Show Formulas mode, hold down the Ctrl key while pressing the Grave (Reverse Apostrophe) key (Ctrl+`).

Figure 128

Worksheet in Show Formulas mode

	C
2	789
3	654
4	=C2*RIGHT(C3,1)
5	=C2*MID(C3,2,1)*10
6	=C2*LEFT(C3,1)*100
7	=SUM(C4:C6)
8	

 Tip:

Ctrl+` toggles in and out of Show Formulas mode. To return to a normal spreadsheet, press Ctrl+` again.

Homework Checker

Note that these formulas only work if cell C3 contains a three-digit number.

1. Enter the following formula in cell C4: =C2*RIGHT(C3,1)
   This formula multiplies 789 by the rightmost digit in C3.

2. Enter the following formula in cell C5: =C2* MID(C3,2,1)*10
   This formula uses the MID function. MID(C3,2,1) starts at the second position in C3 for a length of one character. This will multiply the 5 in 654 by 789. You have to multiply this result by 10 to properly line up the answer with C5.

3. Enter the following formula in cell C6: =C2*LEFT(C3,1)*100
   This formula uses the LEFT function to take the first character from the left of the 654. It multiplies the 6 in 684 by 789 and then multiplies that product by 100.

4. Enter the following formula in cell C7: =SUM(C4:C6)
   This formula sums the results of the formulas in C4 through C6.

The trick will be to make sure that your students complete the work first before they use the homework checker! This last version has the added benefit of letting them figure out where they went wrong.

The homework checker can be adapted to check addition, subtraction, and various other problems.

Magic Squares

Opportunity

You would like to have your students work on some problem-solving skills while at the same time having some fun in the computer lab. Also, you want them to be doing math without realizing it! A Magic Square might just be what you are looking for.

Solution and Overview

You will make a Magic Square worksheet that can be used on the computer so that the sums are automatically calculated, or you can print out the worksheet so that the students will have to do the math themselves. For the computer worksheet, you will lock in the formatting and formulas so that they can not accidentally be changed.

Creating the Solution

1. Set the row height.
   Click on the left side of the worksheet on the row heading 8, and drag down to also highlight rows 9 and 10. Right-click and select Row Height. In the box, type in 48, and click OK. This will make these three rows the same as the standard column width.

Magic Squares

Figure 129

Setting row height

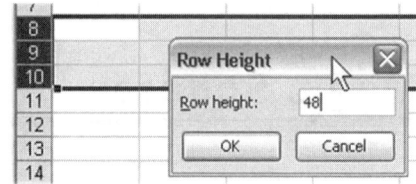

2. Select and format the range.
   Now go to cell D8, left-click and drag right and down to cell F10. You should have nine cells highlighted. While they are still highlighted, right-click and select Format Cells. You will make several changes to the cell format.

   a. Click on the Border tab; from Presets, select Outline and Inside.

Figure 130

Formatting cell borders

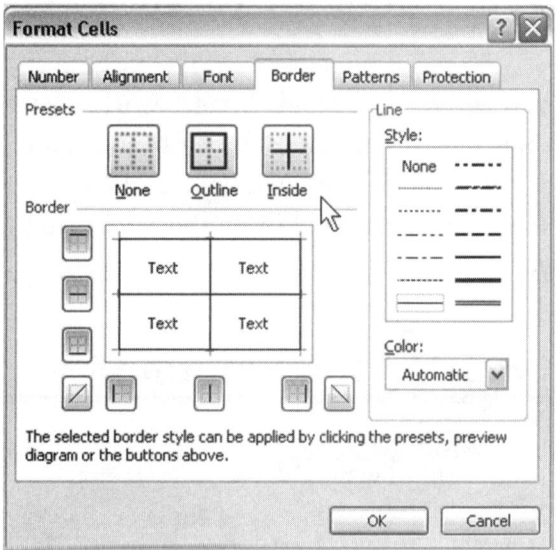

   b. Click on the Alignment tab, and set both Horizontal and Vertical Text Alignment to Center.

Excel for the Math Classroom

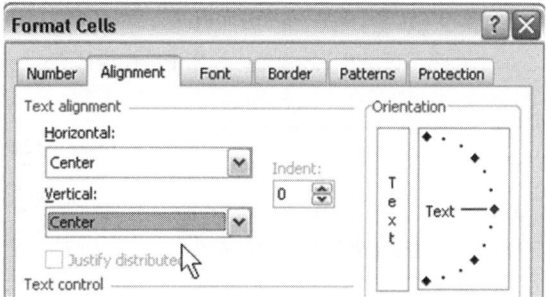

Figure 131
Centering text alignment

c. Click on the Font tab, and change Font to Arial and Size to 20.

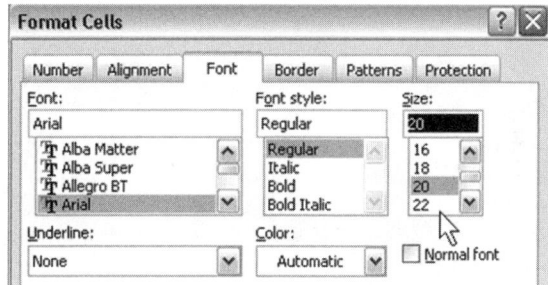

Figure 132
Setting text font and size

d. Click on the Patterns tab, and click on any of the light colors in the bottom row. (I'm partial to blue.)

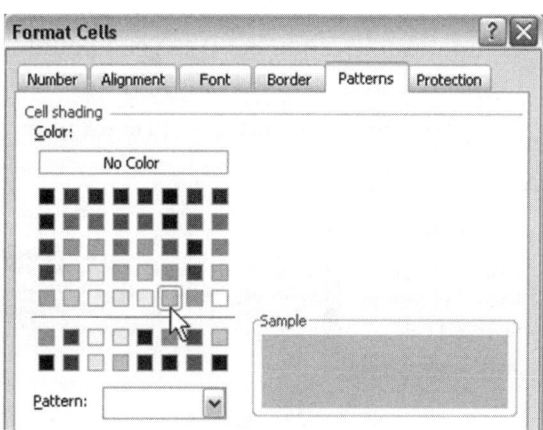

Figure 133
Selecting pattern for cell shading

Magic Squares

e. And last (finally!) click on the Protection tab; uncheck the box next to the word Locked. Click on OK to exit.

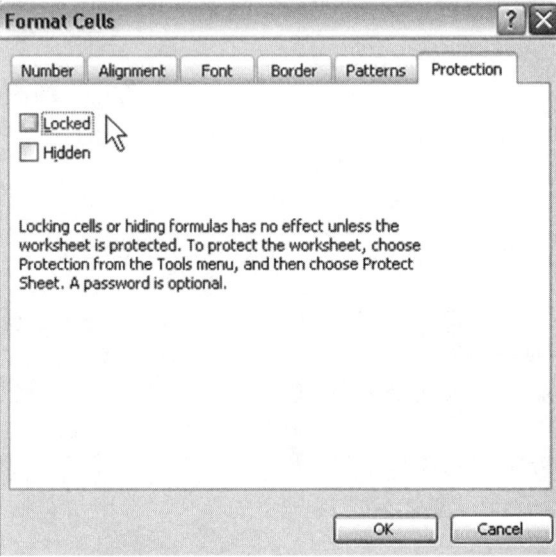

Figure 134

Protecting cells from changes

3. Fill in the nine boxes with the digits 1 – 9.
   For now, it doesn't really matter where they go.

4. Use AutoSum in D11.
   Click on cell D11. From the tool bar at the top of the page, click on the AutoSum icon symbol (Σ). You should see cells D8:D10 highlighted, and a formula that says: =SUM(D8:D10)
   This is what you want, so press Enter.

Figure 135

Using AutoSum to add values in selected cells

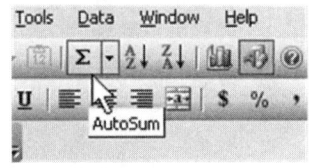

90   Excel for the Math Classroom

5. Format D11.

   Right-click on cell D11 and select Format Cells. Select Alignment, and set Horizontal and Vertical to center. Next set Font to Arial and Size to 20. Click on the down arrow in the Color box, and select Blue from the second row. Now click OK to exit.

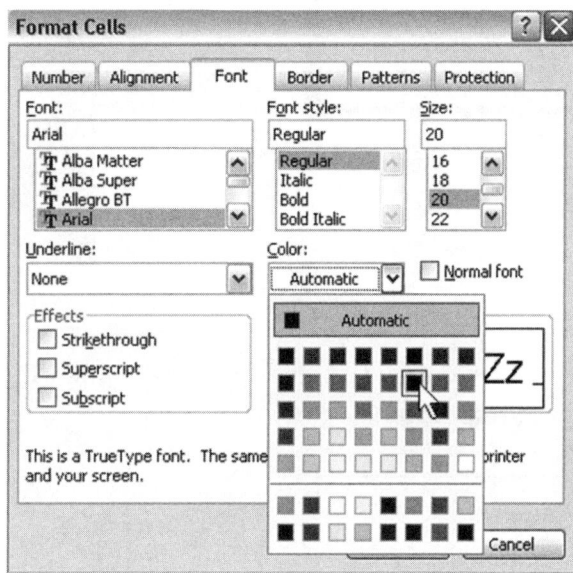

Figure 136

Configuring text font and color

6. Copy down D11's formula and formatting.

   Left-click on the fill handle in the lower right corner of cell D11, and drag to the right to F11.

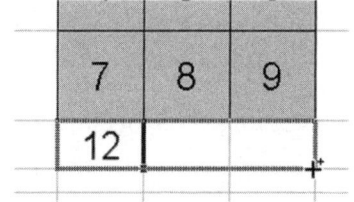

Figure 137

Dragging fill handle to copy formula and formats

7. Use AutoSum on G8 and apply previous formatting; copy down to G10.

   Go to cell G8 and repeat Steps 4 (AutoSum) and 5 (formatting). For Step 4,

Excel for the Math Classroom

however, when you click on the AutoSum icon, you should see =SUM(D8:F8). When you have changed the font formatting, click the fill handle and pull down to cell G10 to copy the formula and formats.

Figure 138

Selecting which cells' formula and formats to copy

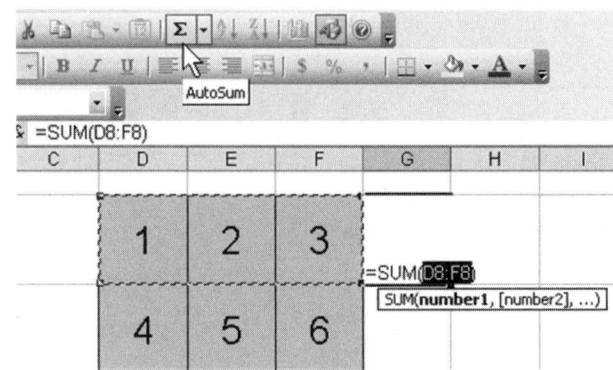

8. Click on cell C11 and type in the following formula: =D10+E9+F8
   Press Enter.

Figure 139

Entering desired formula in cell C11

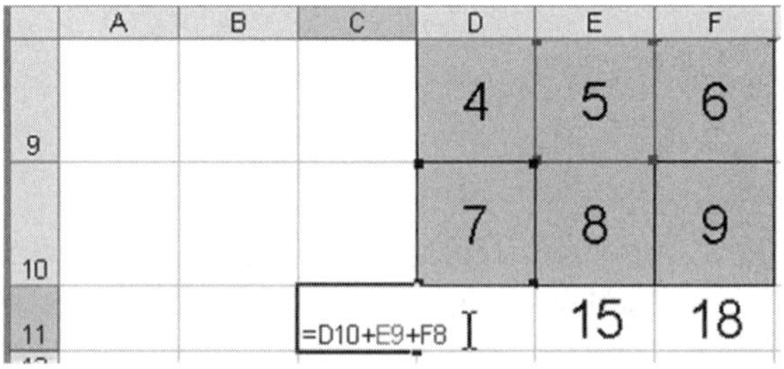

9. Click on cell G11, and type in the following formula: =D8+E9+G10
   Press Enter.

10. Change the formatting in cell C11 and copy down to G11.

   a. Right-click on cell D11 and select Format Cells. Select Alignment, and set Horizontal and Vertical to Center. Next select Font, and select Arial and 20. Click on the down arrow in the Color box, and select Red. Click OK to exit.

b. Now, click on cell C11 and copy (Ctrl+C). Click on cell G11. From the drop down menus, select Edit, Paste Special. From the dialog box, click on Formats and click OK. The font in cell G11 should now match cell C11 for size and color.

Figure 140

Using Paste Special to copy a cell's format

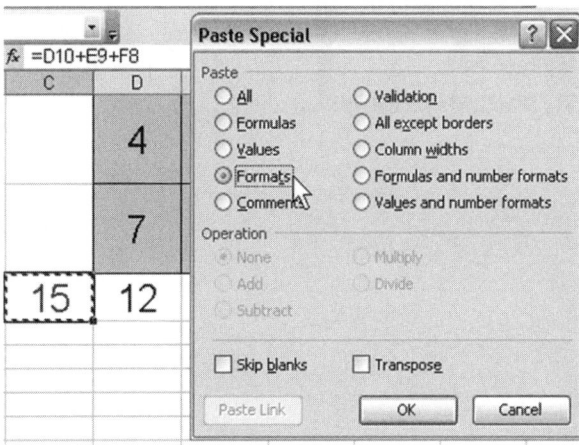

11. Add a title block to the worksheet.

    Move your cursor to the line between rows 1 and 2 on the extreme left until it changes into a plus sign with arrows on the vertical line. Left-click and slowly pull down until the height is 36.

Figure 141

Changing row height by clicking and dragging

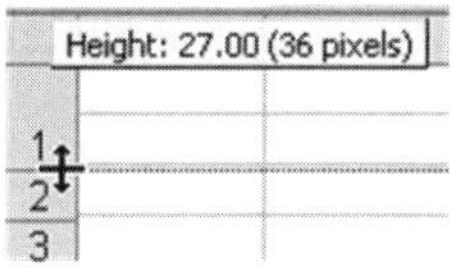

12. Format the title block cells and enter text.

    Go to cell C1, left-click and drag to the right to cell G1.

    a. Right-click and select Format Cells. Select the Alignment tab. Under Text Alignment, select Center for both Horizontal and Vertical. Under Text Control, select Merge Cells.

Magic Squares

    b. Next, click on the Font tab. Change the Font type to Arial with size 20. Click OK. Click on cell C1 and type in: Magic Square

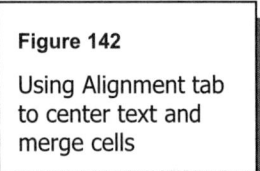

Figure 142

Using Alignment tab to center text and merge cells

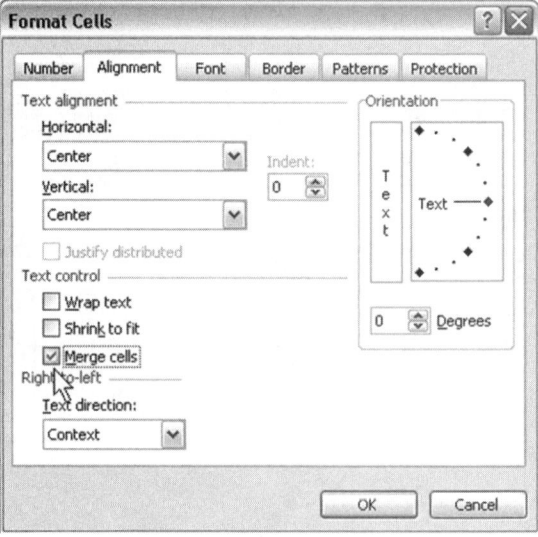

13. Format instructions cells and enter text.
Go to cell C2, left-click and drag down and to the right to cell G6.

    a. Right-click and select Format Cells and Alignment. Select Center for Horizontal and Vertical. Under Text Control, select Wrap Text and Merge Cells.

    b. Click the Font tab, and change to Arial with size 12.

    c. Click on the Border tab and select Outline.
Click OK to exit.

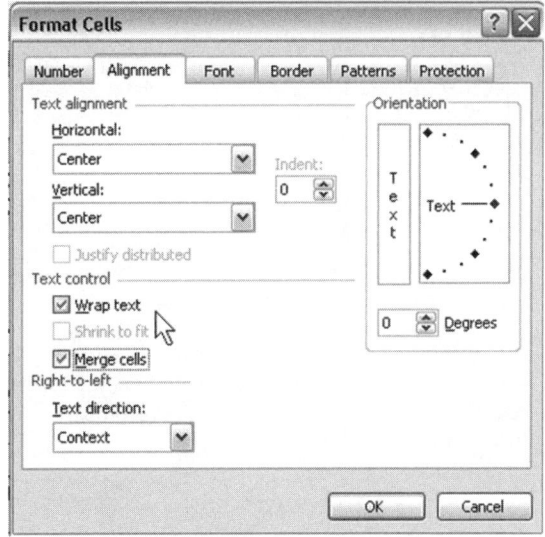

Figure 143

Using Alignment tab to center and wrap text and merge cells

    d. Inside the merged cells, type in the following text:

       Place the numbers 1-9 in the squares below. Use each number only once. The sums in all of the rows, columns, and diagonals must be equal. Have fun!

14. Hide distracting elements.

    From the drop down menus, select Tools, Options, and click on the View tab. Uncheck the boxes labeled Gridlines, Row & column headers, and Sheet tabs. Click OK to exit.

Magic Squares

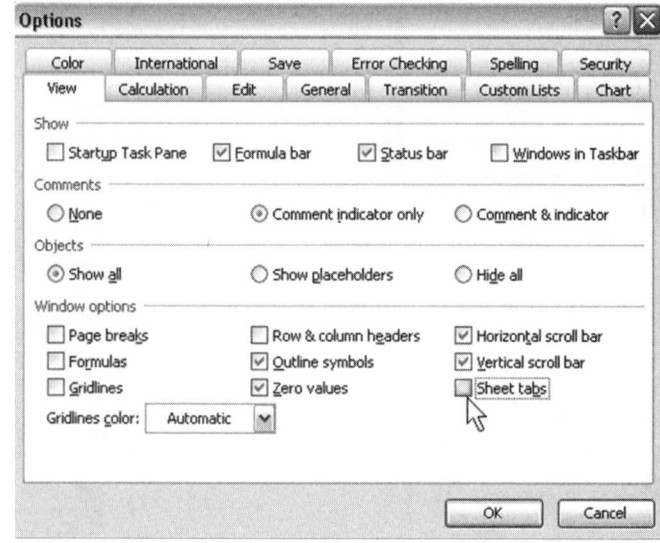

Figure 144

Using view tab to hide gridlines, row and column headers, and sheet tabs

Magic Squares

15. Set up sheet protections.

    From the Tools menu, select Protection and Protect Sheet. Uncheck the box labeled Select locked cells. It is not necessary to use a password, but if you decide to use one, write it down someplace! Click OK to exit.

Figure 145

Using Protect Sheet to make locked cells unavailable to students

16. Save your worksheet as Magic Squares.

Using the Application

Before copying this worksheet onto a computer for students to use, make sure that either the cells are empty, or that it has not been solved correctly. With protection on, the students will only be able to move to one of the nine cells in the magic square, and will not be able to delete any of the formulas, formats, or instructions.

Would you like to make this a pencil and paper activity? Here's how.

1. Go to Tools → Protection → Unprotect Sheet. Remove all the numbers from the cells, and delete the summation formulas.

2. Click on the merged cells with "Magic Square", and pull down and right to highlight the outlined cells.

3. From the File menu, select Print Area → Select Print Area. Then again from File menu, select Page Setup → Margins. At the bottom, click on the box marked Horizontally, and click OK. This will center the Magic Square left to right, and give lots of scribble room at the bottom for calculations.

If you have never worked with a Magic Square before, they can be pretty tricky unless you know the key. One hint is that the middle cell must have the number 5, and that all of the outside corners are even numbers. If you want to see one solution, visit the "secret" website at the following location: http://www.mrexcel.com/mathfiles.html

Do an internet search for "magic square solution" and see what you can find.

Magic Squares

Excel Extras

I had used Magic Squares before, but I discovered quite a bit about them while doing research for this chapter. Once you have a Magic Square built, you can add, subtract, multiply or divide every number in the square by the same number and still have a magic square. You can also build a magic square using any nine consecutive numbers.

To do some investigation into this, make another magic square just off to the right a couple of columns or so, and fill it up with the same number. You can build formulas into the new square so that all you have to do is type in one number, and all the other cells will automatically fill in the same. For example, if your new square has the upper left hand corner in cell J8, type in =J8 in all the other cells.

If you want to add a 3 to all the numbers in your solved magic square, do the following:

1. Type a 3 in cell J8, and then highlight all the cells with a 3 in them.

2. Select Edit, Copy, (or press Ctrl+C) and then click on cell D8 (the upper left corner of the Magic Square).

3. Then select Edit, Paste Special, and check the boxes for Values and Add, and click OK. All the cells in the Magic Square have just been increased by 3.

4. In the Paste Special dialog box, you can check Add, Subtract, Multiply, or Divide.

Have your students build a magic square, and then investigate. Try to build a new magic square by transposing the rows and columns of a square they have solved. See if they can come up with a reason as to why the sums remain the same even though the numbers are being changed.

Coordinate Grid Matching

Opportunity

You are teaching the basics of coordinate grid locations using maps or games, and you would like something fun for both remediation and practice. You can make a game-like grid that will randomly place a smiley face within the grid and then let your students guess the smiley location and have Excel tell them whether they are right or wrong.

Solution and Overview

You will make a 5 x 5 grid in the upper left corner of a worksheet. (You can make this larger, if desired, by slightly altering the instructions.) You will generate random numbers, use the ADDRESS function to generate a cell location, and then employ some tricks with circular references to allow the students to check their answers. Each cell requires a unique formula, so copy and paste is not an option. Work carefully and follow the instructions, and you should be fine.

Creating the Solution

1. Set row height.
   Start by moving your cursor to Row 1 on the left edge of the screen. The cursor will turn into an arrow. Left-click and drag down to highlight rows 1 through 5. Move your cursor back up to the line between rows 1 and 2. Your cursor will turn into a plus sign with a vertical arrow. Left-click and drag down until the row height reads "48.00 (64 pixels)". Release the mouse button and the five rows will change height.

Coordinate Grid Matching

Figure 146

Making the five selected rows all the same height

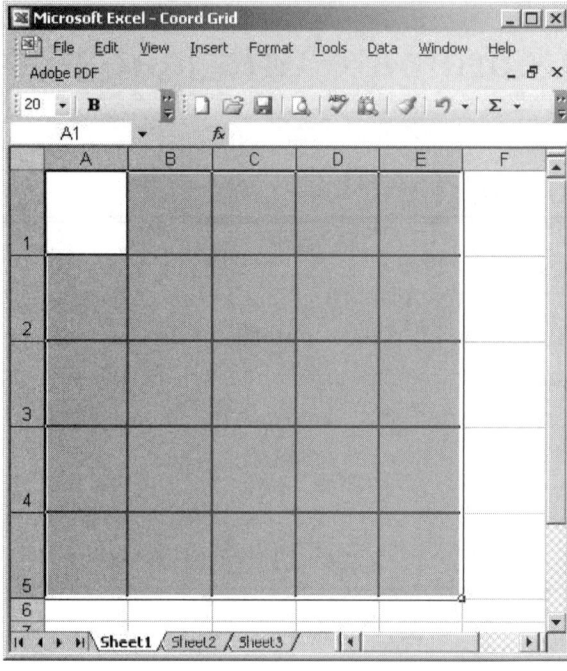

Coordinate Grid Matching

2. Format cells.

   Move your cursor to cell A1. Left-click and drag to the right and down to cell E5 and let go. All the cells should be gray. Press Ctrl+1 to go to the Format Cell dialog box, where you will make several changes to cell format.

   a. Click on the Alignment tab. Under Text alignment, change Horizontal and Vertical to Center.

   b. Click on the Font tab. Change Font to Wingdings and Size to 20.

   c. Click on the Border tab. Under Presets, click on Outline and Inside.

   d. Click on the Patterns tab. Under Color, choose a pale pastel from the bottom row, such as green, by clicking on the color square. Click OK at the bottom to exit.

Figure 147

Using the Format Cells dialog to format the selected range

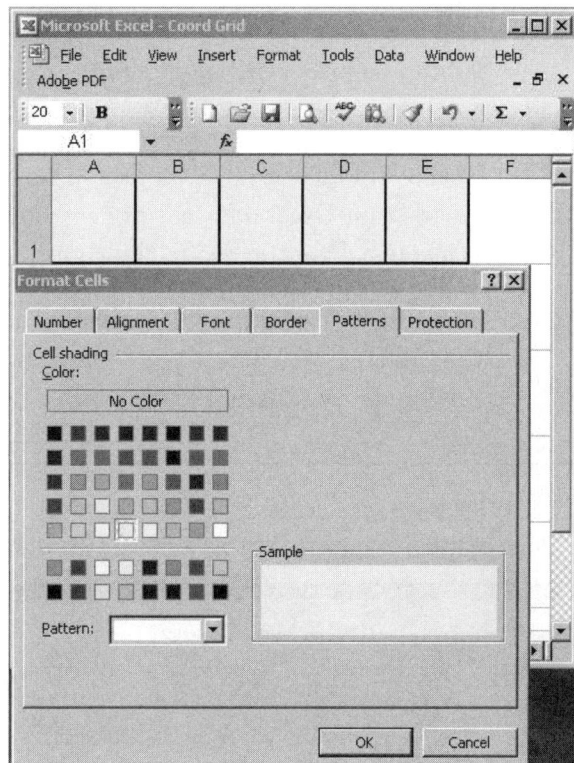

3. Apply conditional formatting to smiley face cell.
   Click on any of the newly colored cells and type in a capital letter J. You should see a smiley face in the cell. To make this cell stand out a bit more, you can use conditional formatting.

   a. Highlight the cell range A1:E5 (all the cells that are green). From the drop down menus at the top of the worksheet, choose Format and then Conditional Format.

   b. A dialog box will appear. Keep the default value in the first box of "Cell Value Is". Click on the down arrow in the second box. Notice all of the different conditions that you can choose from. Select "equal to".

Coordinate Grid Matching

c. The box to the right is currently empty. You can have Excel look at the value in another cell or you can type in the value that you want. Type in a capital J, as shown in the following figure.

d. In the middle is a large rectangle that says "No Format Set". This means that Excel does not know what to do if the condition you typed in exists. Click on the box to the right marked "Format…".

e. You will see a modified version of the Format Cells dialog box. Click on the tab marked Patterns and then click on the bright yellow square in the fourth row down from the top. Click OK twice to exit.

Figure 148

Using conditional formatting to make Smiley Faces stand out

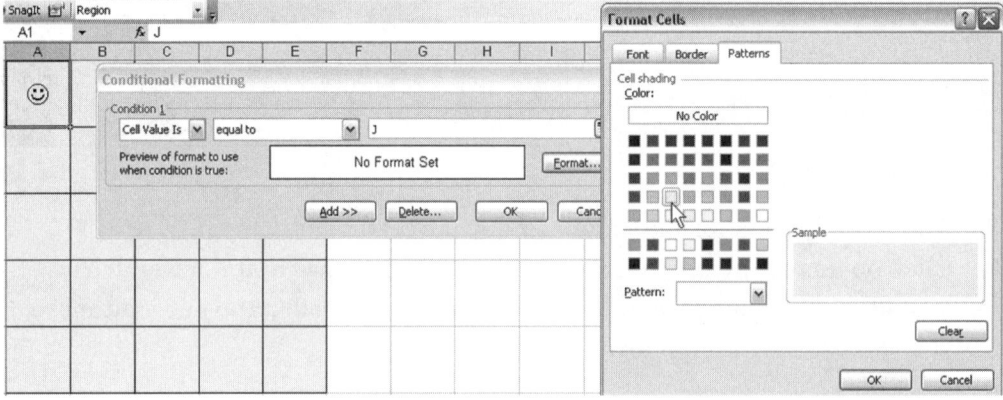

f. Now go back to any of the green shaded cells and type in a capital J. You will now get a yellow smiley face.

Figure 149

Yellow smiley face appears

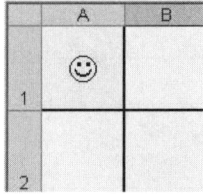

4. Set row height.
Move your cursor to Row 8 on the left edge of the screen and left click to highlight the entire row. Move your cursor down slightly to the line between rows 8 and 9. Your cursor will turn into a plus sign with a vertical arrow. Left-click and drag down until the row height reads "27.00 (36 pixels)". Release the mouse button and row 8 will change height.

The formula that you will enter next requires you to first make some changes in the way Excel handles a circular reference, which is a formula that refers back to its own cell. Normally, this is not allowed, but you can tell Excel to only calculate the reference one time by using the results of the previous iteration (a repeated calculation).

5. Enter the circular reference formula.
From the Tools drop down menu, click on Options and then the Calculation tab. At the top, click on Manual. Click on the box next to the word Iteration and change the number of Maximum iterations to 1. Click OK to exit.

Figure 150

Allowing a circular reference

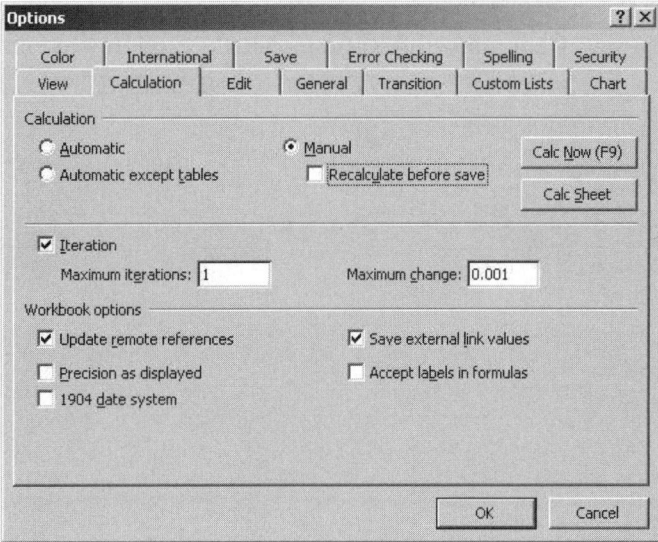

Coordinate Grid Matching

 Note:

The function you will use to generate the random numbers, RANDBETWEEN, is not a standard Excel function, but is, instead, part of something called the Analysis ToolPak. To have this and other functions available, you need to do the following: From the Tools menu, select Add-Ins. When the dialog box opens, click on the boxes next to Analysis ToolPak and Analysis ToolPak –VBA. Click OK to exit.

See page 53, Creating the Solution for more details.

6. Enter a formula to randomly pick one of the 25 cells in your grid.
   You will use three different Excel functions;

   - ADDRESS – Creates a cell address, or location, based on row and column numbers that are supplied.

   - RANDBETWEEN – Returns a random number between any two integers that are given.

   - IF – Tells Excel to do one task if a certain condition is met or to do something else if it is not.

   a. Click on cell A8 and carefully type in the following formula:
      =IF(D8="?",A8,ADDRESS(RANDBETWEEN(1,5),RANDBETWEEN(1,5),4))

Figure 151

Entering the circular reference formula in A8

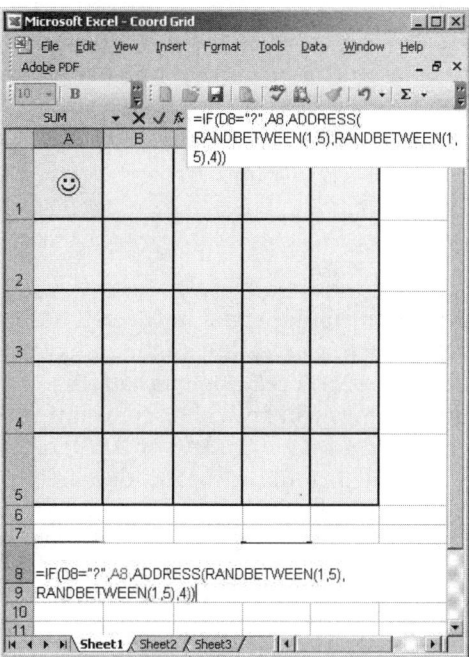

b. When finished, press Enter. This tells Excel to look at cell D8. If it contains a question mark (we'll get to this later), keep whatever value is already in cell A8. However, if cell D8 is empty, return a random column number and row number and turn it into a cell address.

c. Remember that you have turned off automatic calculation. Excel will now only make calculations when the F9 key is pushed. Push F9 several times to see how the cell location in A8 changes.

7. This step will enter the formulas into the grid, which will tell Excel where to put the smiley face, based on the result of the formula in cell A8. Unfortunately, there is no way to copy the formula after you have written it once. Each of the 25 cells in the grid will require their own version of the formula. Fortunately, the change for each cell is minor and can be done fairly easily. Also, remember that you have changed the font type in the grid to Wingdings, which means that, as you type, you will just see some very

Coordinate Grid Matching

strange pictures appearing in the cell. To avoid confusion, watch your typing in the Formula bar at the top of the worksheet.

a. Go to cell A1, and type in the following formula: =IF($A$8="A1","J","")
   Press Enter.

 Note:

Notice the dollar signs in the cell designation A8 ($A$8). These denote an *absolute reference* to that cell, which means that the reference will not change as you copy the formula. A *relative reference* has no dollar signs (A8). The row and column designators will both change, relative to the original cell, as the formula is copied. In a *mixed reference* ($A8 or A$8), either the row or column designator will change when the formula is copied, depending on where the dollar sign is located.

For additional details, see pages 47-48.

Translation: The IF statement says that if cell A8 contains a reference to this cell (A1), put a capital J (the Wingding smiley face) in A1. Otherwise, put nothing.

b. The formula for the rest of the cells in the grid will be almost identical, with one crucial difference. The reference to cell A1 needs to be changed to whatever cell the formula is in. In other words, the formula will look something like this:

=IF($A$8="this cell","J","")
Where "this cell" will be replaced with the cell in which
the formula is being written.

Don't forget to include the quotation marks around the cell designation!

Figure 152

Entering the smiley face formula

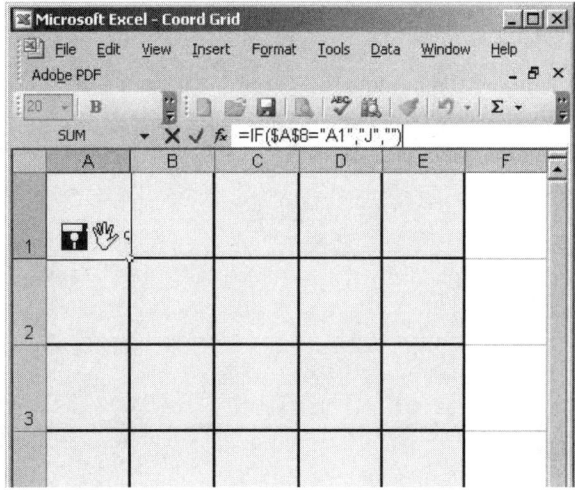

8. Copy the formula into the rest of the grid.

    Go to cell A1, left-click on the fill handle in the lower right corner, drag down to cell A5, and let go of the left button. Immediately left-click on the fill handle in cell A5, and drag right to cell E5. Check to see that each cell in the grid has the same formula.

Coordinate Grid Matching

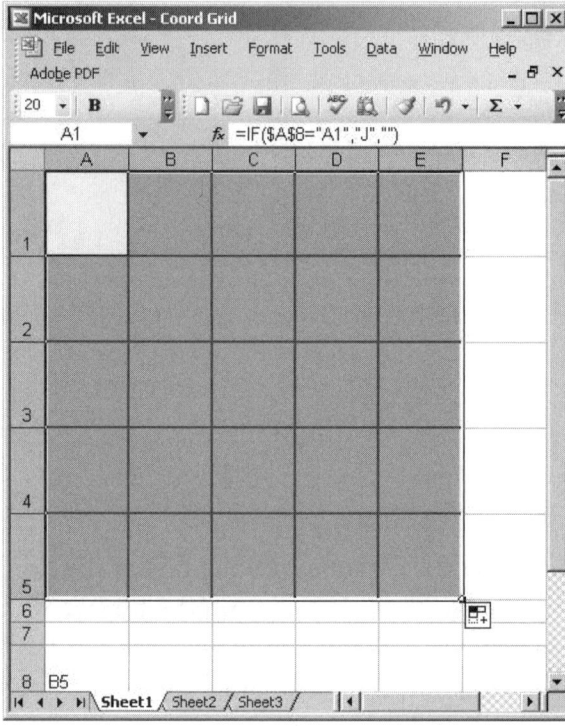

Figure 153

Copying the formula to the other cells

9. Now, one cell at a time, do the following:

   a. Click on a cell, and then click on the formula bar. Use the arrow keys or mouse to move the blinking cursor bar to the "A1" in the formula. (That's the second one, NOT the one with the $).

   b. Change "A1" to whatever cell you are in. If you are in cell B1, change A1 to B1. Remember to KEEP the quotation marks on both sides of the cell designation. When you are done, press Enter and move to another cell.

   c. Repeat this step until you have changed the formula in each of the cells. When you are done, press F9. Look at the contents in cell A8, and make sure that the smiley face appears in that cell in the grid.

Coordinate Grid Matching

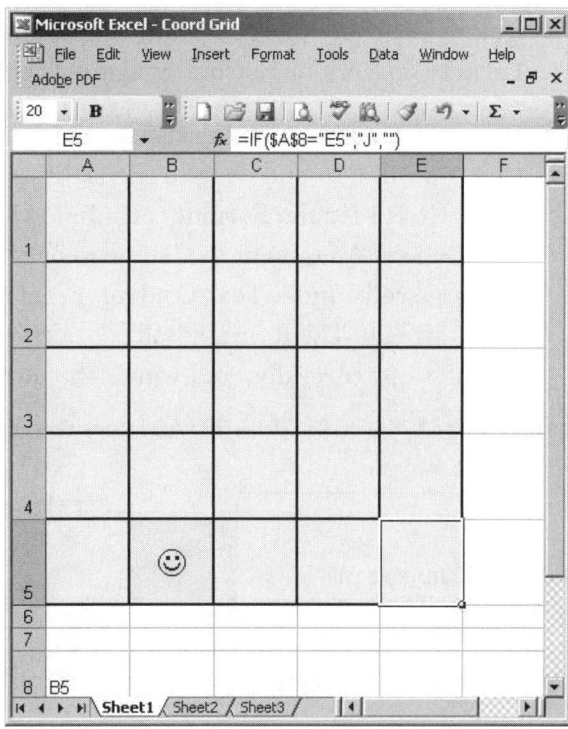

Figure 154

Smiley face appears in cell specified in cell A8

10. Format student answer and response cells.

Go to cell B8. Use the instructions in Step 2 to access the Format Cell dialog box to change the font to Arial, the size to 20, to center the text horizontally and vertically, and to change the cell color to red. Additionally, click on the Protection tab, and remove the check mark from the box next to Locked. Click OK to exit, and then do the same for cell D8, except make the cell blue.

This next formula will allow a student to enter his/her answer into cell B8 and have Excel display a phrase telling him/her whether or not the answer is correct. The difficulty of this is that Excel can not compare the student's response until he/she presses F9. Pressing F9, however, will change the location of the smiley face, and the student's answer will be wrong. You need to tell Excel to change the value of cell A8 (and the location of the

Excel for the Math Classroom 109

Coordinate Grid Matching

smiley face) only under certain conditions. In essence, you will be forcing Excel to do circular reasoning against its better judgment. Here you go!

11. Enter a formula to display the response to a student's answer.
Click on cell B10 and drag to the right and down to highlight cells B10:D11. Press Ctrl+1 for the Format cells dialog box. From the Alignment tab, change Text Alignment to Center in both directions and click the box next to Merge cells under Text Control. From the Font tab, change the font to Arial, size 20. The formula will contain what are called nested IF statements. Copy carefully, and watch the punctuation! Here is the formula:

=IF(D8="","",IF(D8="?",IF(B8=A8,"Very Good!","Try Again.")))

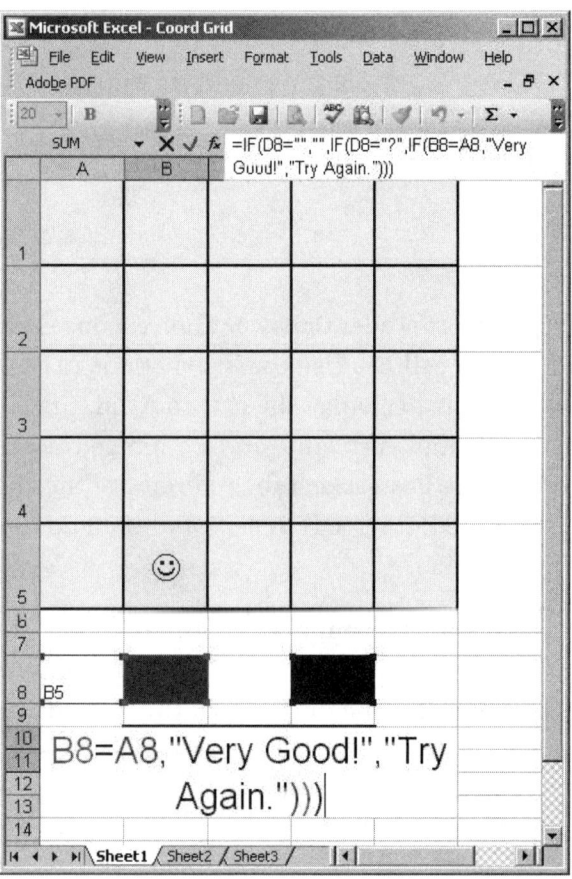

Figure 155

Nested IF formula will provide conditional response to answer student put in B8

Here's the translation: If cell D8 is empty, then display nothing in the merged cells B10:D11. However, if D8 contains a question mark, compare the value in A8 with what the student has entered in B8. If they are the same, display "Very Good!" If they are different, display "Try Again.". Do nothing, however, until F9 is pressed to allow the necessary calculations.

12. Now you will do some conditional formatting on the merged cells to add color, depending on the cell value.

    a. Highlight cells B10:D11. From the Format drop down menu, select Conditional Formatting. In the box containing the word "between", click on the down arrow and select "equal to".

    b. In the empty box to the right, type in the following words:
    Very Good!
    You need to make sure that what you type here is identical to what you typed in the formula in Step 11. Click on the box marked Format, then the Patterns tab. Click on a bright green, then click OK to exit.

    c. Back on the Conditional Formatting dialog box, click on the box marked Add>>. You now have a Condition 1, which you have already configured, and a Condition 2, which needs to be filled in. Change "between" to "equal to", just like you did before.
    In the empty box, type in the following words:
    Try Again.

    d. Click on the Format box, and then Patterns. Click on a light pink color, and then click OK to exit. Click OK again to close the Conditional Formatting box.

Coordinate Grid Matching

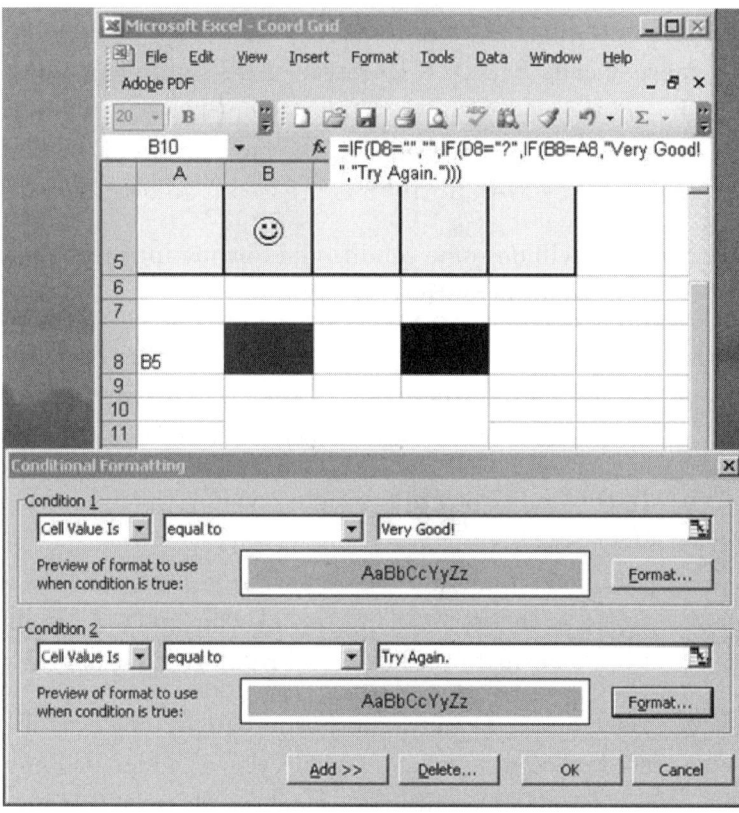

Figure 156

Setting up conditional formatting for responses to student answers

13. Now let's see if this works.

    a. Press F9 to move the smiley face. Type in the cell location of the smiley face in cell B8, then type a question mark in cell D8. Press F9 again. You should get a positive response from Excel in a green cell.

    b. Change the answer to a wrong one in B8, and press F9.
       Now you should have the negative response in a pink cell.

14. This step is important, because it will hide the correct answer from the students!

    a. Click on cell A8, and press Ctrl+1. Click on the Font tab.

112   Excel for the Math Classroom

b. In the section named Color, click on the arrow next to the word Automatic, and then click on the white square in the lower right hand corner. Click OK to exit.
This "white-on-white" format will make the text in cell A8 invisible.

15. Now you need to add some instructions on how to use this worksheet.

   a. Click on cell G1, and drag to the right to cell K1. Access Format Cells. From the Alignment tab, center the text, and put a check mark next to Merge Cells.

   b. From the Font tab, select Arial, size 20. From the Border tab, select Outside, and from the Patterns tab, select a bright yellow. Click OK to exit.

   c. Type the following text inside the merged cells: **Find Smiley!**

16. Format the range of instructions.
Click on cell G2, and drag down and to the right to select K3. Access Format Cells. From Alignment, select Left for Horizontal and Center for Vertical, and check the boxes next to Wrap Text and Merge Cells. From the Font tab, select Arial, size 10. Format the Border and Patterns the same as in Step 14.

17. Type in the following instructions.
However, when you get to the end of a sentence, do not use the Enter key to start a new line. Instead, just press Alt + Enter to move the cursor to the next line. Pressing the Enter key does not make a paragraph; it just stops text input and moves you to another cell.

   1. Press the F9 key to move Smiley to a different location.
   2. Put your answer in the RED box with the column letter first and the row number second.
   3. Type a ? in the BLUE box, press ENTER, and then F9 to see if you were right.
   4. Delete your answer and the ?, and try again.

Coordinate Grid Matching

 Tip:

If for some reason the text doesn't fit in the merged cells, you can adjust the width of one or more columns.

18. You can make this worksheet look nicer by making some changes.
    Select Tools → Options → View tab. Uncheck Gridlines and Sheet tabs. Press OK to exit.

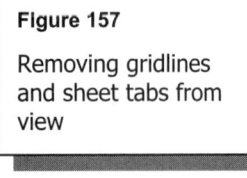

Figure 157

Removing gridlines and sheet tabs from view

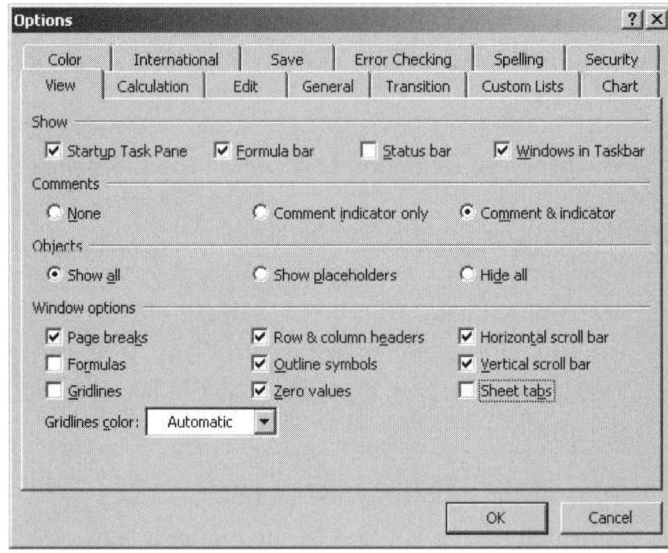

19. If you are going to have students work on this on a computer, you need to protect the worksheet from accidental changes.
    Select Tools → Protection → Protect Sheet. Remove the check mark from the box labeled Select locked cells, and click OK to exit.

Figure 159

Protecting the sheet from accidental changes by students

 Note:

You have the option on this page to select a password (which is entirely optional) before you click OK. Just remember that if you do decide to enter one, make sure that you write it down and store it in a safe place.

Figure 158

Final result

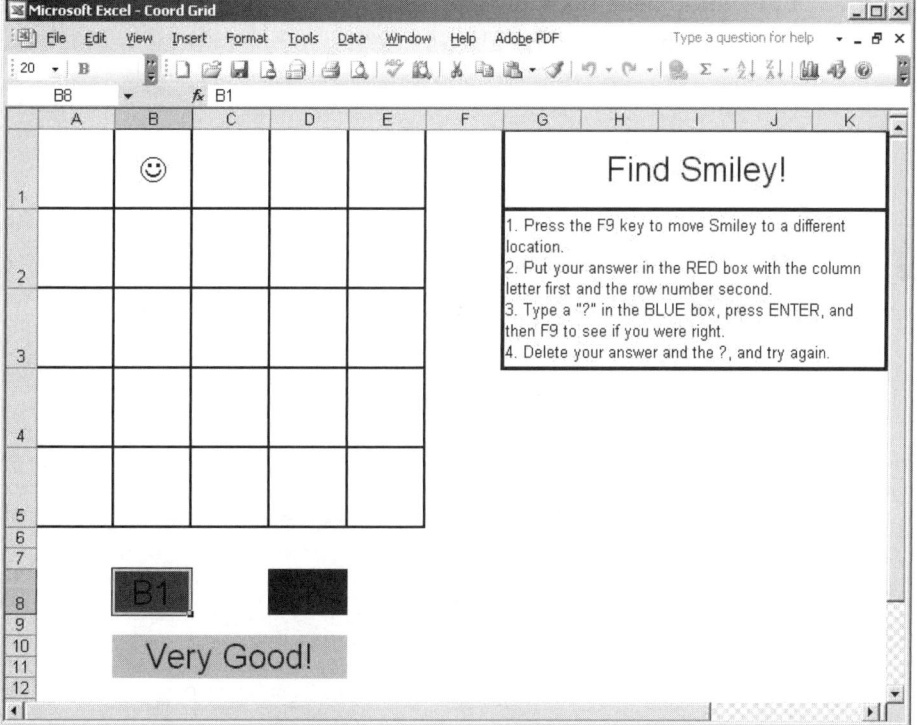

Coordinate Grid Matching

Using the Application

This application was designed for third or advanced second graders. With instruction from you, they should be able to figure out the sequence of what to do. This can also be used one-on-one with an adult doing the typing, or with the use of an overhead projector for the computer.

Excel Extras

I was not really sure how big to make this grid challenging without being intimidating. You, of course, know your students a lot better than I do. With a little tweaking, this can be made just about any size you want it to be. The only restrictions would be to make sure that both the grid and the cells for the answer and Excel's response are visible on the screen without scrolling. Simply alter each formula based on what size your grid will be. Also, you may need to tweak column width and row height a little if you are making a much larger grid.

Math Art

Opportunity

If you need a quick one or two day lesson for those days when you and your students need a little break, try doing some mathematical art with Excel. Both string art and tessellations are bona fide mathematical concepts, and Excel can be used to turn out some surprisingly artistic results. Doing a little internet research for both will turn up a large amount of reference material and design ideas.

Solution and Overview

You will learn how to use the built-in Drawing tools that come with Excel to draw lines and basic shapes and how to change their colors.

Creating the Solution

String Art

You will set up a square grid that will be used as a guide for drawing the lines. The only real consideration here is the age of your students and their level of patience. Younger students may feel overwhelmed by anything larger than a 15 x 15 grid. Older students could easily deal with a 25 x 25 or larger.

1. Begin by making a 25 x 25 grid. (You can easily make this either smaller or larger.)

a. Move your cursor to the extreme left edge of the worksheet to the box that has the 1 in it for Row 1. Your cursor will change to a right-pointing arrow. Move it down towards row 2 and it will change into a plus sign with vertical arrows. Left-click, and you will see how high your rows currently are. It should say "Height: 12.75 (17 pixels)". If it is different, that's OK; just remember the pixel size.

b. Now move your cursor to the A in the rectangle above cell A1 and it will change into a down-pointing arrow. Left-click and slowly drag to the right. Notice that as you drag, Excel counts the number of columns (1C, 2C, 3C, etc.). When you reach the 25th column, which is column Y, stop.

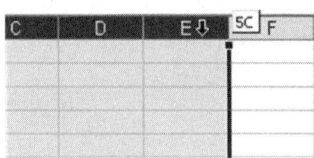

Figure 160

Excel counts the columns as you drag

c. Now move your cursor to the line between column X and column Y until your cursor turns into a plus sign with horizontal arrows. Left-click and drag to the left until the pixel size is 17 (or whatever you discovered your row height to be). Press the Home key on your keyboard to return to cell A1. You now have 25 columns that are the same size as your row height.

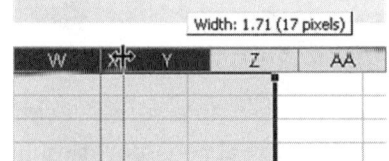

Figure 161

Making columns the same width as the row height

2. Draw a border around the grid.

   a. From the View drop down menu, select Toolbars and click on Borders. A small toolbar will appear somewhere on your worksheet. On the left there is a small grid and pencil icon. Highlight it, and click on the down arrow on the right edge.

b. Click on the words "Draw Border". Your cursor changes to a pencil icon. Move your cursor to the upper left corner of cell A1. Click and drag to the right and down until you get to cell Y25. Your grid should now have a border around it. Move your cursor to the Borders toolbar and click on the X in the upper right hand corner to remove it from your worksheet.

Figure 162

Selecting Draw Border and using its pencil icon to draw a border around a grid of cells

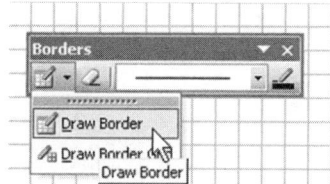
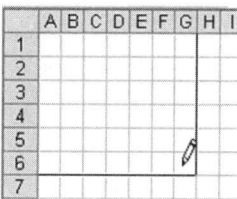

3. Make sure that all the lines you draw line up with the row and column divisions of your grid.
   Go to View → Toolbars, and make sure Drawing has a check mark by it (if there is no check mark, click on Drawing). The Drawing toolbar should appear at the bottom of your worksheet. Click on the word Draw at the extreme left, and then Snap. Click on the To Grid icon.

Figure 163

Using Snap To Grid to make sure lines are properly aligned to rows and columns of a grid

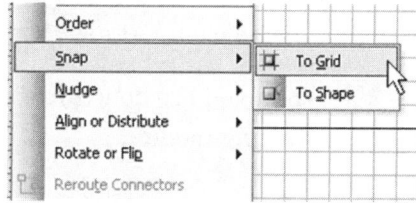

Math Art

4. Draw the string art.

   Next to the word AutoShapes there is a Line icon. Double-click on it and move your cursor up onto the worksheet. It should now look like a small plus sign. This is the Drawing Tool cursor.

   a. Move your cursor to the upper left corner of cell A1. Left-click and drag down to the lower right corner of cell A26 and let go.

   b. Go back to the Drawing toolbar and click on the line icon again. Unfortunately, you only get to draw one line per click. Now draw another line from the upper left corner of A2 to the lower right of B26.

 Tip:

If you double-click the Line icon, it will stay activated. You can then draw multiple lines. To exit Line Drawing mode, click the Line icon once again.

   c. Continue the pattern of moving down one row to start the line, and across one column to finish the line. Remember to start in the upper left corner of the first cell, and end in the lower right. After you draw the line from upper left of A26 to lower right of Z26, the pattern will change. You will move across one column, and up one row. The next line will start in the LOWER left of A26, and go to the UPPER right of Z26. The pattern will change slightly as you get to each corner. However, you don't need to worry about total exactness. The pattern will still look good if you miss a line or two. And remember, if you make a mistake, you can easily "erase" it by clicking Ctrl+Z (undo).

   d. When you are done drawing lines, single-click the Line icon to exit Drawing mode.

Figure 164

Selecting and using the line AutoShape to create string art

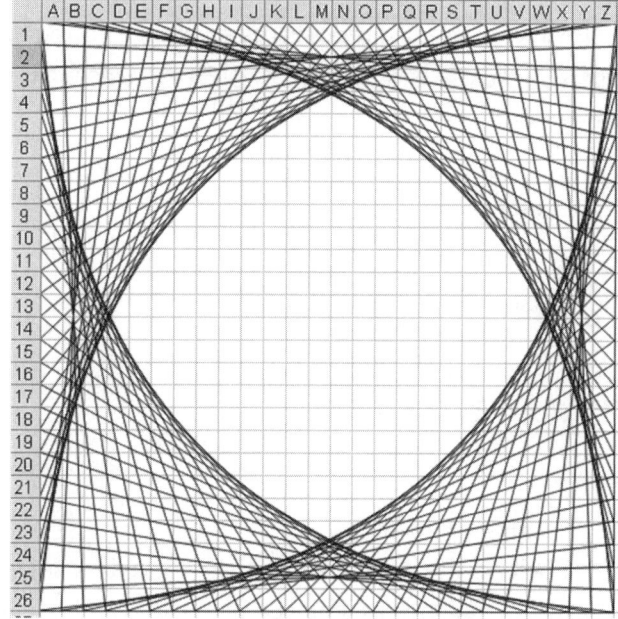

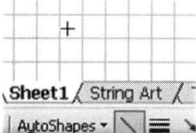

Tessellations

1. Locate tessellating shapes.

   Make sure the Drawing toolbar is visible by going to View → Toolbars and clicking on Drawing. Clicking on the word AutoShapes displays many sub-menus, each of which contain several shapes. Some of the shapes that will tessellate can be found in Basic Shapes (Diamond, Hexagon, Cross, Cube), Block Arrows (Chevron), Flowchart (Decision, Punched Tape, Stored Data), and Stars and Banners (Wave and Double Wave).

Figure 165 Selecting basic shapes suitable to drawing tessellations

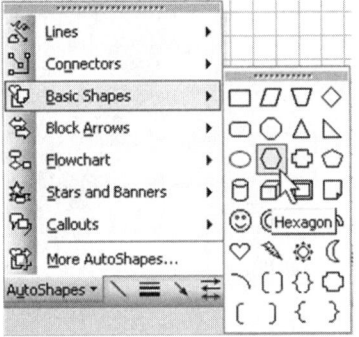
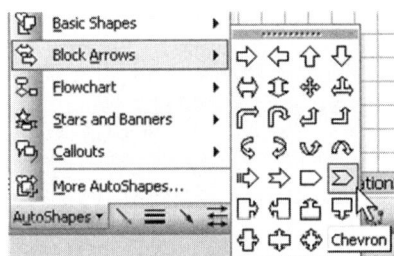

2. Disable Snap.
   Click on the word Draw at the left edge, select Snap, and make sure that neither of the two choices is highlighted. If one is, click it to deselect.

3. Select shape to tessellate; insert and resize.
   To choose a shape, click on AutoShapes, click the submenu you want, and click on the shape. When you move your cursor to the worksheet, it will have changed to a small plus sign.

   a. Move the cursor to the upper left corner and click. The shape will appear. For some reason, the default size of some of the shapes is very small or squashed in one direction. Use one of the circular grab handles to pull it to a size and proportion you like.

   b. While the grab handles are still visible, press Ctrl+C to copy the shape and Crtl+V to paste it. It will end up on top of the first shape.

   c. Move your cursor to the copy. When your cursor changes to a plus sign with arrows in both directions, click and drag the shape to its new position. Unfortunately, this is not a precise step. You have to "eyeball" the new position, and may have to fiddle with it until you are happy. The good news is that all you have to do to continue your design is to press

Ctrl+V, move the new shape, and repeat until your design covers the page.

Figure 166

Copying and coloring basic shapes

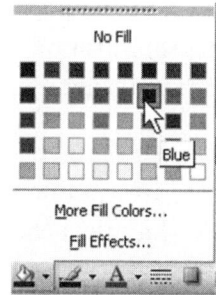

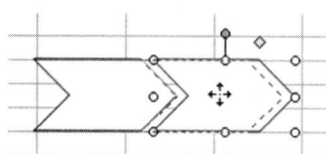

4. Add color to the tessellations using the Paint Can icon.

   a. Click on the arrow next to the Paint Can, and select the color you want from the palette. Go to your design and click on one of the shapes, then click the Paint Can icon.

   b. You can alternately change the color of several shapes all at the same time. Click on one shape to highlight the grab handles. Now press and hold the Shift key. Continue clicking on all the shapes that you wish to color the same.

   c. When you are done, click on the Paint Can icon and all the highlighted shapes will be the same color. Have your students use no more than three colors and make sure that no two shapes that are touching have the same color.

5. For printing, use the same instructions as the ones for string art. The main difference, though, is that tessellations look best in color. If you do not have a color printer you may not want to print them. You could, however, tell the students NOT to fill with color, print them out, and use colored pencils or markers to add color. Also, depending on your students' designs, they may print better in Landscape mode rather than in Portrait.

Using the Application

You can change the look of a string art design by altering the pattern by going farther around the corner when you make the first line. You can also add color to the design, but it is a somewhat tedious process.

1. You can only change the color of a line after you have drawn it. After you draw a line, and while it is still selected (each end has small circular grab handles) click on the Paintbrush icon on the Drawing toolbar. Your line will change to whatever color it currently shows.

2. To change the color, click on the down arrow next to the Paintbrush icon and select any color from the palette. The line color will stay whatever you choose until you change it again. If you have a student with a lot of patience, they should be able to make a pattern of changing colors as they go around the grid.

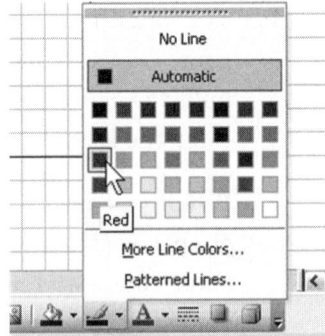

Figure 167

Selecting line colors from the drop down menu

Figure 168

Magnifying the page makes it easier to select individual lines

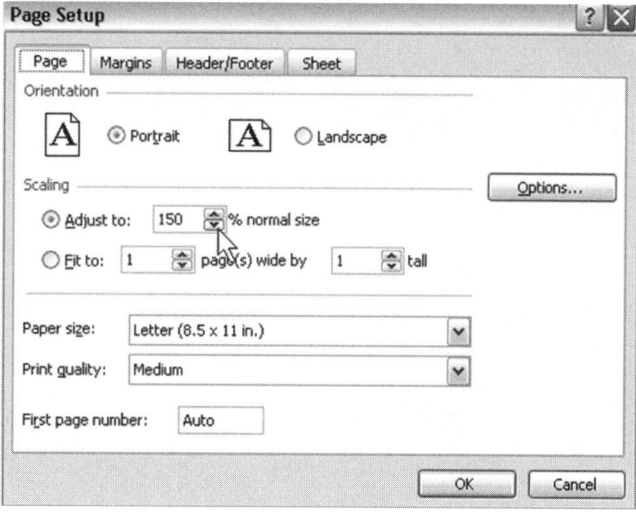

3. For printing out the designs, go to File → Page Setup. Click on the Margins tab and put a checkmark next to Horizontally and Vertically at the bottom of the page. Unless the student has made a very large grid, you probably will not have to change the margins.

4. Click on Print Preview at this point to see how the design will fit on a page. If the design looks too small or too big, click on the Setup box at the top of the Print Preview page and click the Page tab. Under Scaling, click on the radio button next to "Adjust to", and then change the percent in the box by clicking on the up or down arrows. Click OK to exit and check your results. Continue until you are pleased with how the design fits on your paper.

Math Art

Candy Bar Fractions

Opportunity

You are starting your unit on fractions and you would like to have a worksheet that could be used to show the fractional parts of a rectangular candy bar. This could be something that you could display to the class using the overhead or that the students could do individually on the computer.

Solution and Overview

You will make a "candy bar" with twelve pieces so that students can have practice with halves, thirds, fourths, sixths, and twelfths. (For older students, you may want to expand this to 24 or 36 pieces.) You or the student will type the fraction they want to make into one of the cells. Then, they will type "X's" into the cells of the candy bar to make a picture of the fraction. When they think they have the correct solution, they can type a question mark into another cell, and Excel will display the appropriate response, depending on whether they are right or wrong.

Creating the Solution

1. Set the column width.
   Begin by moving your cursor to the very top of column B. The cursor will change to a downward pointing arrow. Left-click and drag to the right, stopping at column G. Columns B through G should be grayed in. Now move your cursor between columns F and G until it changes to a plus sign with horizontal arrows. When you left-click, you will see the current column

width of 8.43 (64 pixels). Hold down the left mouse button and move to the right until the pixel size is 90, and let go. All of the highlighted columns will now have the same width.

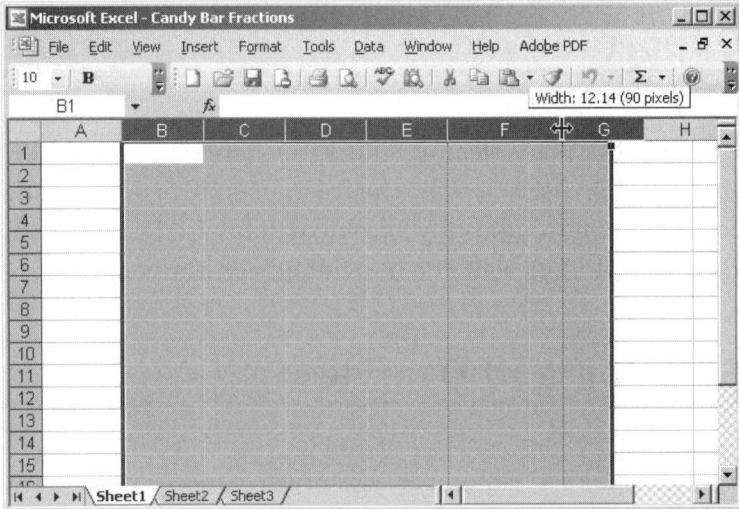

Figure 169

Setting the width of columns B:G to 90 pixels

2. Set row height.

Now move your cursor to the extreme left edge of row 12. The cursor will change to a right-pointing arrow. Left-click and drag down to highlight row 13. Now move the cursor to the line between the 12 and 13 and the cursor will change to a plus sign with vertical arrows. Left-click, and you will see the current row height of 12.75 (17 pixels). This could be different, depending on your default font. As you did in Step 1, left-click and pull down until the pixel size is 90. These two rows should now be the same height.

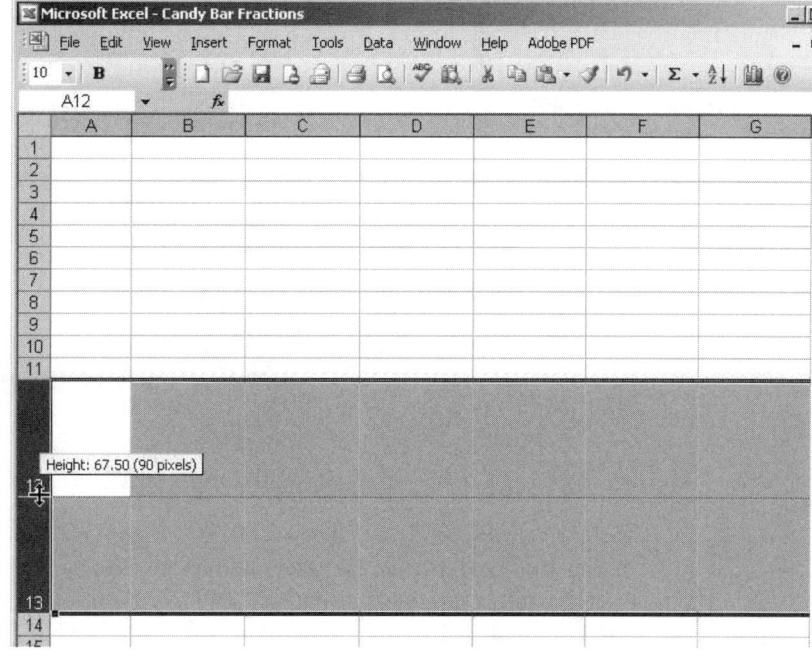

Figure 170

Setting the height of rows 12 and 13 to 90 pixels

3. Format range B12:G13.

    Move your cursor to cell B12. Left-click and drag to the right and down to highlight the range B12:G13 and let go of the mouse button. Press Ctrl+1 to access the Format Cells dialog box. You will make three changes:

    a. Click on the Font tab. Change Font to Arial and Size to 72.

    b. Click on the Border tab. Click on the Inside Preset at the top of the page. Next, under Line Style, click on the thickest line in the right column. Then, click the down arrow in the Color box, and select Brown from the top row of the palette. Now click Outline in the Presets.

Candy Bar Fractions

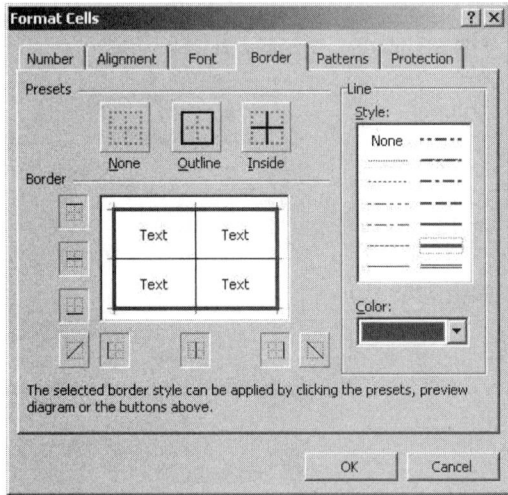

Figure 171

Using the Format Cells dialog to set the font and border options

    c. Click on the Protection tab. Remove the check mark next to the word Locked. Now click OK to exit.

4. Apply conditional formatting to the range.
The twelve cells in the rectangle should still be selected and grayed out. If not, select them again.

    a. From the drop down menus at the top of the page, click on Format and then Conditional Formatting. A dialog box will appear. The second box from the left currently says "between". Click on the down arrow and select "equal to" from the list.

    b. In the large empty box at the top right, type in the letter X. Click on the box labeled Format and then click on the Font tab in the dialog box that appears. Under Color, click on the down arrow and select brown. On the Borders tab, click on the Color drop down menu, and select White from the lower right hand corner, and then click on Outline under Preset. Now click on the Patterns tab and again select brown. Click OK twice to exit.

Figure 172

Using conditional formatting to control screen response to student's answers

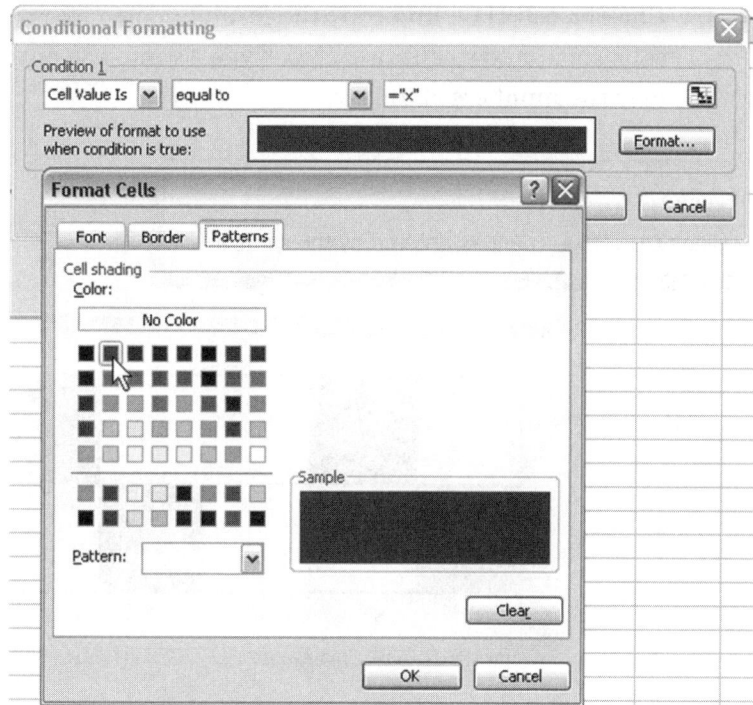

c. Now type an X in one of the cells and the cell and font color should turn brown. You will not be able to see what you typed. If you type in anything else, the cell will not change.

5. Enter a formula to count Xs and copy it down.

a. Go to cell H12 and type in the following formula:
=COUNTIF(B12:G12,"X")
Press the Enter key.

COUNTIF is one of several built-in Excel statistical functions that allow us to count the contents of a cell that contains a specific value. In

Candy Bar Fractions

this case, you want Excel to count the Xs for you. This particular function is not case sensitive, so it will count both upper and lower case letters.

b. Click on cell H13, and copy the formula down by pressing Ctrl+D. Both cells should now contain zeros. Type Xs into the outlined cells to see how the numbers change.

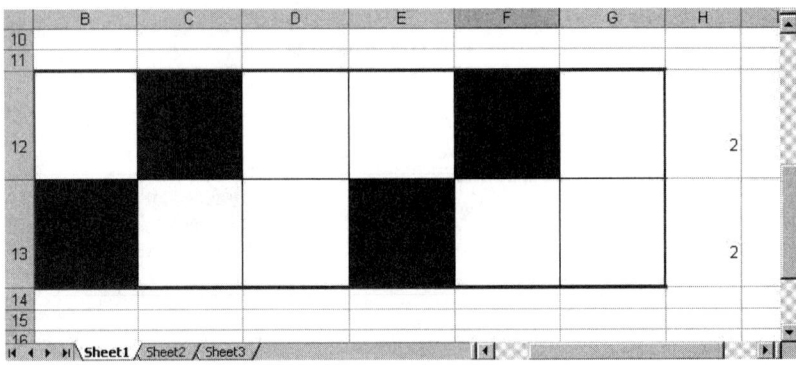

Figure 173

Using COUNTIF to count Xs entered by the student

6. Use AutoSum to sum the number of Xs.

Click on cell H14, and then click on the Greek letter sigma (Σ) on the toolbar at the top of the page. This is the SUM function. Excel should highlight cells H12 and H13, and display =SUM(H12:13). This is the formula you want, so press the Enter key. For now, you are through with these three cells, but you will come back to them later to hide the cell display.

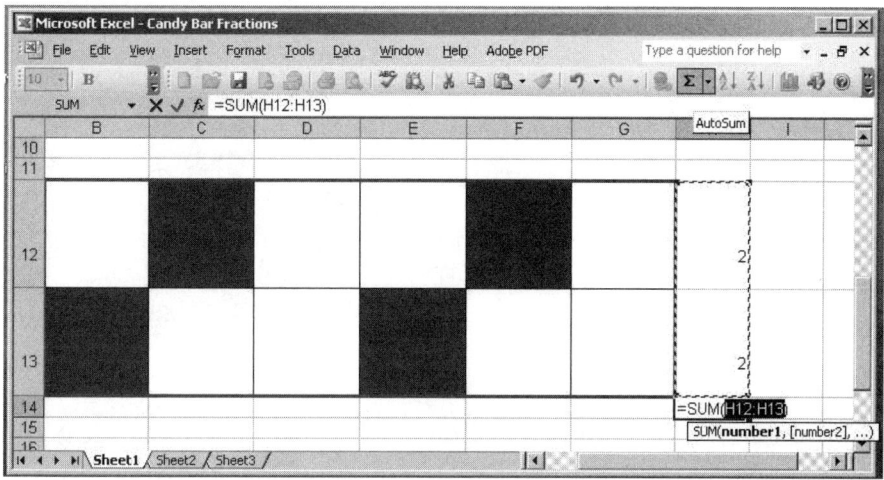

Figure 174

Using AutoSum to add the two rows of Xs entered by the student

7. Change the height of row 10.

    Move your cursor to the extreme left edge of row 10. Click on the line between rows 10 and 11 and, as you did earlier, change the row height of row 10 to only 34 pixels.

8. Format B10.

    Click on cell B10 and press Ctrl+1 to access Format Cells. You will make six changes:

    a. Number tab: Select Fraction; from Type, select "Up to two digits".

    b. Alignment tab: Under Text Alignment, change Horizontal to Center.

    c. Font tab: Change Font to Arial and Size to 20.

    d. Border tab: Click on Outline under Presets.

    e. Patterns tab: Select Pale Yellow from the bottom row.

    f. Protection tab: Remove the check mark from Locked. Click OK to exit.

Candy Bar Fractions

Figure 175 Cell B10 formatted as described in Step 8

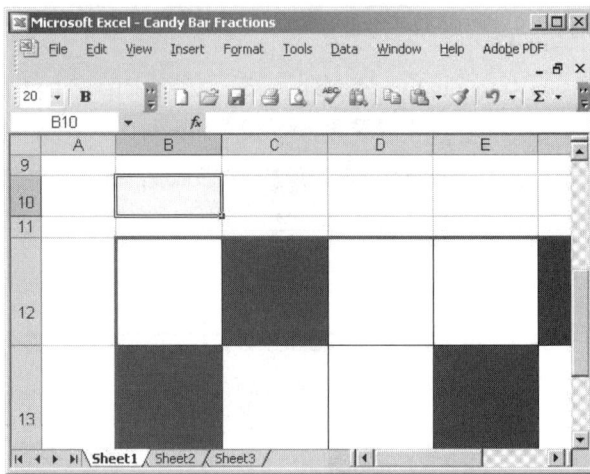

9. Format G10.

   Click on cell G10, and press Ctrl+1. Make no changes on the Number tab, but make all of the other changes you made for cell B10, except, on the Patterns tab, select a Light Blue color. Click OK to exit.

Figure 176 Cell G10 formatted as described in Step 9

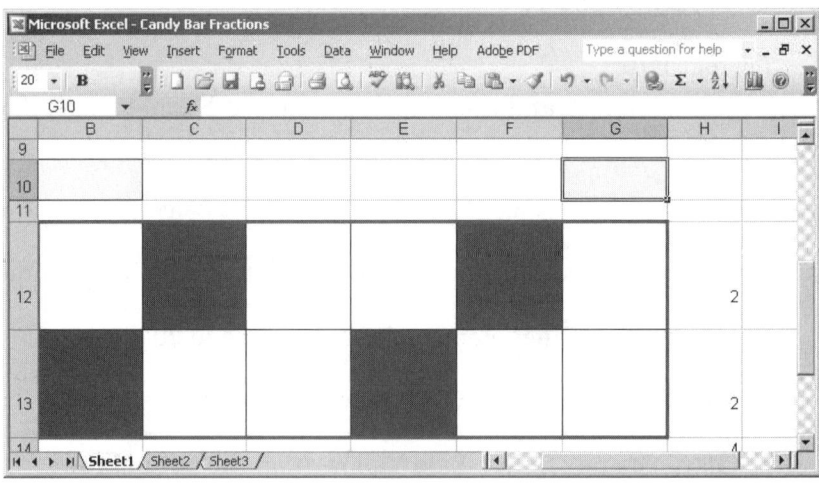

Candy Bar Fractions

134   Excel for the Math Classroom

10. Merge and format cells D10 and E10.

    Click on cell D10 and drag to the right to also select E10. Press Ctrl+1 and make the following changes:

    a. From the Alignment tab, change General under Horizontal to Center. Under Text Control, click on the box next to Merge Cells.

    b. Change the Font type to Arial, size 20. Click OK to exit.

11. Now you will make some conditional formatting changes to the merged cell D10:E10.

    a. From the drop down menu, select Format, and then Conditional Format. As before, change the word "between" to "equal to" on the drop down menu.

    b. In the large rectangle, type in the following: **Correct!**
        Click on Format, and select a green color from the second row from the bottom of the palette. Click OK.

    c. You need to add a second condition, so click on the box with "Add >>". As before, change "between" to "equal to", and then type in the following words: **Try again.**

    d. Click on Format and select Pink from the bottom row. Click OK twice to exit.

Figure 177

Adding a second conditional format

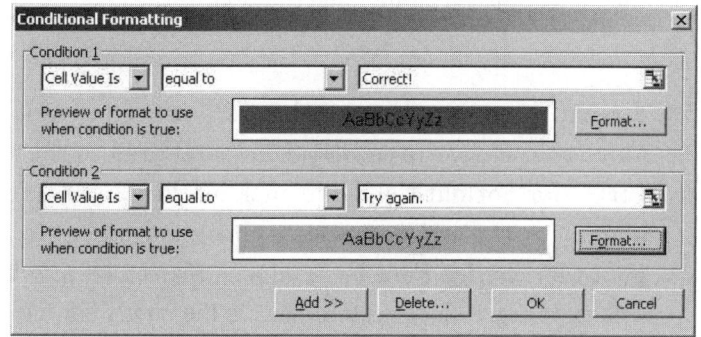

Candy Bar Fractions

12. Hide the text in H13 and H14.

    Remember back in Step 6, when you left some work to come back to at a later time? Now is the time! Click on cell H12 and drag down to highlight cells H13 and H14. Press Ctrl+1. Click on the Font tab. Under Color, click on the down arrow next to the word "Automatic" to view the color palette. Click on the white color in the lower right hand corner. Click OK to exit.

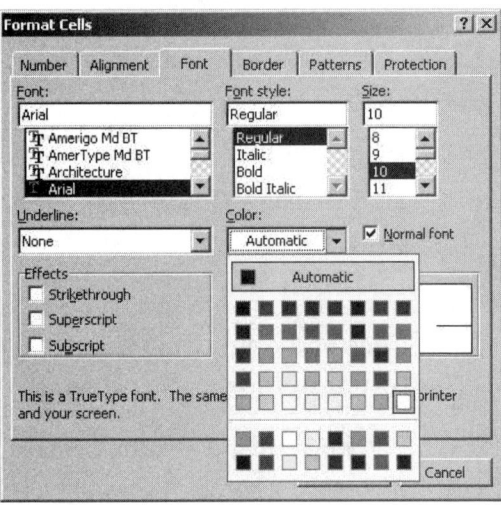

Figure 178

Using a white font color to hide text

Candy Bar Fractions

Note:

Notice that when you click on one of these cells you can see the formula in the Formula bar, but you cannot see the text in the cells.

13. Format the cells and enter the text for the first set of objectives.

    Move your cursor to cell B1. Click and drag to the right to cell G1. Press Ctrl+1 for Format Cells and click on the Alignment tab. Change Horizontal alignment to Center and put a check mark next to Merge cells. Click on the Font tab; change Font to Arial and Size to 18. Click OK to exit. Inside the cell, type the following text: **Divide the candy bar into fractional parts.** Press Enter.

14. Format the cells and enter the text for the second set of objectives.
Move your cursor to cell B2. Click and drag to the right to cell G2. Again, press Ctrl+1 to Format Cells. Make the same changes as in Step 13. When finished, type the following text: Use halves, thirds, fourths, sixths or twelfths. Press Enter.

Figure 179

Entering student instructions

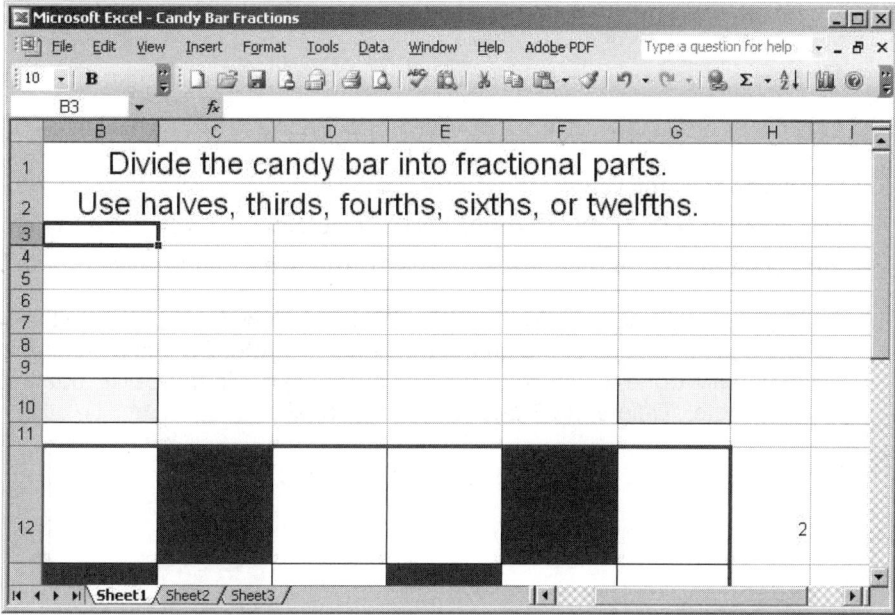

15. Put a border around the objectives.
Move your cursor back to cell B1. Click and drag down one row to select the two sections of merged cells. Find the Border icon in the toolbar at the top of the page, and click on the down arrow next to it. In the bottom row, click on the small icon that shows an outside border.

Candy Bar Fractions

16. Format the cells that will hold the instructions.
    Move your cursor to cell B4. Click and drag down and to the right to cell G8. Press Ctrl+1, and make the following changes.

    a. Select the Alignment tab. Change both horizontal and vertical text alignment to Center, and click on Wrap text and Merge cells.

    b. Select the Font tab. Make sure that Arial is selected and change the size to 12.

    c. Select the Border tab. Change color to Automatic and select the bottom left line style. Click Outline.

    d. Select the Patterns tab. In the bottom row, select Beige. Click OK to exit.

17. Enter the text for the instructions.
    The merged cells (B4:G8) should still be selected. If not, select them and then type in the following text. Press Enter when you have finished:

    To begin, type a fraction into the YELLOW box below. Next, move to the candy bar and color in the pieces to match the fraction you wrote. Do this by typing in an X. When you are done, check your answer by typing a ? in the BLUE box and pressing Enter. Delete the ? and X's, and try again.

18. Delete any Xs you may have entered in cells B12:G13.

Figure 180

Entering student instructions

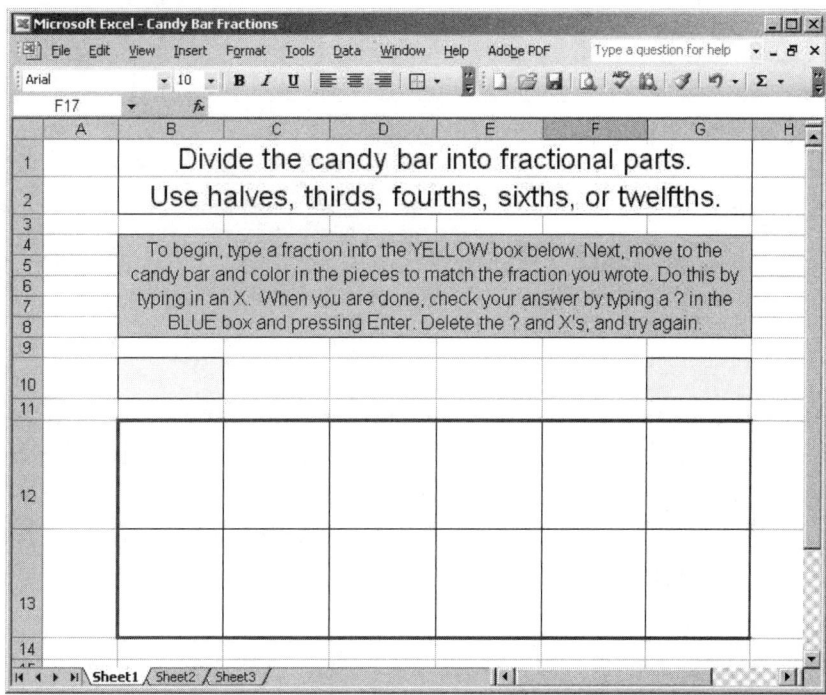

19. Now you will hide some of the Excel distractions.

    From the drop down menus at the top, select Tools and Options. Select the View tab. Click on Gridlines, Row & column headers, and Sheet tabs to remove the check marks. Click OK to exit.

Candy Bar Fractions

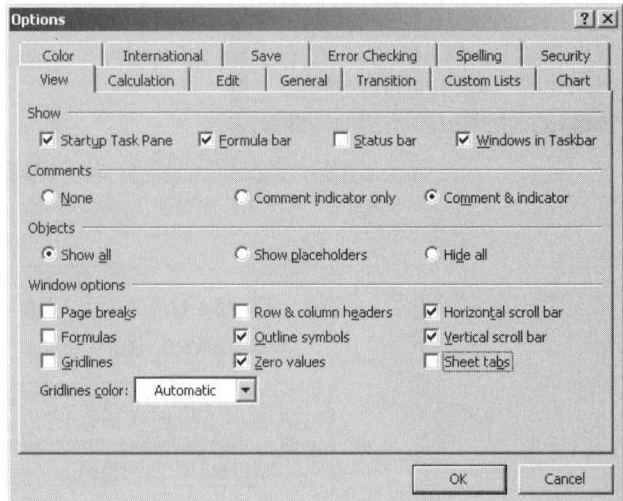

Figure 181

Hiding gridlines, row and column headers, and sheet tabs from view

20. To protect the worksheet from accidental changes, click on Tools → Protection → Protect Sheet. Click on Select locked cells to remove the check mark. You can put a password in at the top if you wish, but it should not be necessary. If you do, remember to write it down and store it in a safe place. Click OK to exit.

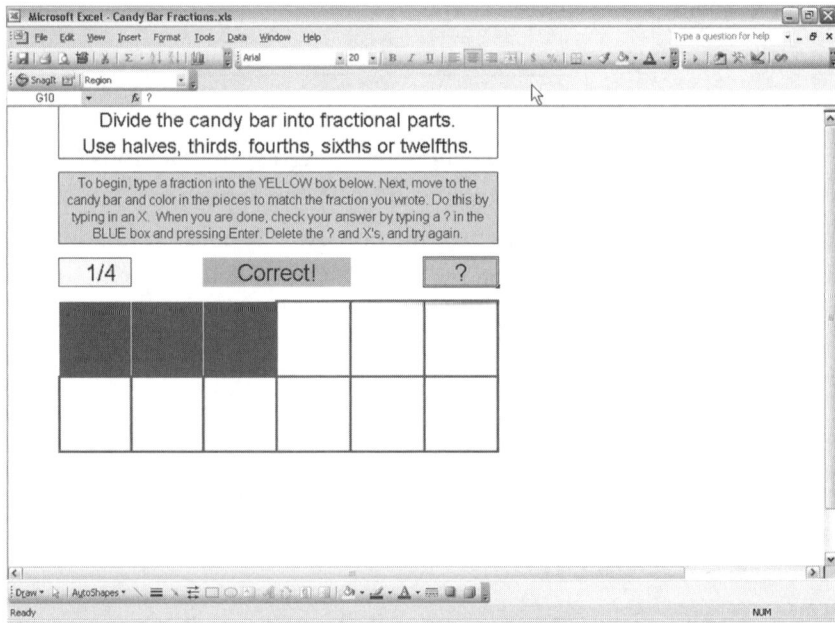

Figure 182

Final version provides student feedback

Using the Application

This worksheet can be used with an overhead by the teacher, or by the student, individually or in small groups. After typing in the desired fraction, X's need to be typed into the "candy bar" to represent that fraction. When the student believes he/she has the correct answer, they can type a question mark (?) into the blue box.

Candy Bar Fractions

Math Facts Game

Opportunity

You would like to have a game for your students to play that will test their math facts mentally and at the same time work on a skill that will be useful for factoring trinomials of the form $x^2 + bx + c$ in algebra. It would be nice if this was something the students could do on their own, in a small group, or with the entire class. The "Math Facts Game" shows the sum and product of two numbers and then asks the students to guess the correct numbers.

Solution and Overview

You will create an Excel spreadsheet to play "The Math Facts Game". Excel will randomly generate two numbers using parameters of your choosing (numbers between 1 and 5, for example, or integers between –10 and +10). The student arrives at the answer by using paper and pencil or mental math, and then enters the numbers into the spreadsheet. Excel will then tell the student if their answer is right or wrong, and can also give the correct solution. This is another worksheet that uses circular references and manual calculations.

Creating the Solution

There are actually only five cells that have any type of formula, ranging from very simple to relatively complex. You will build all the parts of the worksheet first, and then finish by putting in the formulas.

1. Set the row height.

    Move your cursor all the way to the left edge of the page where it changes to a right arrow. Move it to the line between rows 1 and 2 and it will change to a plus sign with vertical arrows. Left click, and you will see a message that says "Height: 12.75 (17 pixels)". Move your mouse down until it reads "Height: 25.50 (34 pixels)" and let go.

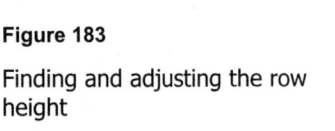

Figure 183

Finding and adjusting the row height

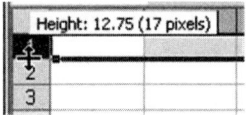

2. Format the cell range C1:G1.

    Click on cell C1, and drag to the right to highlight the range C1:G1. Push Ctrl+1 to open the Format Cells dialog box and make the following changes:

    a. Alignment tab: Change Horizontal and Vertical Text Alignment to Center. Click on the box next to Merge cells.

Figure 184

Centering text and merging cells

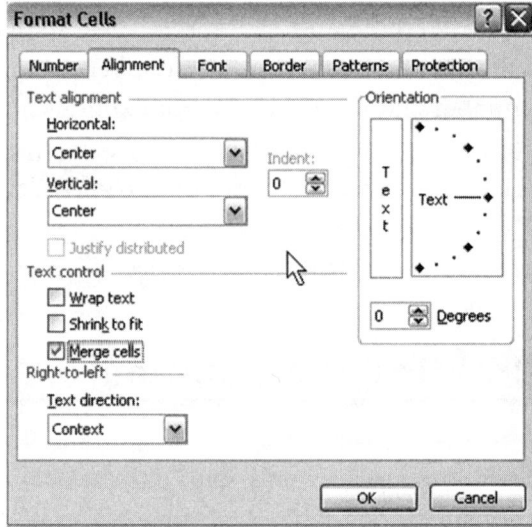

    b. Font tab: Change the Font to Arial and Size to 18.

c. Border tab: Under Presets, click on Outline.

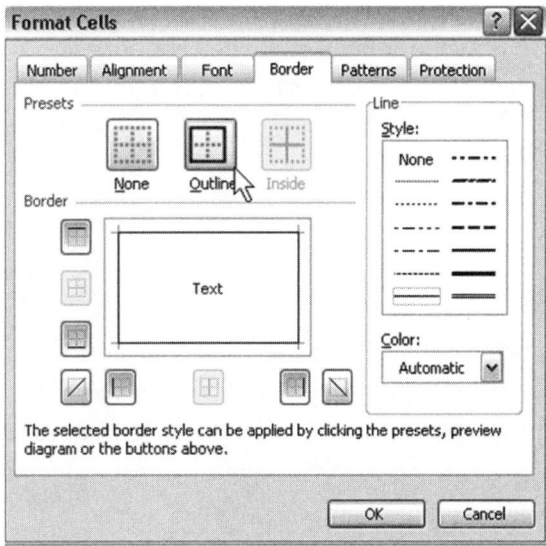

Figure 185

Selecting an outline border

d. Patterns tab: Choose a light color, such as pale yellow. Click OK to exit.

3. Enter title block text.
   Click on the merged cells and type in the following text:
   The Math Facts Game

4. Make four text boxes to hold the instructions.
   Click on cell B3. Hold down the left mouse button and drag to the right and down to select the range B3:H6; release the mouse button. Push Ctrl+1 to open the Format Cells dialog box and make the following changes:

   a. Alignment tab: Under Text control, select Wrap text and Merge cells.

   b. Font tab: Change the Font to Arial and Size to 12.

   c. Patterns tab: Select the same color you did in Step 2d. Click OK to exit.

5. Make the other three "text boxes" in B7:H9, B10:H12, and B13:H14.
   For each, click on the first cell in the range. Hold down the left mouse button and move to the right and down to the last cell in the range and release

Math Facts Game

the mouse button. Press Ctrl+1, and make the same changes that you did in Step 4 to each text box.

6. Put borders around the text boxes.
   Click on the first text box; hold down the left mouse button and drag down to select all four text boxes. Select the Borders icon in the toolbar at the top of the page and click on the down arrow. Click on Outline Borders.

7. Before you begin typing, you will need to make some changes to the way Excel automatically tries to figure out what you want to type. Usually this is helpful, but for this exercise it will just prove to be annoying! From the drop down menus, select Tools and then Options and click on the Spelling tab. At the bottom of the page, click on AutoCorrect. Uncheck the box next to "Capitalize first letter of sentences" and click OK twice to exit. When you are done with this exercise, you may want to change it back.

Figure 186

Configuring AutoCorrect options

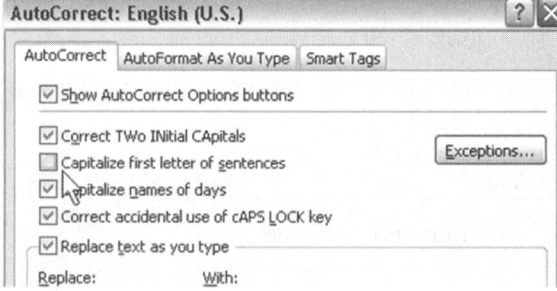

8. Type the following in the text boxes you just made.

   a. In the top text box, type in:

   > 1. The numbers in the GREEN boxes below are the sum and product of two other numbers. When you think you know what the numbers are, type them into the RED boxes.

 Tip:

For extra emphasis, you can highlight the names of colors, and change the font color to match the word. Use the Font Color icon in the toolbar at the top of the page.

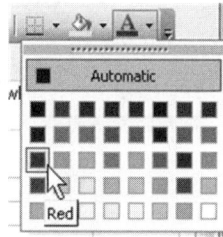

Figure 187

Selecting color to match text to word it represents

    b. In the second text box, type in:

        2. To check your answer, type a ? into the BLUE box, press ENTER and then the F9 key.

    c. In the third text box, type in:

        3. To see the correct answer, type SHOW into the BLUE box, press ENTER and then the F9 key.

    d. In the last text box, type in:

        4. To play again, delete the ? or SHOW and press the F9 key.

9. Change the row height of Rows 16, 19, and 21 to the same height as Row 1 (25.50, 34 pixels).

   Move your cursor all the way to the left edge of the page where it changes to a right arrow. While holding down the Ctrl key, click on each row. Release the Ctrl key and move the cursor to the line between rows 16 and 17 and it will change to a plus sign with vertical arrows. Left click, and you will see a message that says "Height: 12.75 (17 pixels)". Move your mouse down until it reads "Height: 25.50 (34 pixels)" and let go.

10. Select and format cell D16.
    Push Ctrl+1 to open the Format Cells dialog box.

        a. Alignment tab: Change Horizontal to Center.

        b. Font tab: Change the Font to Arial and Size to 18.

        c. Border tab: Select Outline.

        d. Patterns tab: Select Light Green. Click OK to exit.

Math Facts Game

Figure 188

Selecting shading color for cell

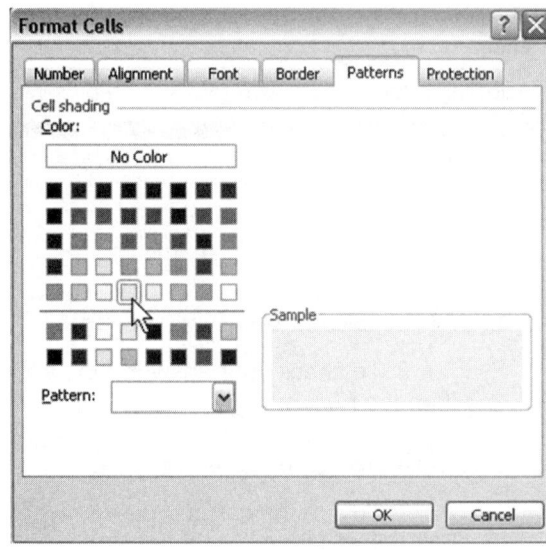

11. Copy format from D16 to F16.
    With cell D16 still selected, press Ctrl+C to copy. Click on cell F16, and push Ctrl+V to paste. Both cells now have the same formatting.

12. In cell D16, type in this formula: =A1+A2
    Press Enter. The cell will read "0".

13. In cell F16, type in this formula: =A1*A2
    Press Enter. This cell will also read "0".

14. In cell D17, type in the following word: SUM
    In cell F17, type in the following word: PRODUCT
    Change the Alignment to Center in both cells by clicking on the Center icon in the toolbar at the top of the page.

Figure 189

Your results should look like this

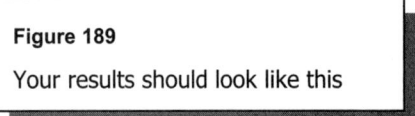
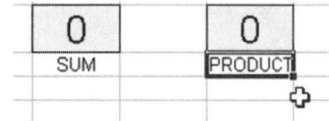

148   Excel for the Math Classroom

15. Select and format cell C19.

    Push Ctrl+1 and make these five formatting changes.

    a. Alignment tab: Change Horizontal and Vertical Text Alignment to Center. Click on the box next to Merge cells.

    b. Font tab: Change the Font to Arial and Size to 18.

    c. Border tab: Under Presets, click on Outline.

    d. Patterns tab: Select Red. Click OK to exit.

    e. Protection tab: *Uncheck* the box next to Locked. This is *IMPORTANT!*

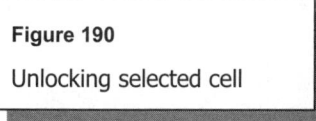

Figure 190

Unlocking selected cell

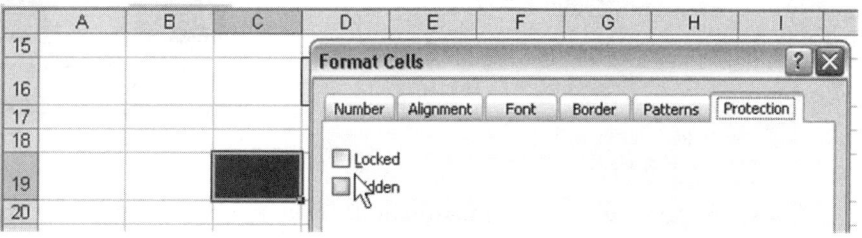

16. Copy the format from cell C19 into cells E19 and G19.

    Select C19. Double-click on the Format Painter icon (looks like a small paint brush). Click on cell E19 and then on G19.

 Tip:

If you don't see the Format Painter icon in your toolbar, you can easily add it. From the menu, select View → Toolbars → Customize. In the dialog box that appears, click on the Command tab, and then select Format in the left column. Scroll down the column on the right until you see the Format Painter icon, and drag it to one of your toolbars. I put mine next to the Paint Can, but any place will do.

Math Facts Game

17. Click on cell G19 and push Ctrl+1. Click on the Patterns tab and change the color to Light Blue.

18. Select and format the range D21:F21.
    Click on Cell D21. Left-click and drag to the right to select the range D21:F21, and release the mouse button. Push Ctrl+1 to open the Format Cells dialog box, and make the following changes:

    a. Alignment tab: Change the Horizontal Text Alignment to Center. Under Text Control, click on the box next to Merge Cells.

    b. Font tab: Change the Font to Arial and the Size to 18. Click OK to exit.

Figure 191

Your results should look like this

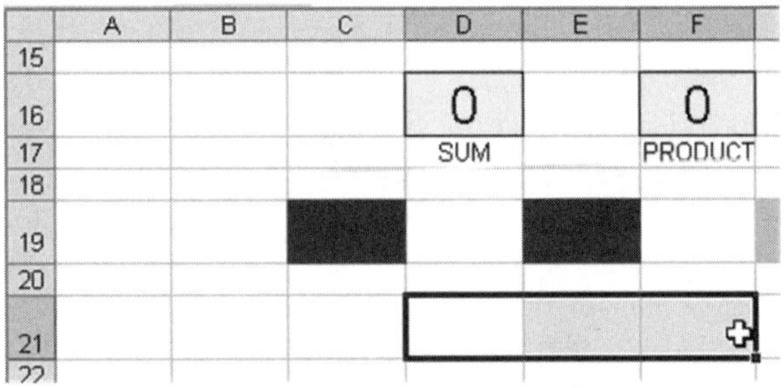

These merged cells will contain the feedback comments to the student, and require the use of IF and AND functions. Very simply, you will have Excel generate one response if the answer is correct, and another if the answer is wrong. Additionally, Excel can generate the correct answer. All of these responses are dependent upon what text has been typed into cell G19.

19. Now, click on the three merged cells in row 21 and carefully type in the following formula.

Note:

Be especially careful of punctuation, upper and lower case, and spaces. Make sure that you type everything as one continuous line with no breaks.

Note that near the beginning of the formula, there are two sets of double quotation marks (they can NOT be apostrophes!).

After A1, there is an ampersand (&) followed by a quotation mark ("). There needs to be a space before and after the word "and" that follows in order to have the correct spacing of text in the merged cell.

Also, there should never be a space after any comma that you type, even though the type-setting of this book may look like there is.

After you finish typing, there will be nothing displayed in the merged cells yet. You still need to add two more formulas.

=IF(G19="","",IF(G19="show",A1&" and "&A2,IF
(AND(G19="?",C19+E19=D16,C19*E19=F16),"Correct!","Sorry! Try again.")))

20. To highlight the answers generated by the last formula, you will format the three merged cells to display a different color for each response.

   a. Select the merged cells. From the drop down menu at the top, select Format, and then Conditional Formatting. The Conditional Formatting dialog box will appear. The first box defaults to "Cell Value Is".

   b. In the second box, click on the drop down menu arrow, and select "equal to".

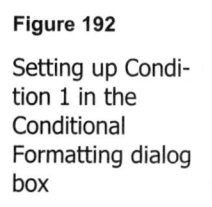

Figure 192

Setting up Condition 1 in the Conditional Formatting dialog box

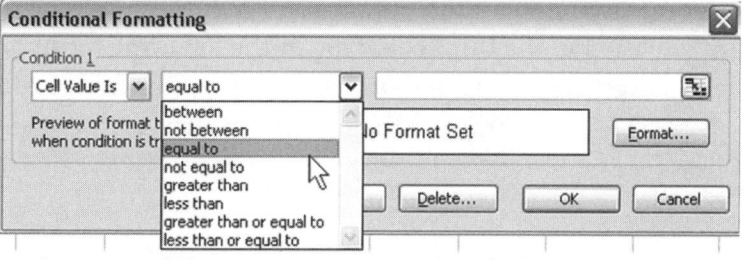

c. In the third box, type in the following text: **Correct!**
Click on the box labeled Format, and the Format Cells dialog box will appear. Click on the Patterns tab and choose a color, such as bright green. Click OK to close just this box.

d. The Conditional Formatting dialog box should still be visible. On the bottom, click on the box labeled Add>>. As before, change the second box to "equal to", and type in the following text in the third box: **Sorry! Try again.**

e. In both of these conditions, it is absolutely imperative that you use the exact phrase that you typed into the formula in Step 19.
Click on the Format box, then on Patterns, and select a color different from the last time, such as pink. Click OK to close just this dialog box.

Figure 193

Setting up Condition 2 in the Conditional Formatting dialog box

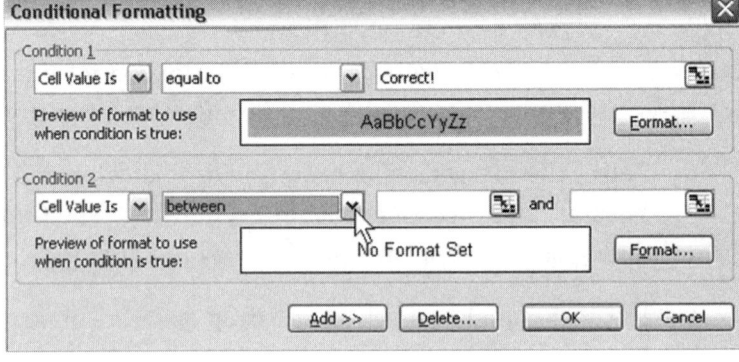

f. Click on the Add>> box again. Change the second box to "equal to". Then in the third box, type in the following formula: =A1&" and "&A2
Again, make sure that, when you type in this phrase, it is identical to the same phrase in the formula in Step 19.

 Note:

If there is any difference, no matter how slight, in the three phrases you just typed from how they appeared in the Step 19 formula, the cell will not change colors correctly.

Math Facts Game

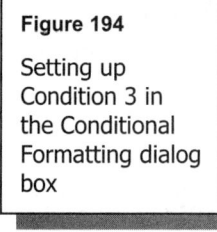

Figure 194

Setting up Condition 3 in the Conditional Formatting dialog box

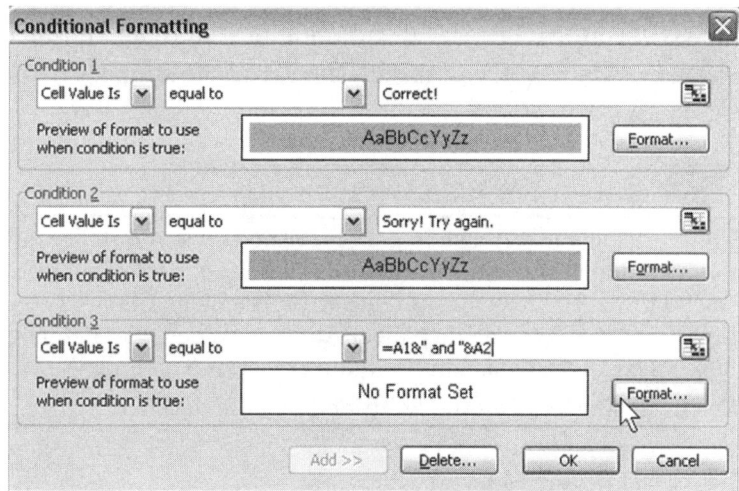

21. Before you enter the last two formulas, you need to get Excel ready to accept circular reasoning and manual calculation.
    From the Tools menu, select Options. Click on the Calculation tab and click on the radio button next to Manual. This means that Excel will no longer automatically calculate any formula until the user presses the F9 key. Make sure that the "Recalculate before save" box before is clear. Next, click on the box next to the word Iteration, and change the Maximum iterations to 1. Click OK to exit.

Figure 195

Setting up Calculation options to allow circular reasoning and manual calculation

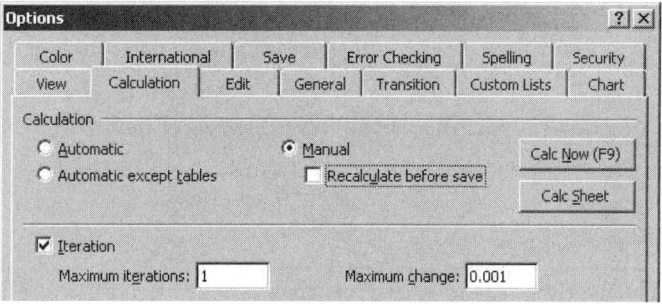

22. Click on cell A1. You will type in a formula that will generate a random number using the RANDBETWEEN function as long as cell G19 is empty. Because there are two different commands that the user can type into cell

Excel for the Math Classroom   153

G19, you will use an OR function nested in an IF function. This is also the place where you can decide the range of numbers to use with your students.

 Note:

The function you will use to generate the random numbers, RANDBETWEEN, is not a standard Excel function, but is, instead, part of something called the Analysis ToolPak. To have this and other functions available, you need to do the following: From the Tools menu, select Add-Ins. When the dialog box opens, click on the boxes next to Analysis ToolPak and Analysis ToolPak –VBA. Click OK to exit.
See page 53, Creating the Solution for more details.

For younger students, you may want to limit the numbers to between 1 and 5. For middle school students who are working on positive and negative numbers, the range could be from –10 to +10. For now, you will use the numbers 1 to 9. Click on A1 and type in this formula:

=IF(OR($G$19="?",$G$19="show"),A1,RANDBETWEEN(1,9))

Very simply, this formula tells Excel to generate a random number in cell A1 unless G19 contains the "?" or "show", in which case to display the last number that was randomly generated.

The dollar signs ($) in the G19 cell reference make it an absolute reference, which means the cell reference will not change if you copy the formula. Normally when you copy a formula to another cell, the cell references change relative to the original cell. For more information, see pages 47-48.

 Note:

Notice that this formula contains a reference to the cell that contains it (A1). This is referred to as a circular reference, and is usually not done. However, putting the check mark in the box next to the word Iteration allows this to happen without an error message.

23. Copy the formula from A1 to A2.

    This formula required a lot of precise typing, so you will just copy it into cell A2. Click on cell A2, and press Ctrl+D. The formula you typed in cell A1 will be copied into cell A2, and the references to cell A1 will change to A2.

 Tip:

Again, to customize this for your students, simply change the numbers after RANDBETWEEN in the formula. The numbers you type are inclusive. Just remember to copy the changes into both cells A1 and A2.

24. At this point, you need to clean up the appearance of the worksheet, but it should work. Perform these steps to make sure.

    a. Press the F9 key and watch the numbers in cells D16 and F16 change.

    b. Type your answer into C19 and E19, and then type ? into cell G19.

    c. Press F9 and notice that the random numbers do not change, but you will get a response in row 21 in the three merged cells.

    d. Type "show" (without quotes) into cell G19 and press F9 again. The correct answer will appear in row 21.

    If things aren't working properly, you need to go back and carefully proofread all your formulas and correct the errors.

25. Now that everything works, you can make some changes to improve the appearance of the worksheet.

    a. First, select cells A1 and A2 by clicking on one and dragging to the other. Press Ctrl+1 to open the Format Cells dialog box, and click on the Font tab.

    b. Under the word Color, there is a drop down menu that currently says Automatic. Click on the arrow and select the white color box in the palette. This will make the text in these cells "invisible". Click OK to exit.

Figure 196

Selecting a white font color makes text invisible

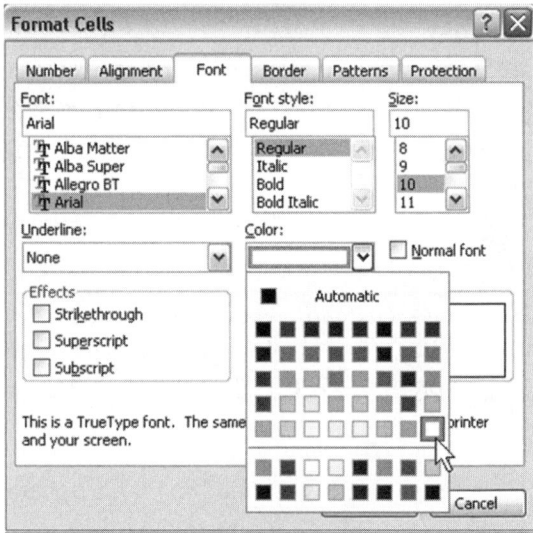

c. From the Tools menu, select Options, and the View tab. Under Window Options, click on the boxes labeled Gridlines, Row & column headers, and Sheet tabs to remove the check marks. Click OK to exit.

Figure 197

Disabling gridlines, row and column headers, and sheet tabs

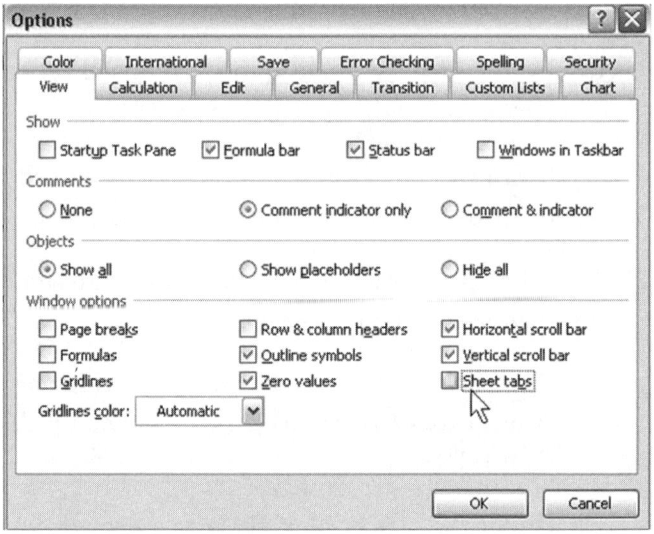

26. Protect the worksheet.

Select Tools → Protection. Click on the top box labeled Select locked cells to remove the check mark. You may enter a password at this point if you want, but it is not necessary unless you are afraid that your students may make changes to the worksheet. Click OK to exit.

Figure 198

Making locked cells inaccessible to students

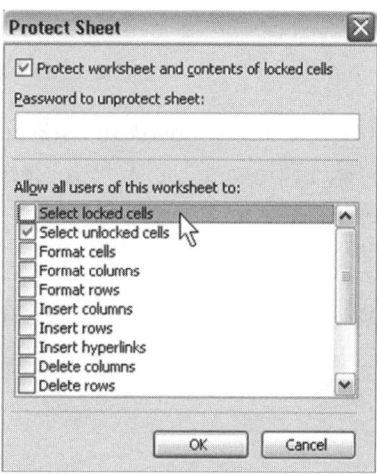

Now the only cells that the cursor will move to are the three cells that the student needs to play the game. Save the file as Math Facts Game, and exit.

Figure 199

Final version of the Math Facts game

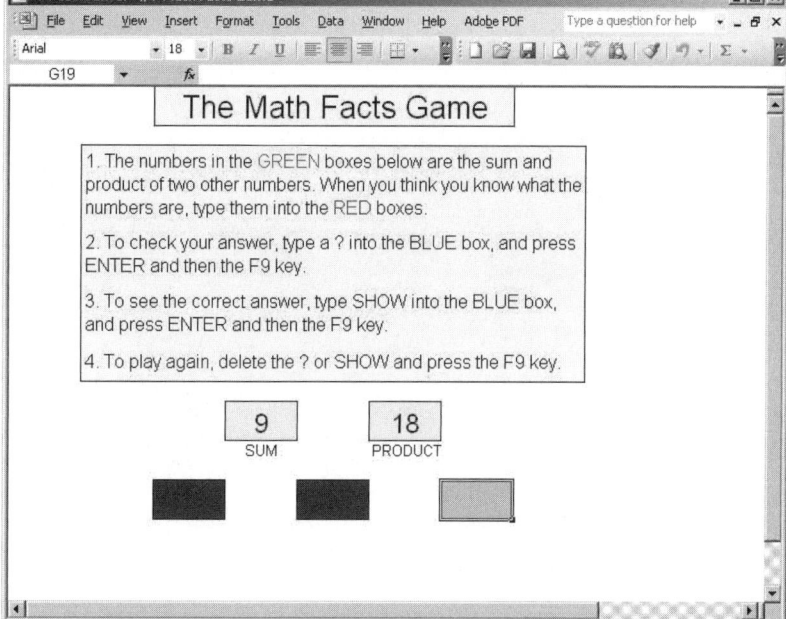

Using the Application

To begin the game, the student (or teacher, if you are using this as a group activity) can delete any answers remaining from the previous game. Then, the student presses F9 to produce a new sum and product. When the student arrives at the answer, they can type the numbers into the red cells, type a question mark into the blue cell, press Enter, and then the F9 key.

If the student needs to correct his or her answer, the question mark needs to stay in the cell, or the problem will change. After a few attempts, the student can discover the correct answer by typing "show" into the blue cell, pressing Enter and then the F9 key.

When you close the worksheet, Excel will ask if you want to save your changes. It is not necessary to do so, but saying yes will not harm anything.

Secret Code Maker

Opportunity

Ralphie in "A Christmas Story" had his Li'l Orphan Annie Secret Decoder Ring. Your students can have their own Excel version of a code maker and decoder, and even learn a little about cryptography in the process.

Solution and Overview

You will use the built-in Excel functions CODE to change letters into their equivalent ANSI (American National Standards Institute) character set number, and CHAR to change those numbers back into text.

Creating the Solution

1. Set column width.
   Start by clicking on the B in column B at the top of the page and dragging to the right to column P. With all these columns highlighted, move your cursor to the vertical line between columns B and C and it will change into a plus sign with horizontal arrows. Left click and drag the vertical line to the left until the column width reads 3.29 (28 pixels).

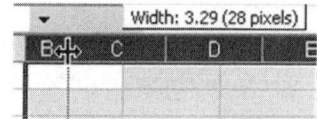

Figure 200

Setting column width

2. Set row height.
   Move your cursor to the horizontal line between row 1 and row 2 at the left edge of the worksheet. The cursor will change into a plus sign, this time with vertical arrows. Left click and drag down until the row height reads 45.00 (60 pixels).

   Figure 201
   Setting row height

   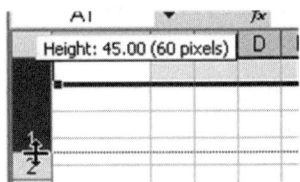

3. Select and format range B1:P1.
   Click on cell B1 and drag to the right to highlight the range B1:P1. With your cursor inside the highlighted area, right-click and select Format Cells from the drop down menu; make the following changes:

   a. Alignment tab: In Text Alignment, change both Horizontal and Vertical to Center by clicking on the down arrow in the menu box. Under Text Control, click next to Merge Cells to add a check mark to that box.

   b. Font tab: Change the Font to Jenkins v2.0 and the Size to 48. If your computer does not have that font style, try Bradley Hand ITC, Papyrus, or Staccato. Find something a little out of the ordinary.

   c. Border tab: Click Outline from the Presets.

   d. Patterns: Select the light green color from the bottom row of the palette. Click OK to exit.

4. Type the following into the text box you just made: **Secret Code Maker**

5. Select and format range A2:Q5.
   Move the cursor to cell A2. Left-click and drag to the right and down to highlight the range A2:Q5. With the cursor inside the highlighted cells, right-click and select Format Cells. Make the following changes:

a. Alignment tab: Change Vertical to Center, and click the box next to Merge Cells.

b. Border tab: Click on Outline.

c. Patterns: Select the light tan color from the bottom row of the palette. Click OK to exit.

6. Type the following into this text box:

Type your message into the grid below, putting one letter into each square. For a blank space between words, press the space bar one time. The secret code will be written out in the grid at the bottom of the page.

7. Add borders to the grid.
Move your cursor to cell B7. Left click and drag to the right and down to cell P13. Click on the Borders icon on the toolbar at the top of the page and select All Borders from its drop-down menu.

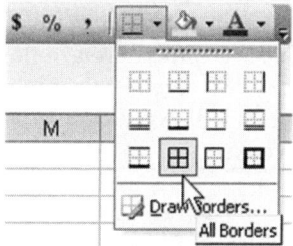

Figure 202

Setting All Borders from the drop-down menu

8. Copy and paste the grid into the worksheet.
While the grid is still highlighted, press Crtl+C to copy. Move your cursor to cell B19 and press Ctrl+V to paste the grid.

9. Select and format range A15:Q17.
Move your cursor to cell A15, left-click and drag right and down to cell Q17. Right-click and select Format Cells. Make the same changes that you made in Step 5.

10. Type in the following in this text box:

Secret Code Maker

>After you type in your message in the grid above, the coded message will appear below. Copy and paste the coded message and give to your friends electronically in an email or text file. Or, you can hand copy the numbers on a piece of paper.

11. You will use the Excel function CODE to change the letters from the top grid into numbers in the bottom grid. Because an empty cell will result in an error message, you will use an IF statement to tell Excel what to do when that happens.

    a. Start by clicking on cell B19. While holding down the Shift key, use the Right and Down arrow keys to highlight the range of cells B19:P25. Any formula that you type will start to appear in cell B19.

    b. Type in the following formula: =IF(B7="","",CODE(B7))
    However, instead of just pressing Enter when you have finished, press Ctrl+Enter to put a similar formula into all the cells.

 Note:

Notice that there are no spaces in the formula. After the second equal sign, there are two sets of two quotation marks separated by a comma. Typing four apostrophes will not work. Type some words into the top grid to make sure the worksheet works.

12. Shift sheet location to the end and delete extra sheets.
    Move your cursor to the Sheet tabs at the bottom of the page and right click on the tab for this worksheet (it's probably named Sheet1) Click on Move or Copy. Now click on (move to end) and the box next to Create a Copy. Click OK. The new worksheet will be named Sheet1(2). Right-click on any other tabs at the bottom of your sheet and select Delete.

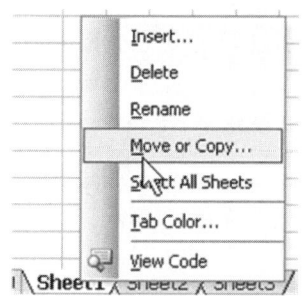
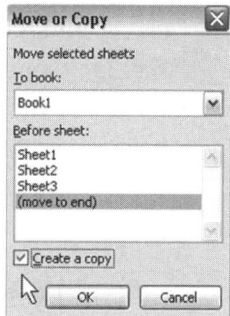

Figure 203

Using Move or Copy to move and make a copy of a worksheet

13. Change sheet names.

    Double-click on the Sheet1 tab to highlight it. Type in **Code Maker**. Click on the other Sheet tab, and then double click to highlight. Type in **Decoder**.

14. Change CODE to CHAR on the Decoder worksheet.

    Click on cell B19 in the Decoder worksheet. Notice that it contains exactly the same formula as the Code Maker worksheet. The new formula will be very similar, except that the function CODE needs to be changed to CHAR. There is a very easy way to do this.

    a. Click on Edit from the drop down menus, and select Replace.
       In the box next to Find what, type in the word **CODE**.
       In the box next to Replace with, type in the word **CHAR**.

    b. At the bottom of the dialog box, click Replace all. Excel will give you a message that says it has replaced 106 instances of "code". Click OK to close that box, and then click Close to exit Find and Replace.

Figure 204

Using Find and Replace to change the CODE to CHAR in the formulas

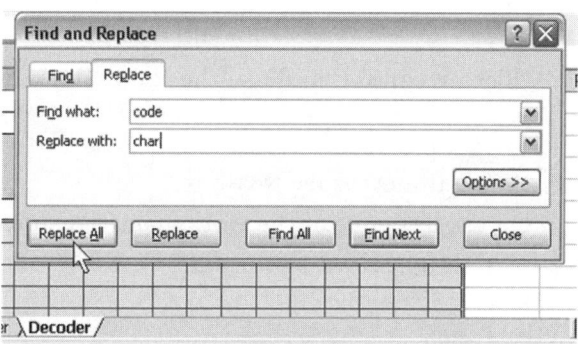

Secret Code Maker

15. Correct and format title block.

    Excel isn't smart enough to know exactly what you wanted. Check the large text box at the top of the page. Where it once contained "Secret Code Maker" it now says "Secret Char Maker". That's OK, because you needed to change it anyway.

    a. Left-click on the merged cells; type in the following text: Secret Decoder Press Enter.

    b. Click on it again, and then click on the Paint Bucket icon on the top of the page. Click on the down arrow to open the palette, and select light yellow from the bottom row.

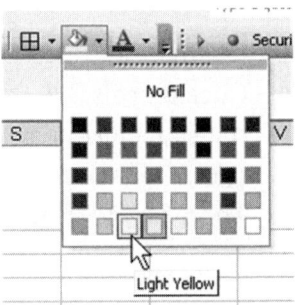

Figure 205

Selecting a fill color for the merged cells

16. Click on the text box that starts in row 2 and change the text as follows:

    To decode your message, you need to copy and paste the message from your friend into the first grid below. Copy the message from the other file using Ctrl+C, and then click on the GREEN box. From the drop down menus, select Paste Special, and click on Text. Or, you can type each number into a separate box in the grid.

17. Click on cell B7, and use the Paint Bucket icon to change the color to a dark green.

18. Delete unnecessary text box.

    On the left edge of the worksheet, click on the 15 in row 15 and drag down to highlight rows 15 through 17. Right-click and select delete. You do not need this text box.

Using the Application

To use the application, the student simply types a message, one character per box, into the grid at the top of the Code Maker. Remember that a space can not be an empty cell; the student has to press the Spacebar key one time.

To send the message to a friend, the student has several options. The numbers can be hand-copied, or can be cut-and-pasted into an e-mail or a word processor such as Word. Cut-and-paste will allow the message recipient to cut-and-paste the numbers into their version of the worksheet, instead of typing them in.

Excel Extras

The code can be made a bit more difficult by adding to or subtracting from the number generated from the CODE function. That number could be the first character in the message, so that the decoding key travels with the message. The formula in cell B19 in the coding grid would simply be =B7. Cell C19, for example, would then have to be changed to the following formula:
=IF(C7="","",CODE(C7)+$B$7)
You can then copy and paste one row at a time to fill in the rest of the grid.

For decoding purposes, you will also need to change the formulas in the decoding grid, but this will take more than find and replace. The new formula for cell C16 would be as follows:
=IF(C7="","",CHAR(C7-$B$7))
Again, this would need to be copied into all the other cells in the bottom grid of the Decoder page. There does not need to be a formula in cell B16.

You can have your students experiment with multiplication and division to change the CODE numbers as well. However, using division may require the use of the ROUND or INTEGER functions in order to make the worksheet work correctly.

Secret Code Maker

**Secret
Code Maker**

Probability with Coins or Dice

Opportunity

You know that theoretical probability does not necessarily predict the actual probability of an event, and that students who are actively engaged in their learning will usually retain more. However, the thought of arming eighth graders with coins or dice that in all probability will become missiles does not sound like an intelligent decision. You can have an Excel spreadsheet toss a coin or a die to demonstrate the difference between actual and theoretical probability.

Solution and Overview

You will build a spreadsheet that will use a random number generator to simulate the toss of a coin or the roll of a die. You can make a visual representation of the coin or die that will change with each toss, and have Excel keep a running total of how many of each outcome have occurred, along with the total number of tosses or rolls.

Both of these workbooks require the use of circular reasoning and manual calculation in order to generate random numbers and keep track of totals. They must be made in two separate files. Otherwise, pressing F9 to calculate results on one worksheet will also calculate results in the other.

Probability with Coins or Dice

Creating the Solution – Tossing a Coin

1. Enable manual calculation and single iteration.
   Open a new workbook. From the Tools menu at the top of the page, select Options and click on the Calculation tab. Click on the radio button next to Manual, and click the box to remove the check mark from "Recalculate before save". Next, click on the box next to "Iteration", and change the number of Maximum iterations in the box to 1 (one). Click OK to exit.

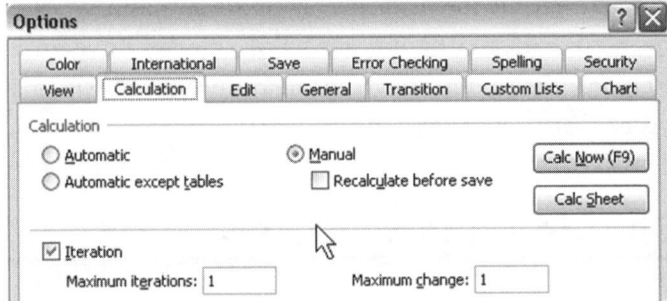

Figure 206
Setting Manual Calculation and Iteration options

2. Type the following words in the indicated cells.
   Cell E3: **Heads**
   Cell F3: **Tails**
   Cell G3: **Total**

3. Enter a temporary number.
   In order to keep the individual counts at zero until you finish, you will need to type a temporary number into the cell that these formulas reference.
   Go to cell E1 and enter a 2.

4. Type in the formulas with circular references.
   In cell E4, enter this formula: =IF(E1=0,E4+1,E4)
   This formula looks at the cell where Excel will generate either a 0 or 1. If there is a 0, Excel will add 1 to whatever number is currently in cell E4. If it is a 1, Excel will keep the count the same.

5. In cell F4, enter this formula, similar to the one above: =IF(E1=1,F4+1,F4)

6. Add the total number of heads plus tails.
   Click on cell G4, and then click the AutoSum icon (∑). You will see the formula =SUM(E4:F4) appear in the cell. Press Enter to accept it.

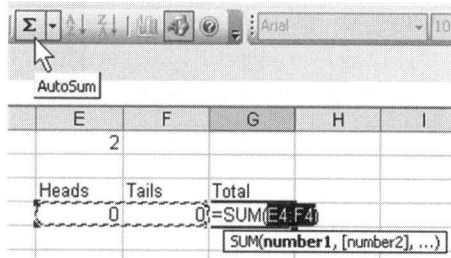

Figure 207

Using AutoSum to generate the desired SUM formula

 Note:

The function you will use to generate the random numbers, RANDBETWEEN, is not a standard Excel function, but is, instead, part of something called the Analysis ToolPak. To have this and other functions available, you need to do the following: From the Tools menu, select Add-Ins. When the dialog box opens, click on the boxes next to Analysis ToolPak and Analysis ToolPak –VBA. Click OK to exit.

See page 53, Creating the Solution for more details.

7. Change E1 so that it will randomly contain either a zero (0) or a one (1).
   Go to cell E1, where you had previously entered a 2. Click on the cell to edit it, and type in the following: RANDBETWEEN(0,1)
   Press Enter.

8. Do not do anything else except to Save your file at this time.
   Name it "Coin Toss".

9. You now have a very "bare bones" worksheet that will toss a coin and keep track of the totals. Try it by pressing the F9 key several times. When you are done, it is CRITICAL that you close WITHOUT saving in order to start again with all zeroes. For a final step later, you can change the properties of this file to "Read-only", to prevent accidental changes.

Probability w/ Coins or Dice

Excel for the Math Classroom

10. Now you can make this workbook look a little nicer.
    Close the workbook. When Excel asks "Do you want to save the changes you made to...." select **No**. Now re-open the file, but do not press F9 until you have saved any new additions to the file.

Figure 208
Do not save changes!

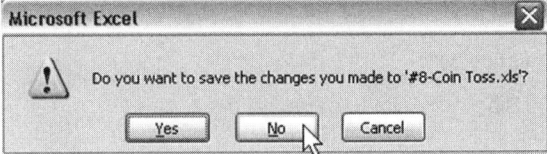

11. Format the head and tail count cells.
    Click on Cell E4. Hold down the left mouse button and drag left and down to highlight the range E4:G5. On the Tool bar, click on the Center text icon. Then click on the arrow next to the Border icon and select All Borders from the drop down menu.

Figure 209
Selecting All Borders

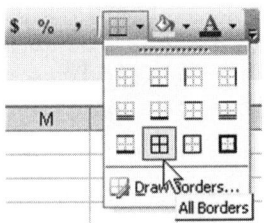

12. Set the row height for the coin simulation.
    Move your cursor to the left until it is on the line between rows 1 and 2. The cursor will change to a plus sign with vertical arrows. Left-click and move down, and watch as the row height changes. When the height equals 48.00 (64 pixels) stop.

Figure 210

Setting row height

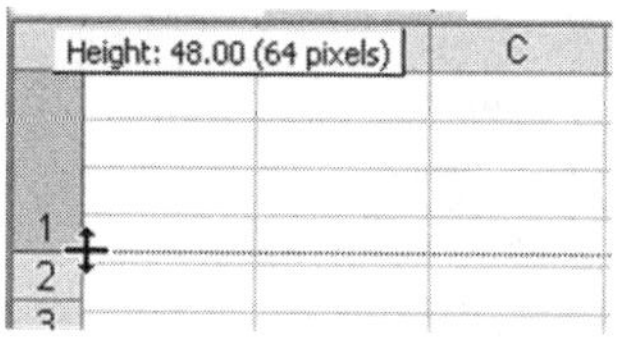

13. Enter the formula for the dice simulation and format its cell.
    Click on cell F1 and type in the following formula:
    =IF(E1=0,"H",IF(E1=1,"T",""))1
    This formula tells Excel that if the random number is zero, to put an H in this cell; if the number is one, to put in a T.

    a. Press Ctrl+1 to open the Format Cells dialog box, and click the Alignment tab. Change Horizontal and Vertical to Center.

    b. Click on the Font tab. Change Font to Arial, and Size to 36. Click OK to exit.

14. SAVE YOUR CHANGES AT THIS TIME.
    Once you have saved the file, if you want to see how this application works, simply press F9 again. Remember, though, when you are done, to be sure to close the file *without saving* before you continue to the next step.

15. Make the output in E1 invisible.
    Click on E1 and press Ctrl+1 to access the Format Cells dialog box. Select the Font tab. In the middle of the dialog box, there is a drop down menu labeled Color. Click on the down arrow, and select White from the palette (it should be in the lower right hand corner). Click OK to exit.

Figure 211

Setting text color to white makes text invisible

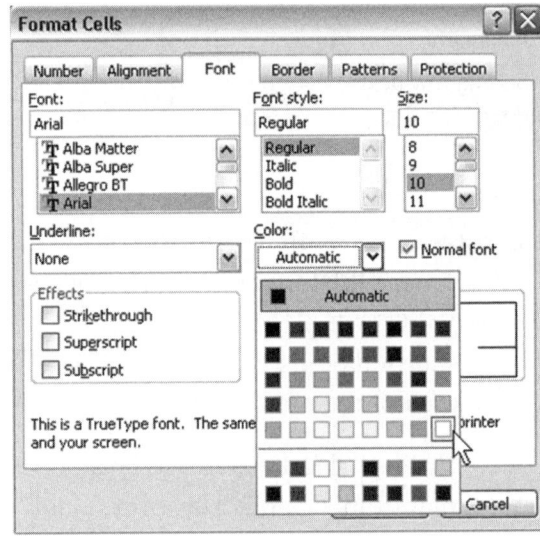

16. Prepare to draw the coin.

    a. From the View menu at the top of the page, select Toolbars. If there is not a check mark next to Drawing, click on it. The Drawing toolbar will be visible on your worksheet.

    b. Click on the arrow next to the word Draw on the toolbar, and then select Snap. Click on To Grid.

Figure 212

Using Snap To Grid ensures that the oval you draw next will line up properly

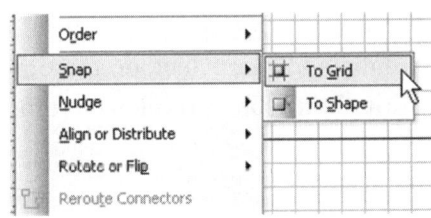

17. Draw and format the coin.

    On the Drawing toolbar, click on the Oval tool. Your cursor will look like a small plus sign. With Snap To Grid selected, drawing a circle inside cell F1 will be relatively easy, but it's not quite an exact science.

a. Move your cursor to the upper left corner of cell F1 and click the mouse. A circular shape will appear somewhere nearby. If you got lucky, it will be the right size to fit exactly inside cell F1. If not, you may need to move it and/or resize it.

b. Notice that, as you move your cursor across the oval, it changes shapes. If you need to move the oval, you want the cursor to look like a plus sign with arrowheads. When it does, you can click and drag the oval to where you want it. After you have it mostly inside cell F1, move your cursor to the small open circle handle on the bottom or side. Click and drag one at a time until the oval is inside cell F1 and appears circular.

Figure 213

Selecting the Oval icon and re-sizing the circle

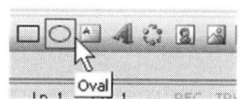
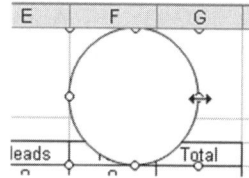

c. Click on the circle to highlight it, and right click your mouse. Select Format AutoShape, and click the Colors and Lines tab. Next to the word Transparency, there is a slide bar. Move it all the way to the right until the box at the right reads 100%. This setting allows you to see the "H" or "T", but keeps the coin white against a white background.

Optionally, you can select any color that you want, or try your hand at making a custom color. Experiment with the transparency levels with colors other than white, but 50% should work. You want to be able to see the "H" or "T" in the center of the circle. Click OK to exit when you are done.

Probability with Coins or Dice

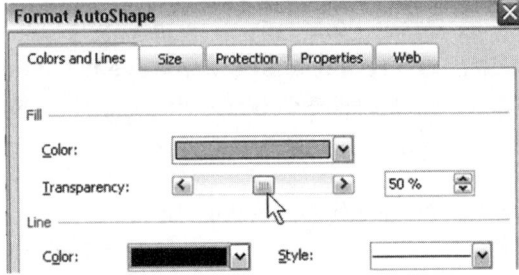

Figure 214

Selecting fill color and transparency level for the oval

18. Add directions.
    Click on cell E6 and drag to the right to cell G6. Press Ctrl+1 to access the Format Cells dialog box. Make the following changes.

    a. On the Alignment tab, change Horizontal to Center, and click the box next to Merge Cells.

    b. On the Font tab, change Size to 12.

    c. On the Borders tab, select Outline.

    d. On the Patterns tab, select Light Yellow from the bottom row.

    Click OK to exit. In the merged cell, type in the following:
    Press F9 to toss the coin.

19. Remove Excel distractions.
    From the Tools menu, select Options and View. Remove the check marks from Gridlines, Row & column headers, and Sheet tabs. Click OK to exit.

174 Excel for the Math Classroom

Figure 215

Disabling gridlines, row and column headers, and sheet tabs

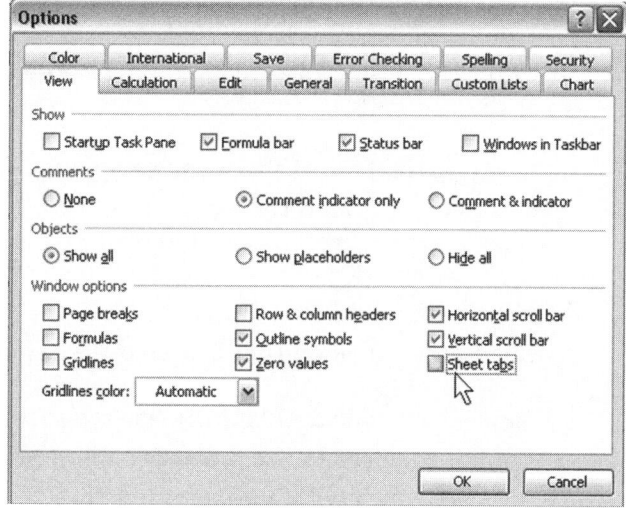

20. Protect your file.

    Click on any empty cell. From the Tools menu again, select Protection, and Protect Sheet. Remove the check marks from Select locked cells, and Select unlocked cells (there should be NO checkmarks on the list). Optionally, if you want to use a password to protect the worksheet from accidental changes, you may do so. Just remember to write it down in a safe place. SAVE YOUR CHANGES!

Figure 216

Preventing students from selecting locked or unlocked cells

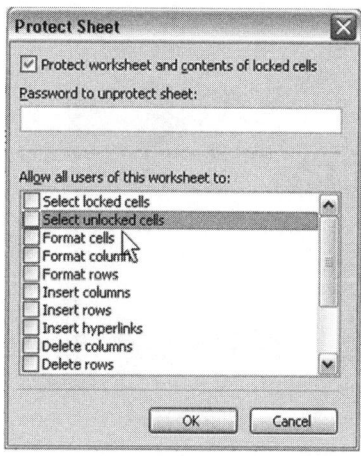

21. Optional: Make your file read-only.

    To completely protect your file, you may want to mark it as Read-only. This is not that difficult.

    a. Open up the folder where you saved your file. Locate this file and right click on it. Click on the word Properties that appears at the bottom of the list.

    b. Next to the word Attributes, you will see an empty box next to the word Read-only. Click on that box, and then click OK to exit.

    Now, if someone accidentally tries to save changes to this file, Excel will prompt the user to use a new file name so that the original file will not be overwritten with changes made to it.

Figure 217

Making file read-only

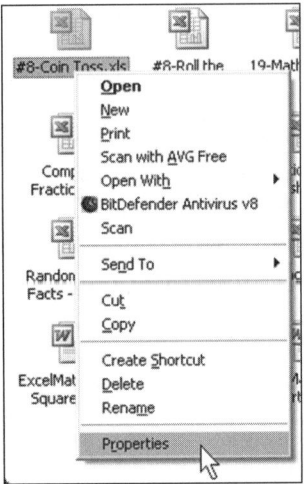

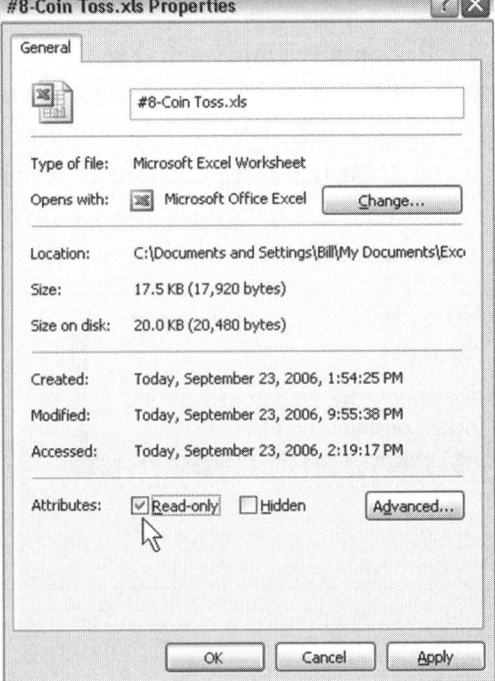

Using the Coin Toss Application

Ideally, this will work best if the file can be opened on several computers at once. The more trials that can be done in a short amount of time, the closer the outcome should be to the theoretical. All the student has to do (in fact, all that he/she CAN do) is to press the F9 key to simulate the tossing of a coin.

Creating the Solution – Rolling a Die

In actuality, you will be simulating the rolling of a "number cube", a die with numbers instead of dots. The process is a lot easier!

1. Enable manual calculation and single iteration.
   Open a new workbook. From the Tools menu at the top of the page, select Options and click on the Calculation tab. Click on the radio button next to Manual, and click the box to remove the check mark from "Recalculate before save". Next, click on the box next to "Iteration", and change the number of Maximum iterations in the box to 1 (one). Click OK to exit.

2. Fill a series with die face numbers (1-6).
   In cell B4, type in the number 1. Right click on the fill handle in the lower right hand corner, and pull straight down to cell B9, and let go. In the dialog box that appears, select Fill Series.

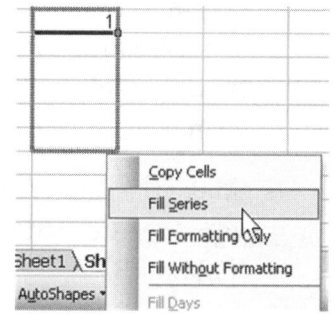

Figure 218

Selecting Fill Series from the right-click drop down menu

Probability with Coins or Dice

3. In cell B10, type in the word: **Total**

4. As you did for the Coin Toss, you need to give Excel a temporary number while you type in the next formulas. Go to cell B2, and type in a 7.

5. Enter and copy down the die face counting formula.

   a. In cell C4, enter the following formula: =IF($B$2=1,C4+1,C4)
      Press Enter. The $ designation makes the B2 cell an absolute reference that will not change as you copy this formula.

   b. Click on cell C4, and then left-click on the fill handle in the lower right corner and pull down to cell C9 to copy the formula into these cells. All of these cells should contain zeroes.

Figure 219

Copying the formula down results in zeroes in all of the cells

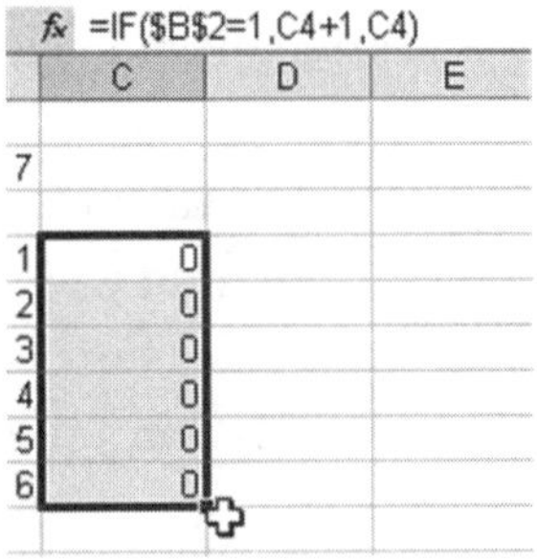

6. Now, one cell at a time, edit each formula using this procedure:

   a. Click on the cell C5, then press F2 to edit the contents. This can be done within the cell, or at the top of the page in the Formula bar. Move your cursor, which now looks like an I-beam, just to the left of the equals sign that follows $B$2. Delete the number one (1) that follows the equal sign, and replace it with a two (2). Press Enter.

   b. Make the same changes to each formula in Column C by changing the number after $B$2= from a 1 to the number that is directly to the left in Column B.

Figure 220

Changing formulas in each cell to match the value in the same row of column B

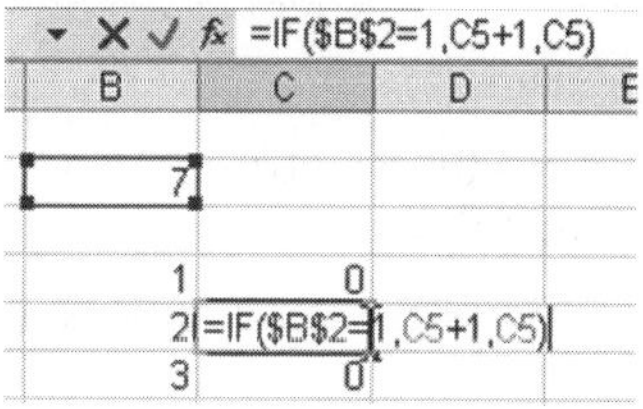

7. Enter a formula to count the throws of the die.
   Click on cell C10, and click on the summation icon (∑) on the toolbar at the top. The formula =SUM(C4:C9) will appear. Click OK to accept it.

 Note:

The function you will use to generate the random numbers, RANDBETWEEN, is not a standard Excel function, but is, instead, part of something called the Analysis ToolPak. To have this and other functions available, you need to do the following: From the Tools menu, select Add-Ins. When the dialog box opens, click on the boxes next to Analysis ToolPak and Analysis ToolPak –VBA. Click OK to exit.

See page 53, Creating the Solution for more details.

8. Change the temporary number to a formula to randomly generate a number from one to six.
   Click on cell B2 and type in the following formula =RANDBETWEEN(1,6) Press Enter. Before doing anything else, save the file as "Roll the Die".

9. As with the Coin Toss, you now have a worksheet that will do what you want it to, but that is not visually attractive. Before you make any changes, press F9 a few times to see it work.
   Close the workbook. When Excel asks "Do you want to save the changes you made to…." select **No**. Now re-open the file, but do not press F9 until you have saved any new additions to the file.

Figure 221

Close the workbook without saving changes

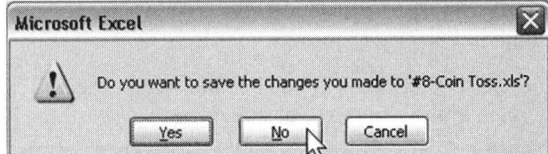

10. Format the die face and die face counting cells.

    Click on cell B4. Hold down the left mouse button and move down and to the right to highlight the range B4:C10. Click on the Center Text icon on the toolbar. Then click on the Borders icon, and select All Borders from the drop down menu.

11. Set the row height for the die simulation cell.

    Move your cursor to the left of the page to the line in between rows 2 and 3. When it changes to a plus sign with vertical arrows, click the left mouse button and move down until the row height reads 48.00 (64 pixels) and let go.

Figure 222

Setting the row height to 64 pixels

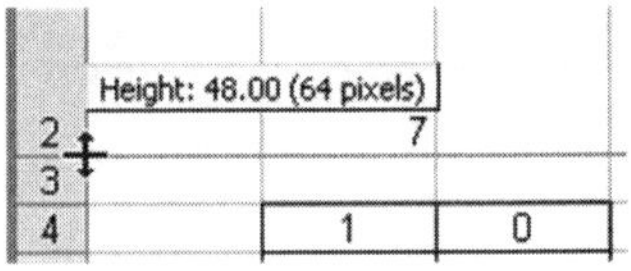

12. Format the die simulation cell.

    Click on cell B2, and press Ctrl+1 to open the Format Cells dialog box and make the following changes:

    a. On the Alignment Tab, change Horizontal and Vertical to Center.

    b. On the Font tab, change the Font to Arial and Size to 36.

    c. On the Border tab, select Outline from the Presets.

    d. On the Pattern tab, select a color for your die. If you choose a dark color, go back to the Font tab, and change the font color to white so you can see it. Click OK to exit.

13. Set row height for instructions.
    Go to the left edge of the page and click on the 12 in Row 12. Hold down the left mouse button and drag down to highlight Rows 12 and 13. Move the cursor (which should look like a plus sign with vertical arrows) to the line between Rows 13 and 14. Left click and hold and move it down to change the row height. When it says 15.00 (20 pixels) let go.

Figure 223

Setting the row height to 20 pixels

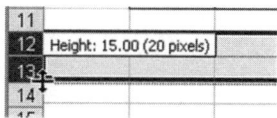

14. Format and enter instructions.
    Move the cursor to cell B12. Left click and drag to the right and down to highlight the range B12:C14. Press Ctrl+1 to open the Format Cells dialog box and make the following changes:

    a. On the Alignment tab, change Horizontal and Vertical to Center. Click the boxes next to Wrap Text and Merge Cells.

    b. On the Font tab, select Arial with size 12.

    c. On the Border tab, select Outline from the Presets.

    d. On the Patterns tab, select Light Yellow. Click OK to exit.

    e. In the merged cells, type the following: **Press F9 to roll the die.**

15. Hide Excel distractions.
    From the Tools menu, select Options → View tab. Uncheck the boxes next to Gridlines, Row & column headings, and Sheet tabs. Click OK to exit.

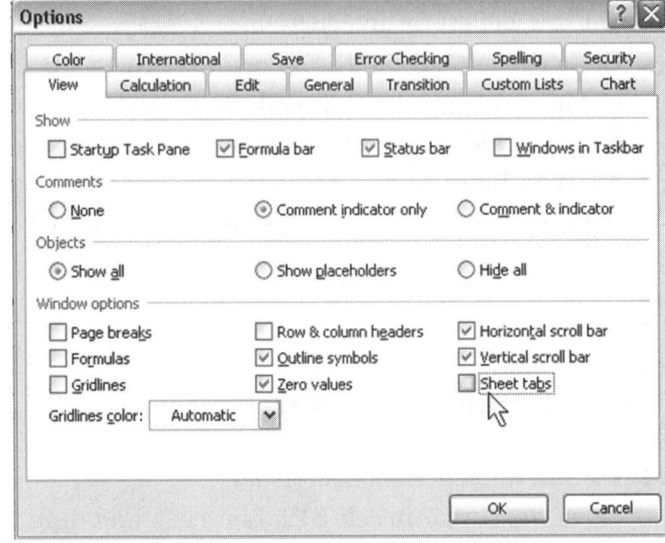

Figure 224

Disabling gridlines, row and column headers, and sheet tabs

16. Protect your file.

    Click on an empty cell. From the Tools menu, select Protection, and Protect Sheet. Uncheck the boxes next to Select locked cells, and Select unlocked cells. You may also select a password at this time if you want to. Click OK to exit. SAVE YOUR CHANGES!

Figure 225

Preventing students from selecting locked or unlocked cells

17. Optional: If you want to completely protect your file, mark it as "Read-only" using the Step 21 on page 176 in the Coin Toss instructions.

Using the Roll the Die Application

This worksheet can be used in the same way as Coin Toss. The teacher can do the "rolling of the die" on the overhead, or the students can work in small groups or independently on a computer. The students would share their data to compile the results.

Excel Extras

Both of these files can be modified without too much trouble. You can change the Coin Toss to simulate the tossing of two coins to figure the probabilities of two heads, two tails, or one of each. This would require the addition of another RANDBETWEEN function in another cell, and the formatting of another cell to look like a coin. Instead of the Heads, Tails, and Total formulas, you would need 2 Heads, 2 Tails, Odd, and Total.

The formula for heads would require an AND function imbedded into the IF function. Both cells with the RANDBETWEEN would need to be zero (0) for the count to increase in 2 Heads. Likewise, both RANDBETWEENs would need to be one (1) for the count to increase in 2 Tails. Assuming the RANDBETWEEN function is in cells C1 and E1 and that the 2 Heads count is in D4, the formula would look like this:

=IF(AND(C1=0,E1=0)D4+1,D4)

The function for 2 Tails would be similar, except the RANDBETWEEN result would be 1.

The formula for Odd (a Head and Tail) turns out to be quite simple once you think it through. In order for the count to increase in Odd, the RANDBETWEEN results need to be different. Or, if the results are the same,

Probability with Coins or Dice

the Odd count remains the same. A simple IF statement when the results are the same would work. Again, assuming the same cell locations as above, with the Odd count in F4, the formula would be:

=IF(C1=E1,F4,F4+1)

You can also change Roll the Die to Roll the Dice by adding another RANDBETWEEN formula for the second die. You would also need to change the table of outcomes to include the numbers 2 through 12. If the RANDBETWEEN formulas were in cells B1 and D1 and the table of results was in column E, a generalized formula would look like this:

=IF(B1+D1=*n*, E*r*+1,E*r*)
where *n* is the total on the two dice, and E*r* is the cell where that total is tallied.

Demonstrating and Comparing Fractions with Charts

Opportunity

In order to teach math standards, you need to help students to visualize fractions.

Solution and Overview

Use an Excel pie chart to draw a circle with a fraction of the circle drawn in. A pie chart is a circle broken up into wedges. Business people typically use pie charts to show the percentage of sales by product line.

You can use pie charts to represent fractions for your students. In the solution, you will create a pie chart with two wedges. One wedge will be colored in to represent the fraction. The other wedge will be formatted to be transparent.

Creating the Solution

1. Enter labels and starting value.
   Start with a blank worksheet. In B1, enter the word "Value" as a heading. In A2 and A3, enter the letters A and B.

   a. The worksheet will be flexible enough to show any fraction. To begin, start with 0.25 in cell B2 in order to represent 1/4. Older students may understand that 1/4 and 25% are the same thing. However, it would be better if the pie chart could have a label of 1/4.

Comparing Fractions in Charts

Demonstrating and Comparing Fractions with Charts

b. Select cell B2. Type Ctrl+1 to display the Format Cells dialog. In the Number tab under the Category list, choose the option for Fraction. If you will only be displaying fractions such as 1/2, 1/3, or 3/8, then it is OK to use the option for Up to 1 Digit. If you might be displaying 1/16 or 1/32, then you might want to use the option for up to two digits.

Figure 226

Entering a decimal value to be represented as a fraction

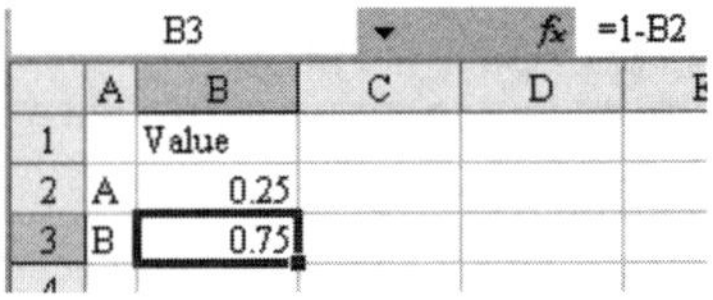

2. In cell B3, enter the following formula: =1-B2

   A pie chart must be comprised of 100% or 1. As you change the fraction in B2, the formula in B3 will ensure that the total value for the pie chart adds up to 100%.

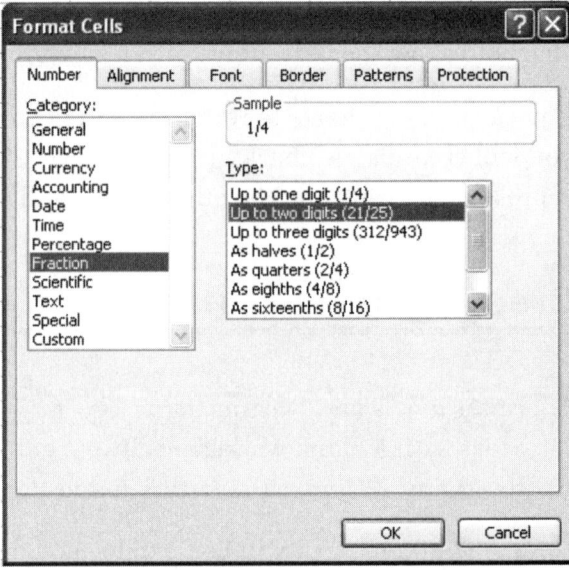

Figure 227

Selecting number of digits for fractions

186   Excel for the Math Classroom

3. Select the range of A1:B3.

Figure 228

Selecting a range to be represented in a chart

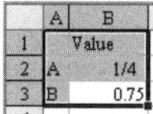

4. Insert the chart.

   a. From the menu, select Insert → Chart. In the chart type selection, choose Pie. There are six pie sub-types. Select the first type.

Figure 229

Selecting a Pie chart and its sub-type

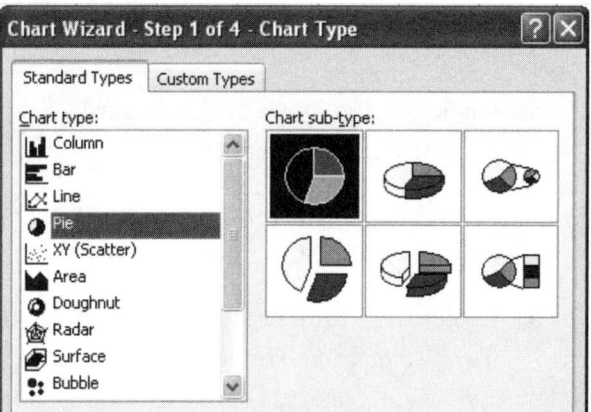

   b. Click Next twice to move ahead to Step 3 of the Chart Wizard. On the Title tab, clear out the title. On the Legend tab, uncheck the Show Legend box. On the Data Labels tab, choose Value.

Comparing Fractions in Charts

Demonstrating and Comparing Fractions with Charts

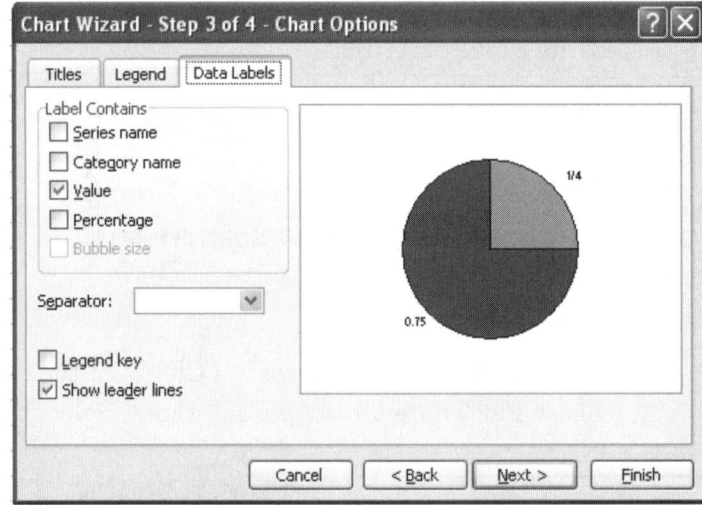

Figure 230

Selecting data label value

c. Click Next to move to the Wizard's Step 4. Choose to create the chart as an object in the current sheet and click Finish.

5. You will turn your attention back to the chart in a minute, but first you should hide some of the extraneous information on the worksheet.

   a. Select the Value heading in B2. In the Formatting toolbar, there is a Text Color icon. The icon contains the letter A over a small (usually red) rectangle. Next to this icon is a dropdown arrow. Click the arrow to display a pallet of available colors. Choose white from the pallet.

Figure 231

Choosing a color from the Text Color icon

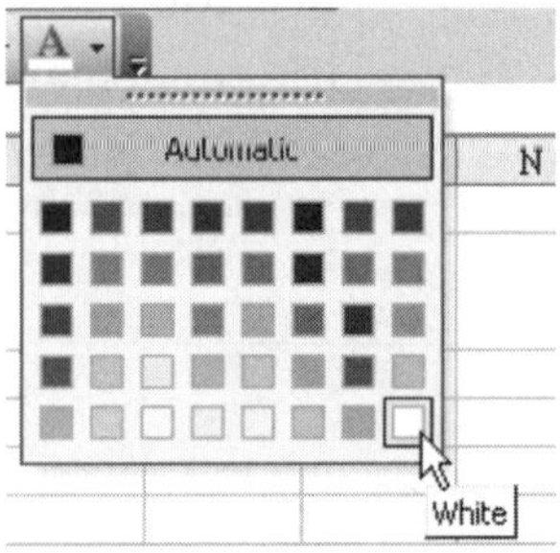

Note that the color of the rectangle of the A icon is now white. You can format additional cells to the same color by simply clicking on the icon.

b. Select cells A2:A3. Click the white text icon. Select the formula in B3. Click the white text icon. If you wish, select the fraction in B2 and change the font to 24 point using the font size dropdown.

Figure 232

Changing font size

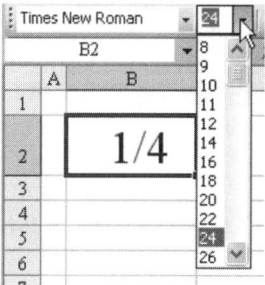

c. Although row 1 and column A now appear to be blank, you can completely hide that row and column.
Select a cell in row 1. Select Format → Row → Hide from the menu. Type the Down-Arrow to move to A2. Select Format → Column → Hide to hide column A.

Making a Worksheet Not Look Like Excel

Many of the elements that make the worksheet look like Excel can be hidden. From the menu, select Tools → Options. You will typically start on the View tab of the options menu. In the Window Options selection, uncheck Gridlines, Row & column headers, Horizontal scroll bar, Vertical scroll bar, and Sheet tabs. Click OK to dismiss the dialog. These settings will only apply to the selected worksheet. They will not affect other workbooks that you might open.

Comparing Fractions in Charts

Demonstrating and Comparing Fractions with Charts

 Caution!

If you really want to go overboard, you can also turn off the Formula and Status bars and hide most of the toolbars. However, these changes will globally affect all future workbooks, so I don't really recommend this!
On the View menu, unselect both Formula bar and Status bar. In the View → Toolbars menu, unselect any checked toolbars.

Customizing a Chart

By default, Excel will draw the chart to take up a certain amount of space on the worksheet. If you are going to be projecting this worksheet onto a screen, you will want the chart to be as large as possible. The chart is comprised of the pie, surrounded by white space and then a black border.

1. Click inside of the white space and eight black handles will appear on the border. You can now click and drag on the white space to move the chart up to just below the fraction.

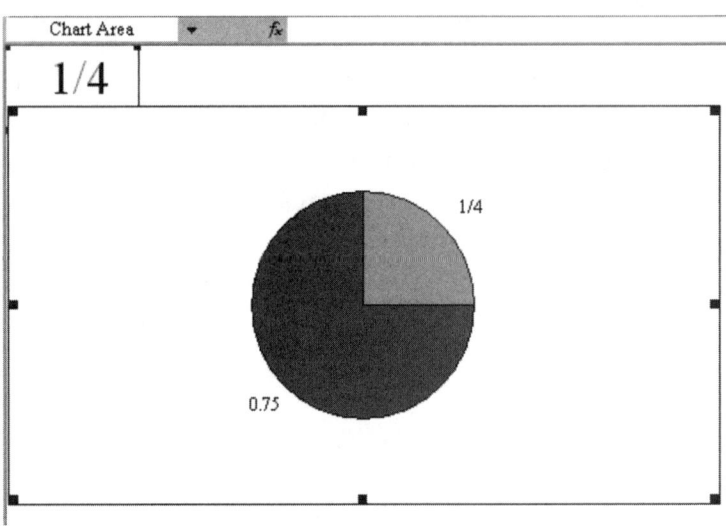

Figure 233
Moving the chart

Comparing Fractions in Charts

190   Excel for the Math Classroom

2. Click on square dot in the bottom right corner of the chart and drag down and to the right so that the chart fills the entire screen.

   For some reason, Excel allocates a lot of room to the white space around pie charts. You can make the plot area of the chart take up more of the chart area.

3. Select the Chart Area dropdown on the Chart toolbar and change the selection to Plot Area.

Figure 234

Increasing plot area size

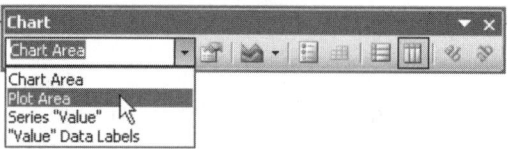

This selection will draw a new bounding box just around the pie.

Figure 235

New bounding box eliminates excess white area around pie

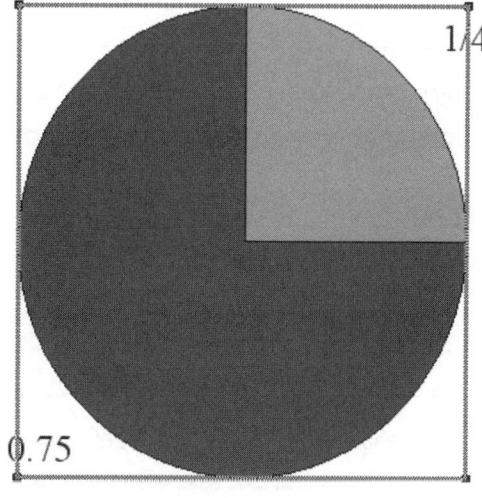

Comparing Fractions in Charts

4. Click on the white space inside this bounding box and drag the pie to the top of the chart area. Next, click on the dot in the bottom corner and drag down and right to make the pie fill most of the height of the worksheet.

5. Now remove the large rectangle from around the chart area.
   In the Chart toolbar, select Chart Area from the dropdown. Right-click on the white space in the chart and select Format Chart Area. Change the Border selection to None.

Figure 236
Removing borders from rectangle around pie

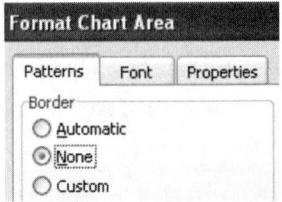

Currently, both wedges of the pie are labeled. The blue wedge is labeled with 1/4 and the other wedge is labeled with 0.75. You want to hide the second label. When you click on the 0.75 label, all of the data labels will be selected. Each label will have a square dot on either side, including the 1/4 label.

Figure 237 Locating square dots on either side of labels

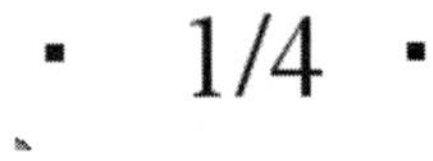

· 1/4 ·

6. After clicking on the 0.75 label, wait a couple of seconds and then do a second single click on the 0.75 label. Now – the 0.75 label is the only label selected and there is a bounding box around just that label. Type the Delete key to remove this label.

Figure 238 Deleting selected label indicated by square dots

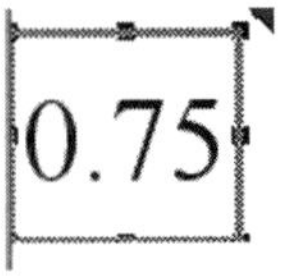

0.75

7. Finally, you will want to change the colors of the pie wedges.

   a. Click on the pie once to select the entire pie. There will be just two square dots on the perimeter of the pie. Wait a moment, and perform a second single click on the larger pie wedge.

   b. The wedge will now be outlined with six square dots. Right-click the larger pie slice and choose Format Data Point.

Figure 239

Format Data Point dropdown menu

   c. Choose a white color for the Area of the data point.

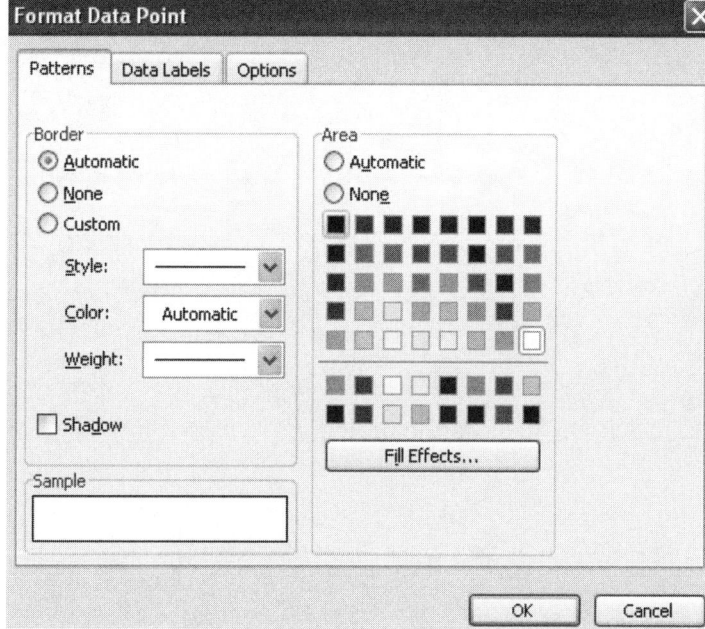

Figure 240

Formatting pie data point color

Comparing Fractions in Charts

Demonstrating and Comparing Fractions with Charts

d. Click OK to close the Format Data Point dialog. Single-click on the smaller wedge to switch the focus to that wedge. Right-click and choose Format Data Point. Change the color to a bright red or yellow color.

8. While you are in the dialog, choose the Options tab. The options tab for pie and donut charts have an interesting setting called angle of first slice. Typically, the first slice will start at the 12 o'clock position. If you would like to rotate the position of the first wedge, you can do so here.

Figure 241
Rotating position of pie wedge

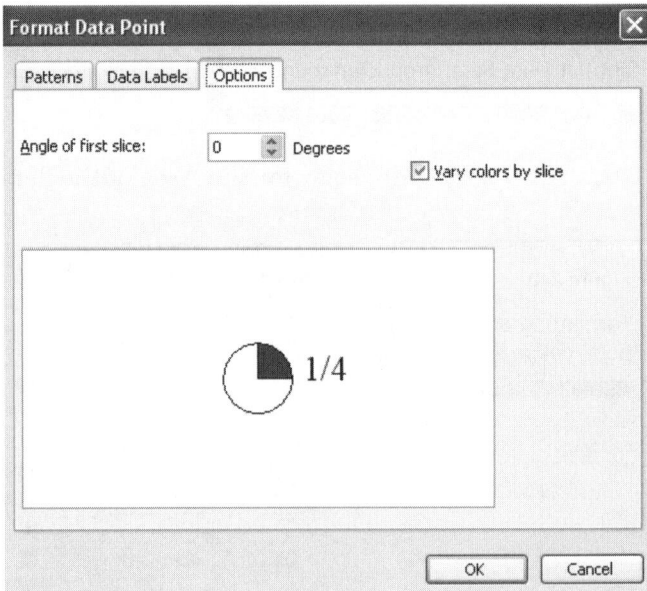

9. Click OK to close the dialog.

Comparing Fractions in Charts

194   *Excel for the Math Classroom*

Using the Application

Select the cell containing the fraction in the upper left corner of the worksheet. Type any fraction here and the pie chart will redraw with that fraction of the circle highlighted.

Figure 242

Typing a fraction in the target cell causes the pie chart to redraw to represent that fraction

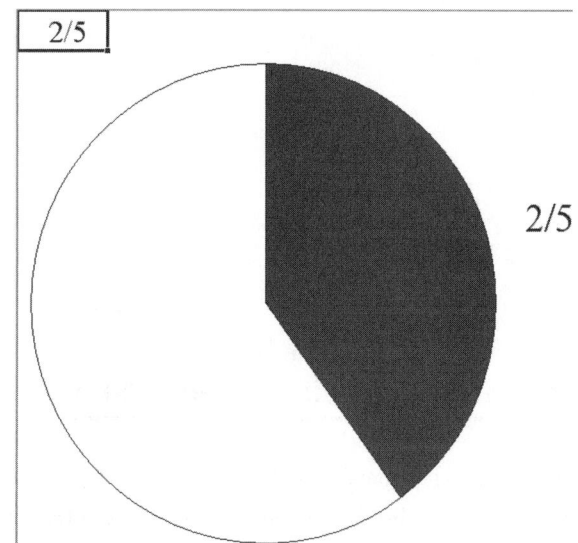

Excel Extras

Pie Chart with Only One Section Filled in

It is also possible to build a pie chart with four equal wedges and only one wedge filled in. Base the chart on a series with four cells, each one containing 0.25. You will have to repeat the steps to delete the data labels for the second, third, and fourth ranges. You will have to individually format the second, third, and fourth slices to change their color to white.

Demonstrating and Comparing Fractions with Charts

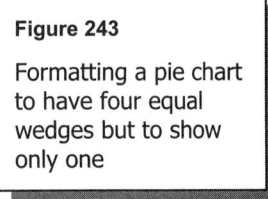

Figure 243
Formatting a pie chart to have four equal wedges but to show only one

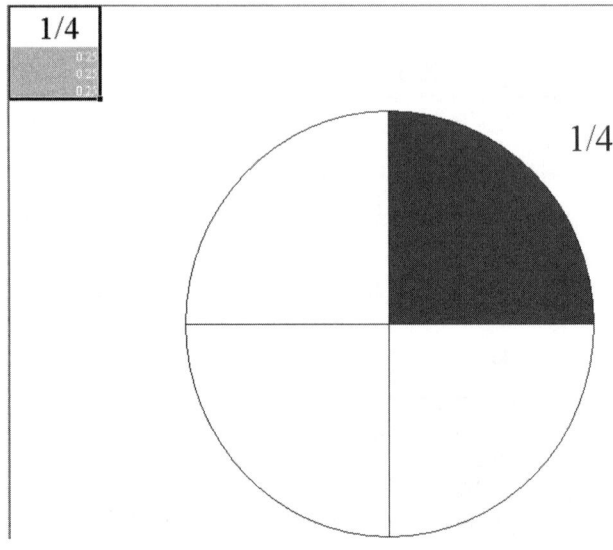

Pie Charts Showing Difference between Two Fractions

With a little extra work, you can change this worksheet so that the student can visually see the difference between two fractions.

1. In the previous instructions under Customizing a Chart on page 190, you made the white space around the chart as large as possible to fit the available space. For this worksheet, you want it to only fill up about half the page going from left to right. On a 17" monitor, that should be somewhere around Column G, but it isn't all that critical.

Comparing Fractions in Charts

Demonstrating and Comparing Fractions with Charts

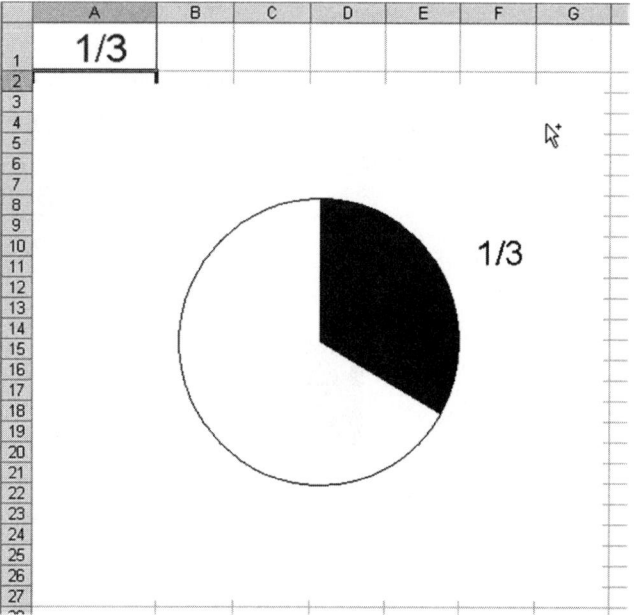

Figure 244

Pie chart with white space taking up about half of the available space

2. Now repeat all the instructions to make a second pie chart and the cell into which you type the fraction that you want displayed. The only difference is that you want to use a different color for the fraction and the pie chart. If you made the first pie chart to display in red, then you may want to use blue for the second pie chart. Then, adjust the size of both charts until they are pretty much identical.

Comparing Fractions in Charts

Demonstrating and Comparing Fractions with Charts

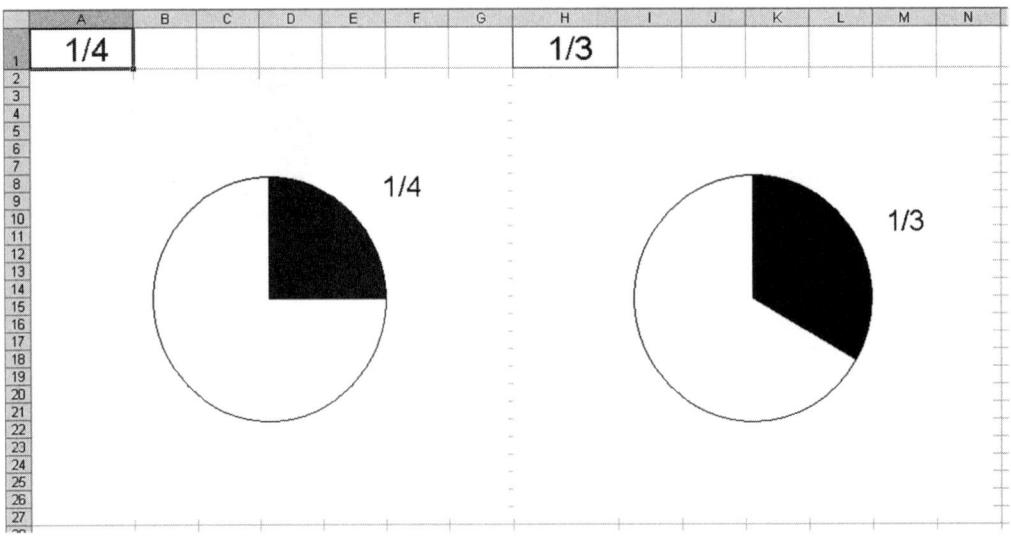

Figure 245

Pie chart with darkened sections comparing two different fractions

3. Next, you need to turn off automatic calculation.
   To do this, go to Tools → Options → Calculation. Click on the radio button next to the word Manual. Now, after you type in the fractions that you want to compare, you will need to press the F9 key in order for the two charts to display the fractions. This will give the student an opportunity to guess which fraction is the larger before Excel displays the charts.

4. To make the worksheet easier to work with, for you or a student, you will need to protect the chart so that you can only move between the two cells that display the fractions you type in.

   a. Select cell A1 (or whichever cell displays the fraction on the left side of the page) and press Ctrl+1 to open the Format Cell dialog box. Click on the Protection tab, and uncheck the box next to Locked. Check the box next to the word Hidden. Click OK to exit.

Comparing Fractions in Charts

Figure 246

Using Format Cells → Protection tab to hide the formula for the left-most fraction

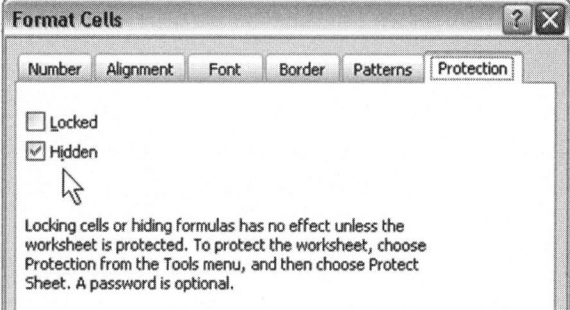

b. Select Tools → Protection → Protect Sheet. Remove the check mark from Select locked cells and click OK.

Figure 247

Preventing students from selecting locked cells

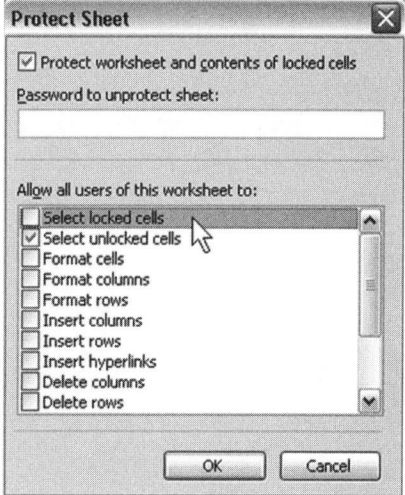

5. To use the worksheet, type in two different fractions in each of the two cells. Have the students determine which is larger, then press F9 to display the two charts.

Comparing Fractions in Charts

Demonstrating and Comparing Fractions with Charts

Comparing Fractions in Charts

Finding Maximum Area and Volume

Opportunity

Guess and check is a legitimate problem solving skill that can be used to allow students to solve some types of problems that normally would use mathematics beyond their current knowledge. Both of the maximization problems in this chapter can be solved using calculus or pre-calculus mathematics. However, students with a basic understanding of area and volume can use those skills in a guess and check process if guided carefully by their instructor. Advanced eighth or ninth graders might also enjoy working on them independently.

With paper and pencil, the process for these problems can be somewhat tedious. Excel allows you to develop the formula for the process and let the computer do the computations.

Solution and Overview – Farmer's Fence

Here is the problem: A farmer has a length of fencing material with which he wants to make a three-sided enclosure against the side of his barn. With that given amount of material, what is the largest area that can be enclosed?

What is the formula for finding the area of a rectangle? How can we come up with a length and a width based on the given total perimeter of 100 ft.? Go through a process of guessing and checking, starting with a width that is one foot away from the building that the fence will be built against, giving you a rectangle that is 1' x 98'. Increase the width in one foot increments, subtracting two feet from the length each time. Depending on your students, you can adapt the increments to incorporate fractional amounts (0.5', 0.25', etc.).

Finding Maximum Area and Volume

You will create a chart that will calculate the area of the fenced-in enclosure using all the possible combinations of length and width using an incremental change of your choice. You will also make a graph to show the change in the area as the dimensions change.

Creating the Solution

1. Enter and format the text as shown below.

    a. Select cells A1-B1 and right-click. Select Format Cells; make the font Ariel, 10 pt, bold and click on the checkbox next to Merge cells under Alignment. Press Enter.
    Enter the following text: Amount of Fence:

    b. In C1, type in 100. You or your students can vary this amount to explore different scenarios.

    c. Select cells J3-K5 and right-click. Select Format Cells; make the font Ariel, bold, 16 and click on the checkbox next to Merge cells under Alignment. Press Enter.
    Enter the following text, pressing Alt+Enter between words to insert a line break: Farmer's Fence:

    d. Select cell A3 and right-click. Select Format Cells and make the font Ariel, 10 pt, bold. Press Enter.
    Enter the following text: Instructions:
    Make the same settings in A8 and enter the following text:
    Further Investigation:

    e. Select cells A4-H6 and right-click. Select Format Cells; make the font Ariel, 10 pt, bold. Click in the checkbox next to Merge cells under Alignment and make Vertical alignment Center. Press Enter.
    Enter the following text, pressing Alt+Enter at each line break:
    A farmer wants to use one side of his barn to make a fenced in area for his livestock.

He has 100 feet of fencing to make the three sides of the enclosure. What measurements must he use to get the largest area inside the fence?

f. Select cells A9-H11 and right-click. Format cells as in previous step. Enter the following text, pressing Alt+Enter at each line break:
Change the amount of fencing by putting a different value in C1.
Does your new answer have any similarities to the original answer to the problem?
What conclusions or predictions can you draw from these examples?

Figure 248

Setting up the amount of fencing and other textual front material

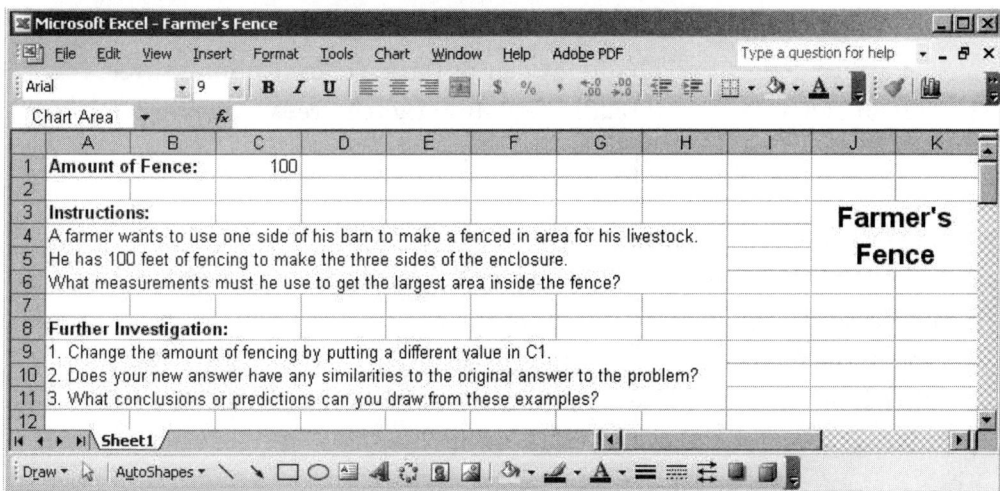

2. Build a barn six columns wide by eight rows tall.
    Select cells H14-M21 and right-click. Select Format Cells and make the following settings:

    a. Alignment: Set Horizontal and Vertical both to Center; under Text control, select Merge cells.

    b. Font: Select Ariel, bold, 12 point.

Finding Maximum Area and Volume

    c. Pattern: Select Cell shading Color of Red (left-most column, middle row). Press Enter.

    d. Type in the following text: **Barn**

3. Build a fence four columns wide by three rows high under the barn. Select I22-L24 and right-click. Select Format Cells and make the following settings:

    a. Alignment: Set Horizontal and Vertical both to Center; under Text control, select Merge cells.

    b. Font: Select Ariel, bold, 10 point.

    c. Border: Select Outline and the thickest solid Line style (one up from bottom right).

    d. Pattern: Select Cell shading Color of Dark Yellow (column three, row two) and a Pattern of 6.25% Gray (top right). Press Enter.

    e. Type in the following text: **Area**

4. Label the Length and Width.
Select H22-H24 and right-click. Select Format Cells; make both Horizontal and Vertical Text alignment Center and click on Merge cells. Press Enter. Type in the following text: **Width**
Select I25-L26 and right-click. Make the same settings as above and press Enter. Type in the following text: **Length**

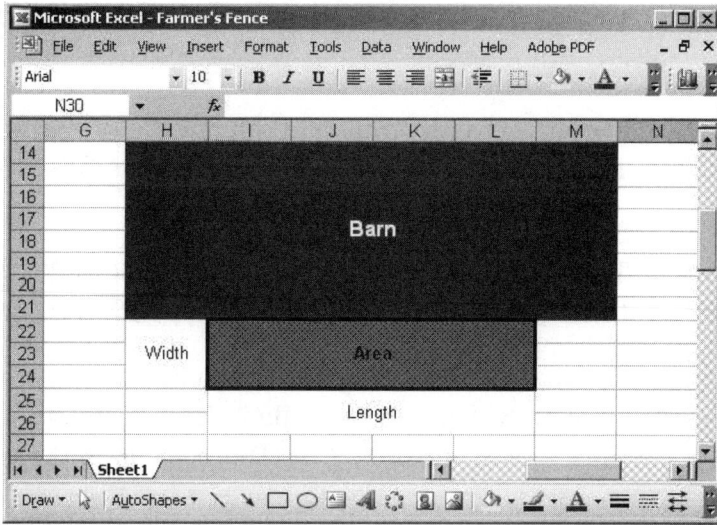

Figure 249

Building and labeling the barn and fence

5. Set up the incrementation value.

   a. Select A14-A15 and select both Outside and Inside borders. Set the font to Ariel, 10 pt, bold and then type in the word Increment in A14.

   b. Type in the incrementation value in A15. In this case, use a one (1). Whatever value you choose (1, 0.5, 1/3, etc.) will be used to increment the rest of the values in this column. This allows you to quickly change the nature of the series. Using a one (1) has the advantage of producing an answer that is a whole number.

6. Build the calculations table.

   a. Select C14 down to E63 and right-click. Select Format Cells.

   b. Set the borders to Outline and Inside.

   c. Select C14-E14 and set the font to Ariel, 10 pt, bold and then type in the following words Width, Length, and Area in C14, D14, and E14, respectively.

Finding Maximum Area and Volume

    d. Type in the starting number at C15. In this example, you will use a one (1).

    e. Set up the width formula in column C.
Type in the following formula in C16: =$A$15+C15

    f. Set up the length formula in column D.
Type in the following formula in D15: =$C$1-2*C15
Click in D16 and press Ctrl+D to copy down the formula to D16.

    g. Set up the area formula in column E.
Type in the following formula in E15: =C15*D15
Click in E16 and press Ctrl+D to copy down the formula to E16.

    h. Select C16-E16; drag the mouse to copy the formulas down to C63-E63.

7. Find the maximum value.
Select C65-D65 and right-click. Select Format Cells and make the font Ariel, 10 pt, bold. Make the horizontal alignment right-aligned and merge the cells. Enter the following text: **Maximum Value:**
Type in the following formula in E65: =MAX(E15:E63)

Finding Maximum Area and Volume

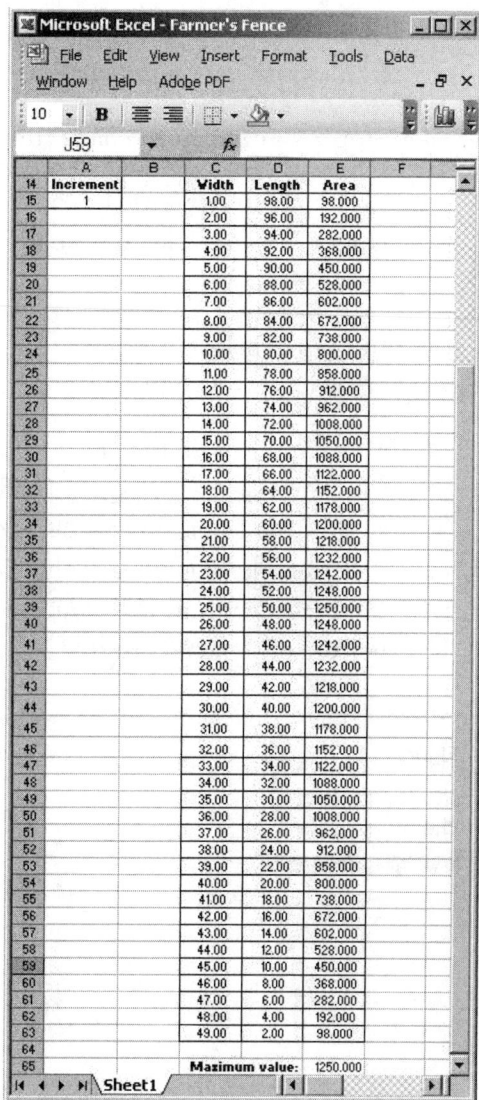

Figure 250

Setting the incrementation value, building the calculation table, and finding the maximum value

8. Create the chart.

   a. Select C14-E63 (the entire calculations table including headings).

   b. Click on the Chart Wizard icon in the Standard toolbar (shows a vertical bar chart). Select the Line Chart type and the middle row, left-most

Finding Max Area and Volume

Excel for the Math Classroom — 207

Finding Maximum Area and Volume

column Sub-type (default). (Push Press and Hold to View Sample to see what your chart will look like.) Press Next.

c. Step 2 shows you the data range selected and the series. Press Next.

d. In Step 3, under Titles, type in a Chart title as follows: **Farmer's Fence** Under Legend, click on the Placement radio button for Bottom. Press Next.

e. In Step 4, select "As object in:" and press Finish. Excel places the finished chart on your worksheet.

f. Move and re-size the chart.
Click on Draw → Snap To Grid. Left-click to select the chart and drag it so that the top is on row 29 under the barn. Use the right and left handles to make the sides of the chart line up with the barn. (It should extend from column H to column M.) Use the bottom handle to drag the bottom of the chart to row 53.

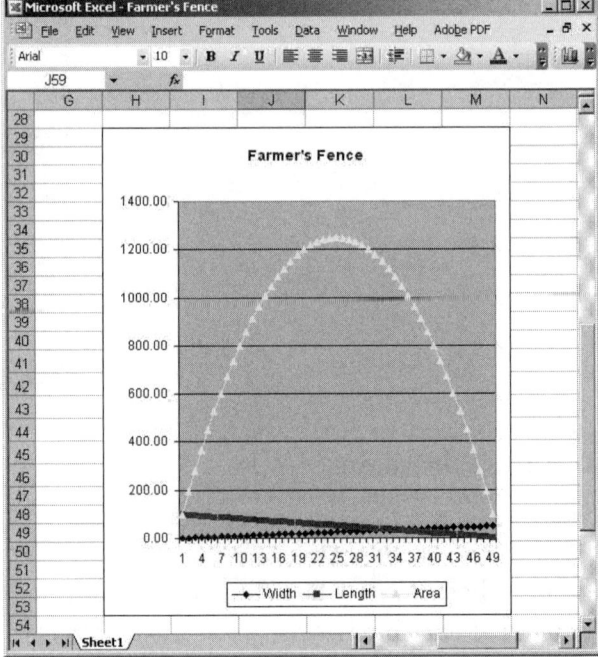

Figure 251

Inserting a line chart

Note:

Once you have the answer for this version, you can feed in some exploratory numbers to see if there is a relationship between the correct answer for this problem and the appropriate answer for other similar problems. That is, is there a basic relationship between width and length of a rectangle that maximizes the area inside this rectangle?

Using the Application

For older students, the difficulty is in figuring out the formula that they need to use. (Instead of the usual A = LW, they need to use A = W (100 − 2W) if the given length of fencing is 100' long, and W is the distance away from the barn.) Once they plug that in, they can just look down the table to find the dimensions that provide the greatest area. They can also do some exploring on their own with different amounts of fence and then tabulate the results on paper and pencil. They can then see if they can draw some conclusions about the ratio – is there a conclusion they can reach about the proportions of a rectangle that would give them the maximum amount of area.

Younger kids can use guessing and checking to come up with the correct answer. You could produce this worksheet as a blank table and use it to guide the students by placing it on an overhead projector and working on it as a teacher-guided activity for the whole class. For these students, you may want to concentrate on the pattern of numbers generated as they fill in the chart: For each unit increase in the width, the length decreases by twice that unit.

Students could work in small groups or individually and, as each discovered the correct answer to one part of the table, that answer could be put on the spreadsheet and shown to the rest of the class.

You could set this up as a table that you provide to the students on paper, which they would need to complete using paper and pencil or calculators. You could also set this up as a spreadsheet, explain the process to the students, and

Finding Maximum Area and Volume

let them work individually at workstations or as a group with an overhead projector.

Excel Extras

You can make the maximum value really pop out using conditional formatting.

1. In the calculation table, select the cells in the Area column, E15-E63. Select Format → Conditional Formatting.

2. Set the condition 1 cell value to "equal to".

3. Type in the following formula in the last text box on the top: =$E$65

4. Press the Format... button and set the Pattern to Yellow. Click OK twice.

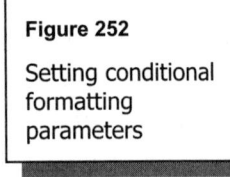

Figure 252

Setting conditional formatting parameters

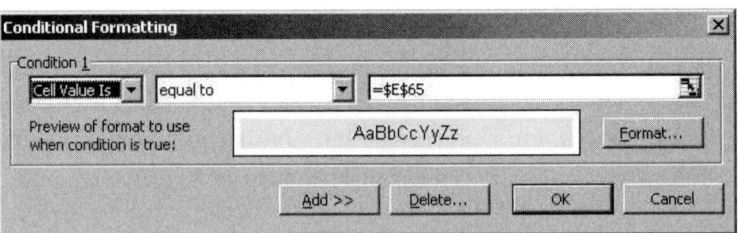

5. Excel highlights cell E39 because it matches the maximum value determined by cell E65.

Figure 253

Cell with maximum value is highlighted

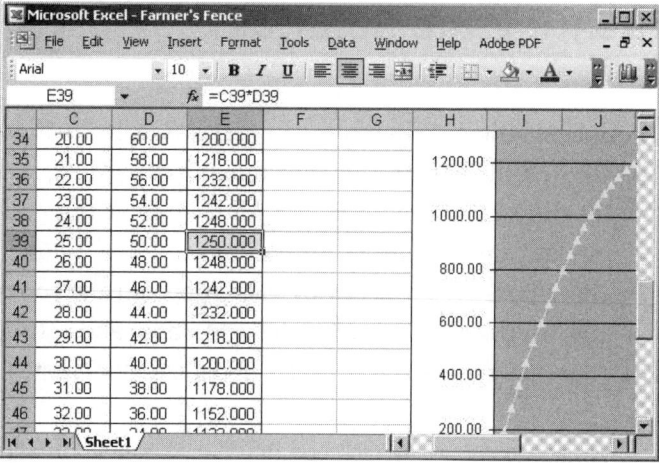

Solution and Overview – Popcorn Box

Here is the problem: A group of students want to sell popcorn as a fund-raiser for their club. They want to make containers for the popcorn from a standard 8½" x 11" piece of paper by cutting squares out of the corners and folding up the four sides. What is the largest volume of popcorn that can fit in a container made this way?

What is the formula for finding the volume of a box? How can we come up with the optimum volume (length, width, and height) based on the given material? Go through a process of guessing and checking. Start by cutting out ¼" squares from the corners and then find the resulting length, width, and height, and volume. Which combination produces the greatest volume? Increase the size of the corner squares in ¼" increments. Depending on your students, you can adapt the increments to incorporate fractional amounts (1/8", 1/2", 1", etc.).

You will create a chart that will calculate the volume of the popcorn box using all the possible combinations of a variable height (the size of the square in each corner), length, and width using an incremental change of your choice. You will also make a graph to show the change in the volume as the height of the box changes.

Finding Maximum Area and Volume

Creating the Solution

1. Select cells A1-H5 and right-click. Select Format Cells; make the font Ariel, 10 pt, and click on the checkbox next to Merge cells under Alignment. Enter the following text, pressing Alt+Enter at the end of each line (twice before the last line) to insert line breaks:
   Your club is raising money by selling popcorn and you want to make boxes to sell it in.
   You are going to start with 8 1/2 x 11 paper and cut squares out of each corner.
   Then, you can fold up the sides and fasten them with tape.

   What size square in each corner will give you a box with the largest possible volume?

2. Select cells J1-M2 and right-click. Select Format Cells; make the font Ariel, 12 pt, bold and click on the checkbox next to Merge cells under Alignment. Enter the following text: The Popcorn Box Problem

Figure 254
Setting up the background information, instructions, question, and title block

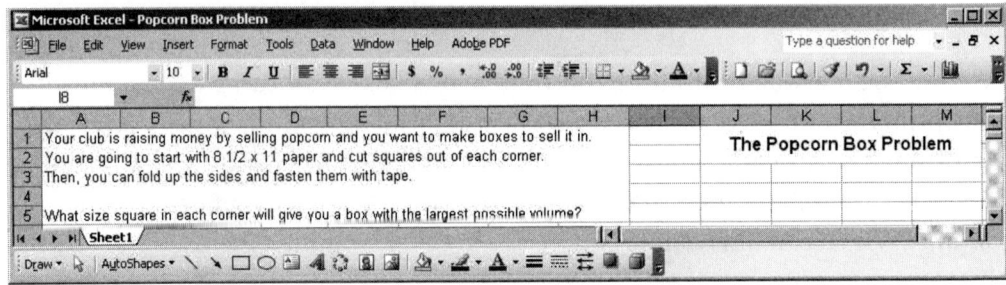

3. Draw the popcorn box layout.

   a. You will use the Drawing toolbar. If this toolbar is not already visible, select View → Toolbars → Drawing. In the Draw drop-down menu, select Snap → To Grid.

b. Use the Rectangle drawing tool to draw a rectangle from J:1-M2 (temporarily covering The Popcorn Box Problem title block). Notice how the rectangle "snaps" into the correct size and position?

c. Select the Rectangle icon again and draw a small rectangle starting one row under the title block. Right-click and select Format AutoShape. Under size, set the Height to 2" and the Width to 2.51". Press Enter.

d. Click in a blank cell. Now click on the rectangle covering the title block, hold down the Shift key, and then click on the rectangle below it. In the Draw drop-down menu, select Align or Distribute → Align Center. The "sheet of paper" rectangle centers itself on the "title block" rectangle. Click in a blank cell, click on the title block rectangle, and press the Delete key.

e. Draw a rectangle inside the remaining ("sheet of paper") rectangle and right-click. Select Format AutoShape; under Size, set the Height to 1.39" and the Width to 1.9". Under Colors and Lines, set the Line color to 50%. Press Enter.

f. With the smaller rectangle still selected, press the Shift key and then click on the larger rectangle. In the Draw drop-down menu, select Align or Distribute → Align Center and then select Align or Distribute → Align Middle. Press Enter. The inner rectangle centers itself on the outer rectangle.

g. Next you will draw the four corners. Click in a blank cell. Using the Rectangle icon, draw a small rectangle off to the side. Right-click and select Format AutoShape. Under size, set the Height and Width both to 0.3". Under Colors and Lines, set the Fill color to 0.25%, the Line color to 50%, and Dashed to the fourth line down (even dashes). Press Enter.

h. Press Ctrl+C to copy this small square. In the Draw drop-down menu, select Snap → To Shape. Hover over the square and so that the cursor becomes four outward-pointing arrows. Left-click and drag to the upper left corner of the large rectangle. When the sides line up, release the left mouse button.

Finding Maximum Area and Volume

i. Click in an empty cell just outside the lower left corner of the largest rectangle. Press Crtl+V to paste the small square. Drag and drop this square to the lower left corner of the large rectangle. Repeat for the upper and lower right corners.

j. Optional: Use the Arrow tool to draw four arrows as shown. Use the Text box tool to make the two "Fold lines" labels. If necessary, drag to correct position. You can also zoom to more easily see what you are doing. Select View → Zoom and either click 200% or Custom to specify the desired level of magnification.

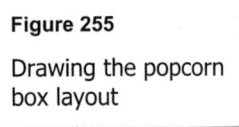

Figure 255

Drawing the popcorn box layout

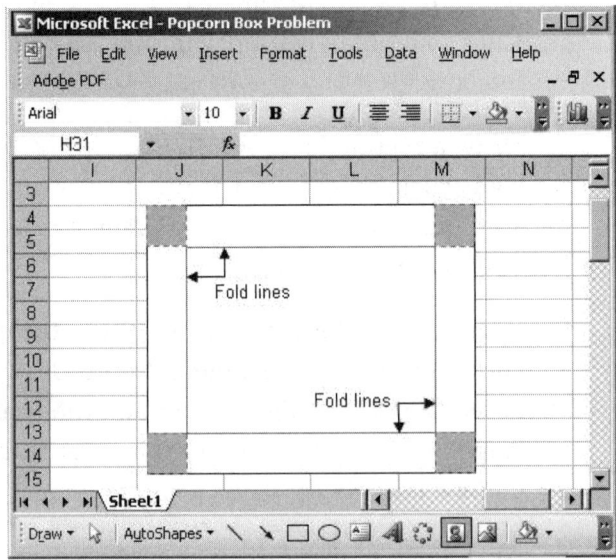

4. Set up the incrementation value.

   a. Select A7 and set the font to Ariel, 10 pt, bold. Type in the following word: Increment

   b. Type in the incrementation value in A8. In this case, use a 0.25 (will display as 1/4). Whatever value you choose (0.25, 0.125, etc.) will be used to increment the rest of the values.

c. Right-click and select Format Cells. Under the Number tab, select Fraction and Up to two digits (21/25). Press Enter.

5. Build the calculations table.

   a. Select C7 down to F24 and right-click. Select Format Cells.

   b. Set the borders to Outline and Inside.

   c. Select C7-F7 and set the font to Ariel, 10 pt, bold. Type in the words Height, Width, Length, and Volume in C7, D7, E7, and, F7, respectively.

   d. Select C8-E24. Under the Number tab, select Fraction and Up to two digits (21/25). Select E8-E24. Under the Number tab, select Fraction and Up to three digits (312/943).

   e. Type in the starting number at C7. In this example, you will use 0.25.

   f. Set up the height formula in column C.
   Type in the following formula in C9: =C8+$A$8

   g. Set up the width formula in column D.
   Type in the following formula in D8: =8.5-2*C8
   Click in D9 and press Ctrl+D to copy the formula.

   h. Set up the length formula in column E.
   Type in the following formula in E8: =11-2*C8
   Copy down to E9.

   i. Set up the volume formula in column F.
   Type in the following formula in F8: =C8*D8*E8
   Copy down to F9.

   j. Select C9-F9; drag the mouse to copy the formulas down to C24-F24.

6. Find the maximum value.
   Select D27-E27 and right-click. Select Format Cells and make the font Ariel, 10 pt, bold. Make the horizontal alignment right-aligned and merge

Finding Maximum Area and Volume

the cells. Type in the following text: Maximum Value:
Type in the following formula in F27: =MAX(F8:F24)

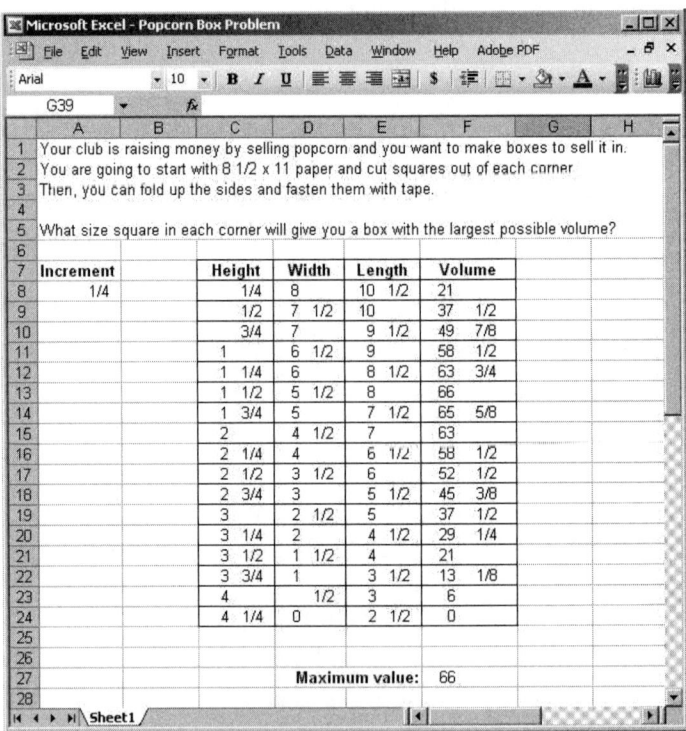

Figure 256

Setting the incrementation value, building the calculation table, and finding the maximum value

7. Create the chart.

   a. Select C7-F24 (the entire calculations table including headings).

   b. Click on the Chart Wizard icon in the Standard toolbar (looks like a vertical bar chart). The Chart Wizard dialog pops up. Select the Line Chart type and the middle row, left-most column Sub-type (default). Press Next.

   c. In Step 2, click on the Series tab. To help the students focus on the two most important elements of the series (height and volume), you can remove the width and length lines. Under Series, click on "Width" and press the Remove button. Do the same for the length. (Want to see how the chart will look? Press Back and then use the "Press and Hold to View Sample" button. Release and press Next.) Press Next.

d. In Step 3, under Titles, type in a Chart title as follows: **Popcorn box** Under Legend, click on the Placement radio button for Right. Press Next.

e. In Step 4, select "As object in:" and press Finish. Excel places the finished chart on your worksheet.

f. Move and re-size the chart. Click on Draw → Snap To Grid. Left-click to select the chart and drag it so that the top is on row 17 under the popcorn box. Use the right and left handles to make the sides of the chart extend from column I to column N.) Use the bottom handle to drag the bottom of the chart to row 36.

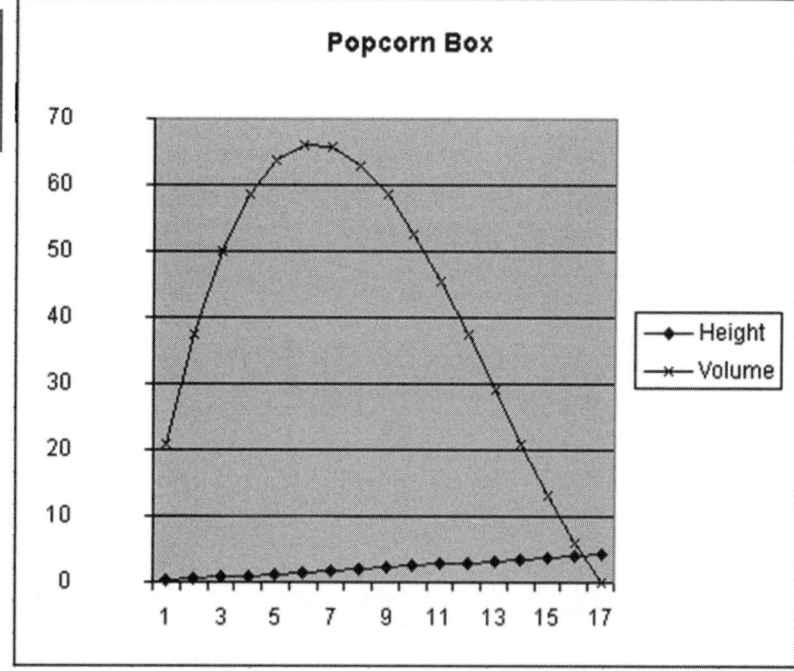

Figure 257

Inserting a line chart

Using the Application

Pass out sheets of graph paper and actually build the varying sizes of popcorn boxes. Try different increment values. Your students will find that, as the interval becomes smaller, they are able to zero in more precisely on largest possible volume.

Solving Systems of Equations

Opportunity

"Tweedledum said to Tweedledee: 'The sum of your weight and twice mine is 361 pounds.' Tweedledee said to Tweedledum: 'Contrariwise, the sum of your weight and twice mine is 362 pounds."
Through the Looking Glass, Lewis Carroll

Sometimes, the minor errors of arithmetic can get in the way of understanding the process of an algebraic algorithm. In solving a system of equations, such as the one presented by Lewis Carroll, the real trick is in figuring out exactly what the equations are. If the student is to solve the system by subtraction, the process involves an understanding of the algorithm, plus some very basic computational skills. Many schools allow the use of calculators in the math classroom. Why not a calculator that requires the student to enter the equations, and then to enter a few additional numbers to make the algorithm work?

Solution and Overview

You will make a worksheet that uses the subtraction method for solving a system of two equations (sometimes known as simultaneous equations). The worksheet will be protected so that the student will have access only to the cells that require user input to solve the equations.

Creating the Solution

You will begin by making the instructions for the worksheet, which requires you to make several "text boxes".

Solving Systems of Equations

1. Change the font style and size for the entire worksheet.
   In the extreme upper left hand corner, there is an empty box just to the left of Column A, and above Row 1. Clicking on that box highlights the entire worksheet. Go to the toolbar at the top of the page and change the Font to Arial and the Size to 12 by clicking on the small arrow to the right of each box and making the correct selection.

Figure 258 Selecting the entire worksheet and changing the font

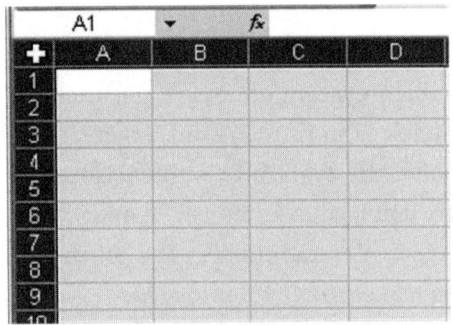 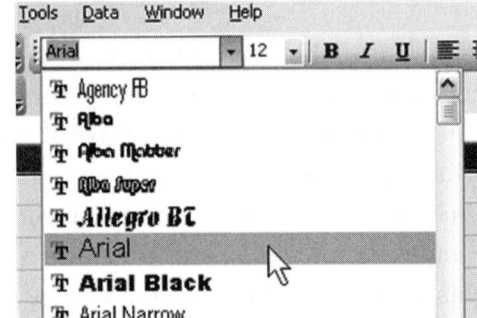

2. Create a title block.
   Move your cursor to cell C1. Left click and drag to the right until you get to cell Q1 and let go. While the cells are still highlighted, and with the cursor inside the highlighted range, right-click to open the Format Cells dialog box. Make the following changes:

   a. Click on the Alignment tab, change the Horizontal Alignment to Center, and click on the box next to Merge Cells under the Text Control Heading.

   b. Click on the Font tab, and change Size to 18. Click OK to exit.

   c. Inside the merged cells, type in the following text:
      Solving a System of Two Equations by Subtraction

3. Format the information box.

   Move to cell B2. Left click and drag to the right and down to highlight the range B2:R6. Open the Format Cells dialog box again by right-clicking, and make the following changes:

   a. Alignment tab: Check the boxes next to Wrap Text, and Merge Cells.

   b. Border tab: Select Outline from the Presets at the top.

   c. Patterns tab: Select the pale blue color from the bottom row. Click OK to exit.

4. Enter the information.

   Normally, when you type into merged cells that are using word wrap, the text will break to the next line when you get to the right edge of the merged cells in much the same way that a word processor works. Making the text go to the next line when you want it to requires the use of a hard break, which, within a merged cell, can be accomplished by pressing the Alt key and then the Enter key.

   Type in the following text, pressing Alt+Enter when you see the paragraph icon (¶).

   This worksheet can be used to solve equations you have written to solve word problems with two unknowns.¶ The solution can be found by multiplying each equation by the y-coefficient of the other equation. Then, subtracting the two equations will yield a third equation with a y-coefficient of 0.¶ The value of x is then found by using the new equation, and dividing by the x-coefficient.¶ This worksheet will then calculate the value of y by substituting the value of x into one of the original equations.

   Right now, both of the two text boxes you just made are probably wider than your screen. That's OK. You will be adjusting some column widths in later steps.

5. Create a series of instruction text boxes.

   a. Click on cell B9 and drag to the right to cell G9. Right-click inside the highlighted cells to open the Format Cells dialog box. Under Alignment, check Merge Cells; under Border, select Outline; and under Patterns,

Solving Systems of Equations

select light green from the bottom row. Click OK to exit.
Inside the merged cells, type in the following text:

1) Enter the coefficients of Equat. 1 in the green boxes.

b. Click on cell B11 and drag to cell G11. Right-click inside the highlighted cells, and make the same format changes you did in Step 5, except for the Pattern. Choose tan, which is the second color from the left on the bottom row.
Inside this box, type in the following text:

2) Enter the coefficients of Equat. 2 in the tan boxes.

c. Click on cell B13, and drag right and down to cell G15. Right-click inside the highlighted cells and make the following format changes:

   i. Alignment: Select Wrap Text and Merge Cells.
   ii. Border: Select Outline.
   iii. Patterns: Select pale yellow.

d. Type in the following text, remembering to press Alt+Enter when you see the paragraph icon (¶). (Do this twice after the first sentence!)

3a) Enter the y-coefficient of Equat. 2 in Box A. ¶ ¶
3b) Enter the y-coefficient of Equat. 1 in Box B.

Figure 259
Instructions entered in merged cells

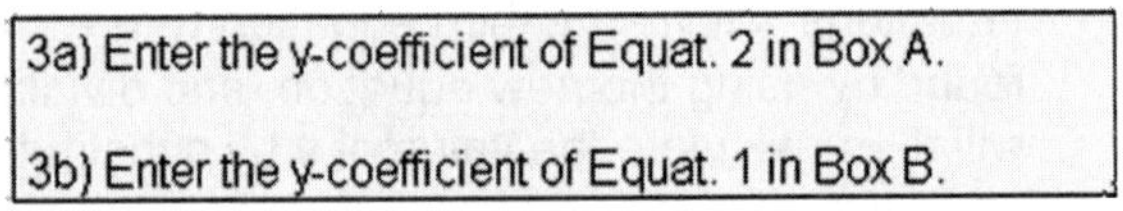

3a) Enter the y-coefficient of Equat. 2 in Box A.

3b) Enter the y-coefficient of Equat. 1 in Box B.

e. Click on cell B17 and drag right and down to cell G18. Change the cell formatting the same as Step 5c, except use light pink for the Pattern color. Type the following text into these merged cells:

4) The y-coefficient in this equation should be zero. If it isn't, you made a mistake in step 3a and/or 3b.

Solving Systems of Equations

    f.   Click on cell B20, and drag right and down to cell G22. Format these cells EXACTLY the same as you did in Step 5c, including the color. Enter the following text in this box:

          5) Enter the x-coefficient from the last equation (the pink one) in Box C. The correct solutions will be shown in the dark blue and red boxes to the right labeled x and y."

    g.   Last text box! Click on cell B24 and drag right and down to cell G25. This box also is formatted EXACTLY the same as Step 7.
Enter the following text in this box:

          6) Compare the results of the check to the right with the original equations. They should be the same."

6.   Enter and format the template for the first equation.

    a.   Move your cursor to cell K8. Starting with that cell, type the following equation, PLACING ONLY ONE character per cell: A x + B y = C

        In order to type in the + and = without Excel thinking you want to enter a formula, you will need to precede each of those characters with an apostrophe. This tells Excel that they are text characters. When you finish, you will be in cell Q8.

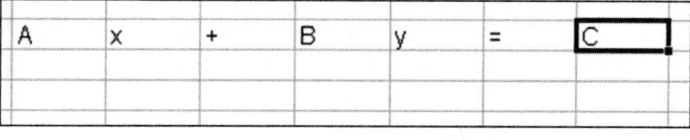

Figure 260

Entering equation, one character per cell

    b.   Starting with cell K8, click and drag to the right to highlight the range K8:Q8. Right-click; select the Borders tab and click Outline from the Presets. From the Patterns tab, select bright yellow (second row from the bottom).

    c.   Now you will change the widths of columns M and P. Move your cursor to the very top, next to the letter M in column M. The cursor will change to a plus sign with a horizontal arrow. Double-clicking at that

Excel for the Math Classroom

point will narrow the width to accommodate the "x" in cell L8. Do the same to column P.

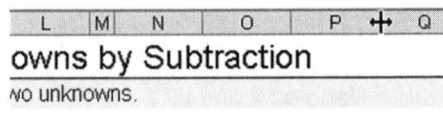

Figure 261
Changing column width

d. Now you will change the widths of columns K, L, N, O, and Q using a neat trick. Click on the K in column K to highlight the entire column. Then, holding down the Ctrl key, click on the M and the Q. This will allow you to change the width of all three columns at the same time. Move your cursor between the K and L until it changes to the plus sign with the horizontal arrows. Then left click and you will see the current column width as 8.43 (64 pixels). Hold down the left mouse button and slowly move to the left until the width is 5.00 (40 pixels). Release the mouse button and all three columns will change width. This width should work for most problems. Once this is complete, if you ever get a cell filled with ###, that tells you that the number in that cell is too big for that width. Make adjustments at that time accordingly.

Figure 262
Changing width of multiple non-contiguous columns

7. Do the formatting for the first equation.

   a. Click on cell L8. While holding down the left mouse button, drag to the right to cell P8. Press Ctrl+C to copy the contents of these five cells. Click on cell L9. From the Edit menu on the toolbar, select Paste Special, Values, and then click OK. The contents of the five cells, without the color, have been copied. Now click on cell N9, and delete the B in that cell.

b. Click on cell L9, and drag to the right to cell P9. Press Ctrl+C to copy the cells. Click on cell L11, and press Ctrl+V to paste the values into the cells. Continue this process (click on a cell, then press Ctrl+V) in the following cells: L13, L15, L17, L23, and L24.

c. You will now change the background colors in some of the cells in Columns K through Q. To make this a bit easier, you will use a similar trick to the one you used to change non-contiguous columns in Step 6d. Change the following cells to light green. Click on cell K9. Hold down the Ctrl key and click on N9, Q9, K13, N13, and Q13. Now right-click and change the Patterns color to the same light green as the text box in row 9. Also, go to the Borders tab and select Outline.

d. Now do the same with these cells (change border and color), except make them the same tan as the text box in row 11. Select cells K11, N11, Q11, K15, N15, and Q15.

e. Cells K17, N17, and Q17 need to be changed to pink, the same color as the text box in rows 17 and 18. Don't forget the border (Outline).

f. Now highlight the range of cells K23:Q23; right-click and change their color to the pale green from Step 7c.

g. Highlight the range of cells K25:Q25, and change their color to the tan color from Step 19.

h. Click on cell L23. Hold down the Ctrl key and click on cell O23, L25, and O25. Press the Delete key to remove the x and y characters in these cells. Press Ctrl+1 to open the Format Cells dialog box and give these cells an Outline border.

i. Click on cell I13. Hold down the Ctrl key again and click I15 and I20. Press Ctrl+1 to open the Format Cells dialog box. Change the Pattern color to pale yellow and place an Outline Border on the cells.

j. Move the mouse cursor in between the I and J at the top of the page. Left click and drag to the left to change the cell width to 3.57 (30 pixels).

Solving Systems of Equations

Figure 263
Changing cell width

k. In cell H13, type an A; in cell H15, a B; and in cell H20, a C. Click on cell H13 and drag down to cell H20. Go to the toolbar at the top, and click on the Right Align icon.

Figure 264
Selecting the Align right icon

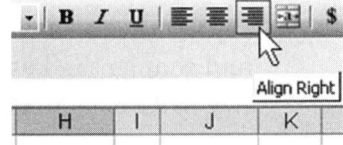

l. Go to cell O20 and type in the letter x. In cell O21, type in the letter y. In cells P20 and P21, type in an equal sign preceded by an apostrophe ('=).

m. Go to cell Q20. Press Ctrl+1. Change the Pattern color to Blue and set the Border to Outline.

n. Go to cell Q21. Press Ctrl+1. Change the Pattern color to Red and set the Border to Outline.

8. Now you will enter the formulas needed to make this work. In order to do that, you will use the equations from the Lewis Carroll quote at the beginning of this section. Translating the paragraph into math sentences gives the following result:

   Tweedledee + 2(Tweedledum) = 361;   Tweedledum + 2(Tweedledee) = 362

   Assigning "x" to Tweedledee and "y" to Tweedledum, gives the following two equations:

   $x + 2y = 361$
   $2x + y = 362$

a. So, before you begin, enter a 1, 2, and 361 into cells K9, N9, and Q9, respectively. Then enter 2, 1, and 362 into cells K11, N11, and Q11. In Box A, enter a 1, and in Box B, enter a 2. This way, you can check to see if you are getting the correct results with your formulas as you go along.

b. In row 13, you need formulas that will multiply the value in Box A by the coefficients in Equation 1. In cell K13, type in the following formula:
   =i13*k9
   This tells Excel to multiply the value in cell I13 by the value in K9. The i13 tells Excel that you have made an absolute reference to I13 that will not change as we copy the formula.

c. Click once on cell K13 and press Ctrl+C to start the copy process. Click on cell N13 and press Ctrl+V, and then click Q13 and press Ctrl+V to paste the copied formula. The three cells should contain the numbers 1, 2, and 361.

d. Now click on cell K15 and type in the following formula:
   = i15*K11
   Press Ctrl+C to copy, and paste into N15 and Q15. These three cells should now contain a 4, 2, and 724.

e. This step subtracts the equation in row 15 from the equation in row 13. Click on cell K17 and type in the following formula:
   =k13-k15
   Copy and paste into N17 and Q17. The cells should contain -3, 0, and -363.

f. Box C is used to tell Excel what you want to use to divide the equation in row 17. Since the x-coefficient of that equation is currently -3, enter that into Box C.

g. In cell Q20, enter the following formula:
   =Q17/Q20
   The number displayed in this cell should be 121.

Solving Systems of Equations

    h. Now that you know the value of x, you can substitute it back into one of the original equations and solve for y. You will use Equation 1 to do this. In cell Q21, enter the following formula:

        =(q9-k9*q20)/n9

    The number displayed in this cell should be 120.

    i. The equations in rows 23 and 25 will put the answers from cells Q20 and Q21 back into the original equations. If the answers are correct, the numbers to the right of the equal sign in rows 23 and 25 will be the same as the number to the right in the original equation. In cell K23, enter the following formula:

        =k9

    You can then copy (Ctrl+C) and paste (Ctrl+V) that formula into N23.

9. In order to maintain the correct cell color, you will need to use Paste Special to copy the formula into cells K25 and N25. To do this, click again on cell K23. Then, from the Edit menu, select Paste Special → Formulas and press Enter. Only the formula will get copied. Then click on cell N25 and do the same. Since the original equations were set up with the same relative spacing of the equations in rows 23 and 25, you can copy the formulas this way without error.

Figure 265

Using Paste special to copy formulas

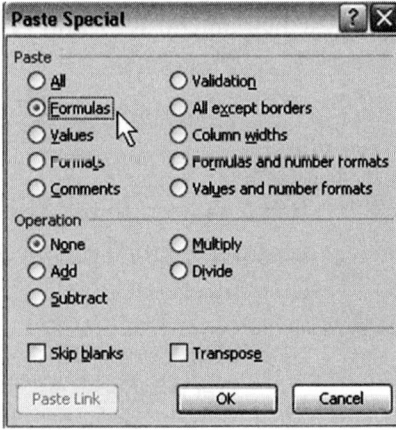

10. Copy the calculated solutions to the system of equations and place them into the cells that will check these answers against the original equation
In cell L23, enter the following formula:
   =q20
Copy and use Paste Special again to copy into cell L25.
In cell O23, enter the following formula:
   =q21
Copy and Paste Special into cell O25.

11. Enter a checking formula.
In order to make sure the worksheet (and student) has calculated the answers correctly, you do not want to simply copy the values from Q9 and Q11 directly into Q23 and Q25. That would give the appearance of a correct answer even if it was wrong. You need a formula that uses the worksheet answers and substitutes them back into the original equations. In cell Q23, enter the following formula:
   =k23*l23+n23*o23
Then use Ctrl+C and Paste Special to copy the formula into Q25.

12. To "student-proof" this worksheet, you are going to use Protection to lock the cells with formulas, while allowing user input where needed.
There are only nine cells that need to be unlocked. Click on cell K9, press and hold the Ctrl key, and then click on N9, Q9, K11, N11, Q11, I13, I15, and I20. Press Ctrl+1 to open the Format Cells dialog box, and click the Protection tab. Click the box next to the word Locked. Click OK to exit.

Figure 266

Using Format Cells to unlock certain cells

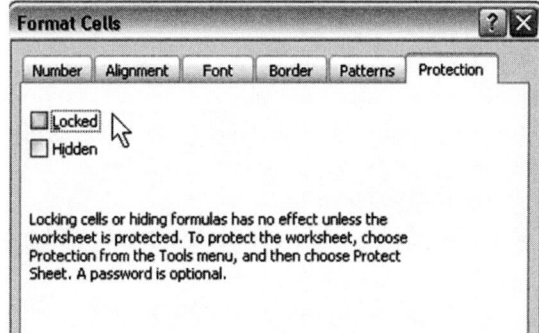

13. Hide Excel distractions.

To make the worksheet look less like Excel, go to Tools, Options, and click on the View tab. Remove the check marks from Gridlines, Row & column headers, and Sheet tabs, and click OK.

Figure 267

Hiding gridlines, row and column headers, and sheet tabs

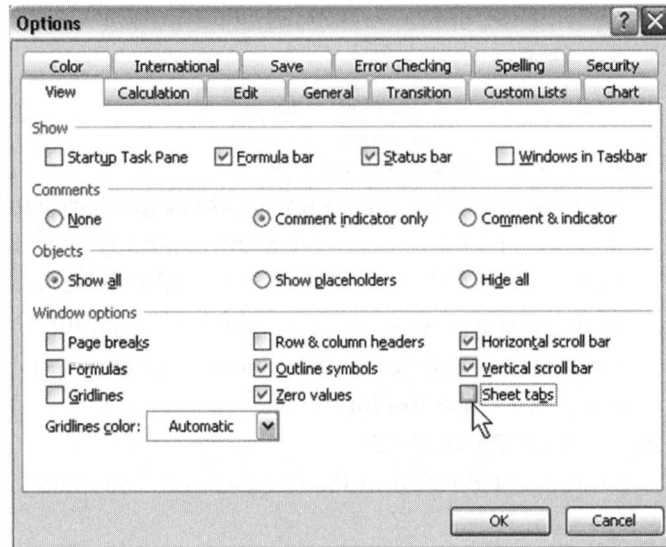

14. Protect the worksheet.

From the Tools menu, select Protect, and then Protect Sheet. Click on the box next to Select locked cells to remove the check mark. You may enter a password at this point to completely protect the worksheet, but remember to write it down someplace in case you need to come back and make changes some day.

Solving Systems of Equations

Figure 268

Protecting locked cells from being selected by students

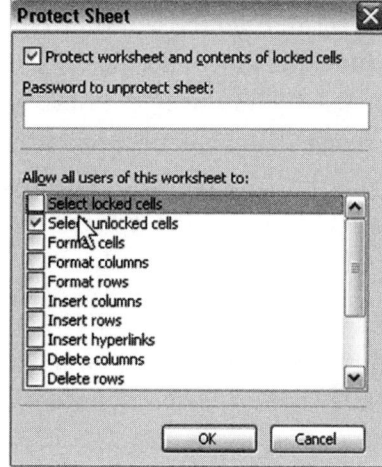

Using the Application

Depending on the class (pre-algebra or algebra) and exactly what your goals are, this application can be used in one of two ways. The first would be as a worksheet to reinforce the process of solving a system of equations with two unknowns. Sometimes, students get bogged down in learning the process because of minor calculation errors. They may have a handle on what they are supposed to do, but are still getting wrong answers. This worksheet would give them an opportunity to practice the process without having to worry about the calculations.

I have used a similar worksheet when the focus of the lesson was on solving word problems where the students not only had to interpret the problem correctly to arrive at the equations; they also had to solve the system of equations correctly. If they made an error, they were unsure if it was because of the equations they had used or because they had made computational errors.

In actual use, the student needs to enter the coefficients of each equation into the first series of cells. Typing in the number and pressing Enter moves the cursor to the next cell that needs input. After the equations are entered, the student needs to decide, by looking at the original equations, what number will be used to multiply the first equation, and what number will multiply the second. The student then enters the number that will divide both sides of the equation to solve for x. Finally, the student must compare the equations at the end of the worksheet with the originals to see if they match, ensuring that the work was done correctly.

You need to decide if you will give the students problems that have a solution, called *simultaneous* equations, or meet one of these two special circumstances:

If the two equations are parallel lines, the system is called *inconsistent*, and will have no solution. As the students enter numbers, everything will appear normal until they are asked to divide by the coefficient of x in Step 5 of the worksheet. At this point, the x-coefficient is zero, and the answer cells will fill with ####. However, upon examining what is displayed above, students will notice that in Steps 3a and 3b, the calculations resulted in identical **left** sides of the two equations, with different values on the **right**.

Another circumstance results in **completely identical** equations after doing Steps 3a and 3b. This is when one equation is actually a multiple of the other, and is called a *dependent* system. As in an inconsistent system, the final step will result in #### being displayed. In this situation, however, instead of no solution, there are an infinite number of solutions. It is up to the student to be able to recognize the difference.

Excel Extras

With some expansion, this worksheet could also be used to solve a system of three equations in three unknowns. However, since the focus of this book is for the middle grades, that particular worksheet is outside the scope of this book.

Solving Systems of Equations

Figure 269

Finished application for solving systems of equations

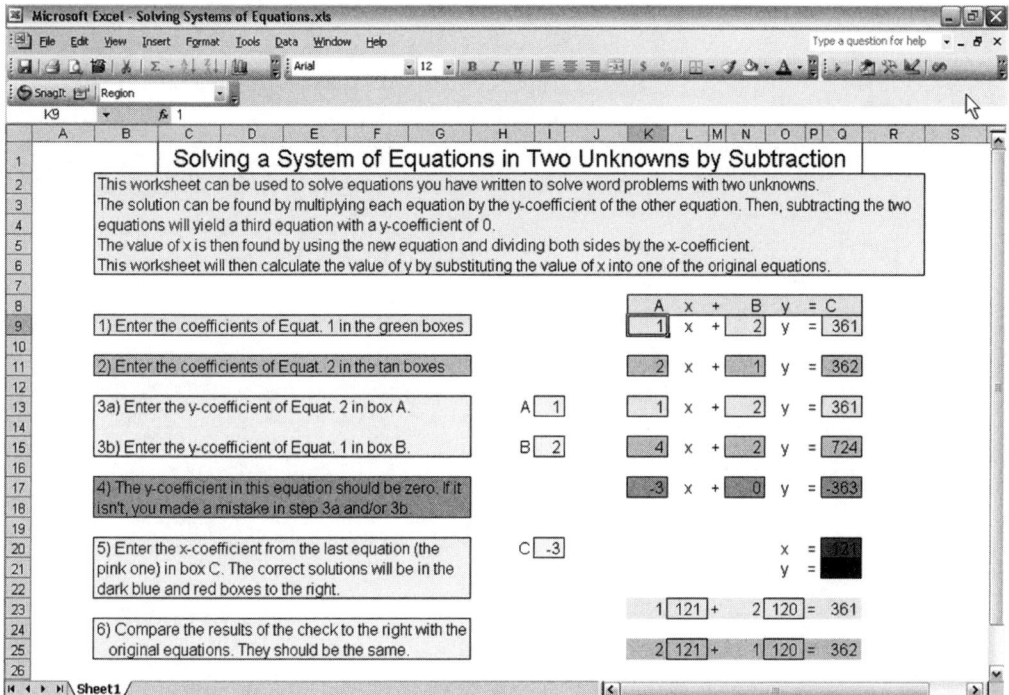

Excel for the Math Classroom

Solving Systems of Equations

233

Solving Systems of Equations

Index

A

Absolute References. *See also* Relative and Mixed References, 49, 154, 178, 227

Addition, 1-3, 5-8, 11, 12, 15, 16, 54-57, 62-67, 73, 84, 86, 183

Alignment, 56, 69, 70, 88, 93, 100, 110, 113, 133-137, 144-150, 160, 161, 171, 174, 180, 181, 220, 221

Ampersand (&), 64

Analysis ToolPak, 53, 54

Answer Keys, 60

Apostrophes, 55, 223, 226

Area Formula, 206, 209

Area of a Rectangle, 201-206, 209, 215

Arrow Key Method, 5-7

Art, 117
   String Art, 117-121, 123, 124
   Tesselations, 117, 121-123

Asterisk, 9, 50

AutoFill, 45

Automatic Calculation. *See also* Manual Calculation, 3, 58, 75, 103, 153, 168, 177, 198

AutoShapes, 39, 40, 120-123
   Align, 119, 213
   Format, 41, 173, 213
   Move, 41, 122, 173
   Resize, 40, 41, 173
   Transparency, 173

AutoCorrect Spelling, Disable, 146

AutoSum, 15-18

Average, 17-18

B

Borders, 22-25, 33, 36, 55, 68, 70, 77, 88, 94, 100, 113, 118, 119, 129, 133, 137, 145-149, 160, 161, 180, 181, 221

C

Calculations, 143
   Automatic, 3, 58, 75, 103, 153, 168, 177, 198
   Manual, 55, 58, 103, 105, 109, 143, 153, 168, 177, 198

Calculus and Pre-Calc, 201

Carat (^), 12, 13, 55, 77

Cartesian Coordinate Grid, 35-42, 99
   Handouts, 41-42
   Insert in Word Document, 35, 40

Cells
   Alignment, 202
   Color, 41, 76, 188
   Copy, 57, 224
   Format, 22-25, 36, 68-70, 78, 81, 88-94, 100, 102, 113, 129, 133, 136, 144-150, 152, 155, 160, 161, 170, 171, 174, 180, 181, 186, 188, 202-206, 212, 214, 215, 220, 221, 225, 229
   Locked and Unlocked, 96, 114, 140, 157, 175, 182, 199, 230
   Merge, 93, 94, 113, 134, 150, 160, 161, 174, 181, 220-222

Center Text, 55, 77

Chart Wizard, 187, 188, 207, 216

Charts, 188, 202, 207, 211, 216
   Customize, 190-193
   Data Points, 193, 194
   Insert, 187, 208, 217
   Labels, 192
   Legends, 187

Index

Charts, cont.
    Line, 207, 208, 216, 217
    Move, 190, 208, 217
    Pie, 185-187, 191-199
        Angle of First Slice, 194
    Plot Area, 191
    Resize, 191, 208, 217
    Series, 216
    Titles, 208, 217

Checking Homework, 75, 76

Circular Reference, 99, 103-110, 143

Circular Reasoning, 109, 167

Coefficients, 221-223, 226-227, 231, 232

Columns
    Headers, Hide, 95, 114, 139, 156, 189
    Hide, 65, 189
    Width, 20, 21, 35, 42, 127
        Adjust Multiple Non-contiguous, 224

Comma as 1000 Separator, 78

Concatenation, 64
    Operator, 64

Conditional Format, 80-83, 101, 102, 111, 112, 130, 134, 151, 152, 210

Conditional Responses, 110, 112, 151

Coordinate Grid, 35-43, 99
    Handouts, 49, 41
    Insert in Word Document, 40

Count, 17

Cubes and Cube Roots, 14

D

Data Points, 193, 194

Data Ranges, 15, 48, 187

Decimal Places, 78

Division, 10

Division Operator, 10

Dollar Signs ($), Enter, 48-50, 154

Drawing Tools, 37-40, 117, 212
    Arrow, 39
    Line, 39, 120
    Oval, 40, 41, 172, 173
    Rectangle, 212

Duplicate Problems, 65, 66

E

Edit mode. *See also* Show Formulas Mode, 74

Equals Sign (=), 1, 3, 6

Equations, Systems of, 219-232
    Dependent, 232
    Identical, 232
    Inconsistent, 231

Exercise Sheets, 53-64

Exponents, 12, 13, 14

Extend a Series, 45-52, 71, 177
    Dates, 52
    Days, 51
    Months, 50
    Periods, 50
    Weekdays, 51

F

Fill Color Tool, 41, 76, 77

Fill Handle, 45, 46, 50-52, 71-73, 91, 92, 107, 177, 178

Fonts, 69, 82, 89, 94, 100, 110-113, 129-133, 135-137, 144-150, 155, 160, 171, 174, 180, 181, 220
    Color, 61
    Size, 56

Format
    Conditional, 80-83, 111, 130, 151, 152, 210
    Copy, 77, 92
    Lock, 87

Formulas
    Copy, 47, 48, 57, 73, 74, 91, 92, 105, 107, 132, 154, 155, 162, 178, 206, 215, 227-229
    Edit, 178
    Enter, 1-8, 104, 110, 131, 179
        Arrow Key Method, 5
        Mouse Method, 3-5
        Touch-Typing Method, 1, 2
    Freeze Results, 87
    Recalculate Automatically, 3, 55, 58, 75, 103, 153, 168, 177
    Recalculate Manually, 55, 58, 103, 105, 109, 153, 168, 177
Forward Slash. *See* Division Operator, 10
Fractions, 10, 127-141, 185-199
    in Pie Charts, 185-199
    Visually Compare, 185, 196-199
Functions
    ADDRESS, 99, 104
    AND, 150, 151
    AVERAGE, 17
    CHAR, 159, 163, 165
    CODE, 159, 162, 163, 165
    COUNTIF, 131
    Enter
        Arrow Key Method, 6, 7
    IF, 79, 80, 104, 106, 110, 150, 151, 154, 162, 165, 168, 169, 171, 178, 183, 184
    INT, 63
    INTEGER, 165
    LEFT, 86
    MAX, 206, 215
    MID, 85
    MOD, 62, 63
    RAND, 66, 71
    RANDBETWEEN, 53-55, 59, 62, 63, 104, 153, 154, 169, 179, 183, 184
    RANK, 66, 72
    RIGHT, 85
    ROUND, 165
    SQRT, 12, 14
    SUM, 15, 86, 90, 92, 132, 148, 169, 179
    VLOOKUP, 66, 72, 73

G

Graphs, Insert in Documents, 40
Grave. *See* Shortcut Keys, Ctrl+`, 72, 85
Grid Paper, 19-35
    Grid Size, 31
Grid Sheet, Isometric, 32-34
Grid, Cartesian Coordinate, 35-40, 99
    Handouts, 41
Gridlines, 22-28, 174, 181, 229
    Hide, 95, 114, 139, 156, 189

H

Handout Sheets, 42, 43
Height Formula, 211, 215
Hidden
    Columns, 65, 189
    Text, 61, 112, 155, 189
Homework Checker, 75-99

I

Incrementation Value, 205, 214
IntelliSense, 15
Isometric Grid Sheets, 32-34
Iterations. *See also* Circular References, 103, 153, 168, 177

L

Landscape Mode, 67, 123
Largest Value, Find, 17
Left-justify Text, 56
Length Formula, 206, 209, 211, 215
Line Break, 202, 203, 212, 221, 222
Line Charts, 207, 208, 216, 217
Literals, 64

Index

M

Magic Squares, 87-98

Manual Calculations. *See also* Automatic Calculation, 55, 58, 73, 103, 105, 143, 153, 167, 168, 177, 198

Margins, 26, 27, 42, 68, 125

Math
Exercise Sheets, 53-59, 63, 64
Operators and Functions, 1, 2, 4-11, 55, 77

Mathematical Art, 117
String Art, 117-120, 123, 124
Tesselations, 117, 121-123

Maximization, 201, 210-215
Area of a Rectangle, 201-206, 209, 210
Volume of a Box, 211-215

Maximum Value, 17

Minimum Value, 17

Minus Signs (-), 3-8, 11

Mixed References. *See also* Absolute and Relative References, 45, 48, 49

Mouse Method. *See also* Arrow and Touch-Type, 3, 5, 12

Multiplication, 9, 11, 45, 47, 59-62, 67, 73, 76-79, 84, 165
Intermediate Steps, 84-86
Operator. *See* Asterisk, 9, 77

Multiplication Tables, 45, 47, 73

N

Nested IF Statements, 110, 151

New Line, 202, 203, 212-222

Numbers, Format, 78, 133, 186, 214, 215

O

Order of Operations, 11
Overridden by Parentheses, 11

P

Page Break Preview, 28

Page Setup, 26, 28, 34, 42, 67, 97, 125

Parentheses, Control Order of Operations, 11

Passwords, 96, 140, 157, 175, 182, 230

Percentages, 167, 185

Pie Charts, 185-199
Angle of First Slice, 194
Show Fractions, 185-188, 192-199

Plus Signs (+), 7, 55, 64, 73

Pound Signs (#), 74, 224

Powers, 12-14

Print Area, Set, 29-34

Print Gridlines, 26

Print Preview, 22, 28, 31, 34, 42, 125

Print Settings, 26, 28, 29

Products, 86, 143, 148

Protection, Files, 96, 97, 114, 140, 157, 175, 176, 182, 183, 198, 199, 230

Pythagorean Theorem, 12, 13

Q

Quizzes, 67-73

Quotation Marks, 55, 56, 106

R

Random Numbers, 53, 54, 66, 67, 71, 72, 99, 104, 153-155, 167, 171

Ranges, 15, 48, 187
Select, 69
Turn on Side, 45, 46, 98

Read-only Files, 169, 176, 184

References
  Absolute, 49, 154, 178, 227
  Mixed, 45, 49
  Relative, 49
Relative References. *See also* Absolute and Mixed References, 49
Right-justify Text, 55, 56
Roots, 12-14
Rows
  Headers, Hide, 95, 139, 156
  Height, 19, 20, 36
  Insert, 59

S

Scroll Bars, Hide, 189
Series, Extend, 45, 50-52, 71, 177
  Dates, 52
  Days, 51
  Months, 50
  Periods, 50
  Weekdays, 51
Shortcut Keys
  Alt+Enter, 202, 203, 212, 221, 222
  Ctrl+1. *See* Cells, Format, 22, 33, 36, 100, 110, 112, 129, 133-137, 144-147, 149, 150, 155, 171, 174, 180, 181, 186, 198, 225, 226, 229
  Ctrl+A, 75
  Ctrl+C, 40, 42, 46, 57, 70, 73, 77, 93, 98, 122, 148, 164, 213, 224, 227-229
  Ctrl+D, 132, 155, 206, 215
  Ctrl+Enter, 48, 162
  Ctrl+V, 42, 57, 70, 73, 122, 148, 161, 224, 227, 228
  Ctrl+Z, 120
  F2, 74
  F4, 49, 50
  F9, 55, 58, 59, 72, 73, 105, 108, 109, 111-113, 147, 153, 155, 158, 167, 169-171, 174, 177, 179, 181, 198, 199
  Home, 118
  Shift+Spacebar, 64
Show Formulas Mode. *See also* Edit Mode, 72, 85
Sigma (Σ). *See also* AutoSum Button, 15

Simultaneous Equations. *See* Systems of Equations, 219, 231
Snap To Grid, 38, 40, 119, 172, 212
Spelling, AutoCorrect, 146
Square Roots, 12-14
Start New Line, 202, 203, 212, 221, 222
Story Problems, 1-18
String Art, 117-121, 123, 124
Subtraction, 3-8, 11, 15, 16, 62-64, 86, 219, 220
Sums, 141
Systems of Equations, 219-233
  Dependent, 232
  Identical, 232
  Inconsistent, 231

T

Tabs
  Copy, 162
  Delete, 162
  Hide, 95, 114, 139, 156, 189
  Move, 162
  Rename, 163
Tesselations, 117, 121-123
Text
  Alignment, 69, 88, 93, 100, 110, 133, 144, 149, 150, 160, 171, 180, 181
  Center, 56, 77
  Find and Replace, 163
  Hide, 61, 112, 155, 189
  Right-/Left-justifying, 55
  Wrap, 94, 113, 137, 145, 181, 221, 222
Touch-Typing Method, 1, 2
Transposition, 45-47, 98

V

Volume of a Cube, 13
Volume Formula, 215

W

Width Formula, 206, 209, 211, 215

Index

Worksheets
    Copy, 162
    Delete, 162
    Format,19-21, 56, 220
    Hide Tabs, 95, 114, 139, 156, 189
    Move, 162
    Protect, 90, 109, 130, 133, 149, 198, 229
    Rename, 163
Wrap text, 94, 113, 137, 145, 181, 221, 222

X

X-axis, 35-41

XYZ Coordinate Grid. *See* Isometric Grid Sheets, 32

Y

Y-axis, 35-41

Notes

Notes

Notes

HOLY MACRO! BOOKS QUICK ORDER FORM

Fax Orders: (707)-220-4510. Send this form.
E-Mail Orders: store@MrExcel.com – Online: http://www.MrExcel.com
Postal Orders: MrExcel, 13386 Judy Ave NW, PO Box 82, Uniontown OH 44685, USA

Quantity	Title	Price	Total
	Learn Excel from Mr Excel By Bill Jelen ISBN 1-932802-12-6 (853 pages – 2005)	$39.95	
	Excel for the Math Classroom By Bill Hazlett with Bill Jelen ISBN 1-932802-15-0 (240 pages – 2006)	$24.95	
	Excel for Teachers By Conmy, Hazlett, Jelen, Soucy ISBN 1-932802-11-8 (236 pages – 2006)	$24.95	
	Excel for Marketing Managers By Bill Jelen and Ivana Taylor ISBN 1-932802-13-4 (172 Pages – 2006)	$24.95	
	Excel for the CEO (CD-ROM) By P.K. Hari Hara Subramanian ISBN 1-932802-17-7 (351 pages – 2006)	$24.95	
	Excel for Auditors By Bill Jelen and Dwayne K. Dowel ISBN 1-932802-16-9 (212 pages – 2006)	$24.95	
	Office VBA Macros You Can Use Today By Gonzales et al ISBN 1-932802-06-1 (433 Pages – 2006)	$39.95	
	Holy Macro! It's 2,200 Excel VBA Examples (CD-ROM) By Hans Herber Bill Jelen and Tom Urtis ISBN 1-932802-08-8 (2200 pages – 2004)	$89.00	
	Slide Your Way Through Excel VBA (CD-ROM) By Dr. Gerard Verschuuren ISBN 0-9724258-6-1 (734 pages – 2003)	$99.00	
	Join the Excellers League (CD-ROM) By Dr. Gerard Verschuuren ISBN 1-932802-00-2 (1477 pages – 2004)	$99.00	
	Excel for Scientists (CD-ROM) By Dr. Gerard Verschuuren ISBN 0-9724258-8-8 (589 pages – 2004)	$75.00	
	Guerilla Data Analysis Using Microsoft Excel By Bill Jelen ISBN 0-9724258-0-2 (138 pages – 2002)	$19.95	
	The Spreadsheet at 25 By Bill Jelen ISBN 1-932802-04-5 (120 color pages – 2005)	$19.95	
	Grover Park George On Access By George Hepworth ISBN 0-9724258-9-6 (480 pages – 2004)	$29.95	
	Your Access to the World (CD-ROM) By Dr. Gerard Verschuuren ISBN 1-932802-03-7 (1450 pages – 2004)	$99.00	
	Access VBA Made Accessible (CD-ROM) By Dr. Gerard Verschuuren (1323 pages – 2004)	$99.00	
	DreamBoat On Word By Anne Troy ISBN 0-9724258-4-5 (220 pages – 2004)	$19.95	
	Kathy Jacobs On PowerPoint By Kathy Jacobs ISBN 0-9724258-6-1 (380 pages – 2004)	$29.95	
	Unleash the Power of Outlook 2003 By Steve Link ISBN 1-932802-01-0 (250 pages – 2004)	$19.95	
	Unleash the Power of OneNote By Kathy Jacobs & Bill Jelen (320 pages – 2004)	$19.95	
	VBA and Macros for Microsoft Excel By Bill Jelen and Tracy Syrstad ISBN 0789731290 (576 Pages – 2004)	$39.95	
	Pivot Table Data Crunching By Bill Jelen and Michael Alexander ISBN 0789734354 (275 Pages – 2005)	$29.95	

Name: _____
Address: _____
City, State, Zip: _____
E-Mail: _____
Sales Tax: Ohio residents add 6% sales tax
Shipping by Air: **US:** $4 for first book, $2 per additional book. $1 per CD.
                  International: $9 for first book, $5 per additional book. $2 per CD
                  FedEx available on request at actual shipping cost.
Payment: Check or Money order to "MrExcel" or pay with VISA/MC/Discover/AmEx:
                  Card #:_____ Exp.:_____
                  Name on Card: _____
Bulk Orders: Ordering enough for the entire staff? Save 40% when you order six or more of any one title.